341%

Rosemary Stanton
vegetables

Rosemary Stanton
vegetables

Illustrations by Nerida de Jong

A SUE HINES BOOK

ALLEN & UNWIN

A Sue Hines Book
Allen & Unwin
9 Atchison Street
St Leonards NSW 2065 Australia
Phone: (61 2) 8425 0100
Fax: (61 2) 9906 2218
E-mail: frontdesk@allen-unwin.com.au
Web: http://www.allen-unwin.com.au

National Library of Australia
Cataloguing-in-Publication data:

Stanton, Rosemary.
Vegetables.
Includes index.
ISBN 1 86508 215 5.
1. Cookery – Vegetables. I. Title.
641.65

Designed by Ruth Grüner
Typeset by J&M Typesetting
Printed by South China Printing Company, Hong Kong

FOR OUR PARENTS, ALAN AND ELIZABETH

Contents

Introduction

Nutritionists are often accused of changing their minds and their messages, but there is one area in which there is total agreement: vegetables. Every health expert agrees we need to eat more of them. And with something that looks and tastes as good as vegetables can if they are prepared with love and respect, it's easy to keep the pundits happy. Consider the beautiful flavour of perfectly steamed asparagus, the crisp sweetness of a freshly picked pea, the crunch of a brilliant orange carrot, the smoothness of perfect mashed potato, the tang of rocket in a well-dressed salad, the flavour of a good tomato dressed simply with basil, olive oil and ground black pepper, or the wonderful aroma of onions frying at a barbecue. And the delights of roasted capsicums, char-grilled eggplant, a celeriac purée or braised leeks.

I have watched children in Crete sitting down to their bitter wild greens, squeezing lemon juice and shaking olive oil over them before tucking in. Families in many parts of Asia enjoy meals based largely on vegetables and you can visit many countries around the Mediterranean and realise only at the end of a wonderful meal that many of the delicious dishes were based on superbly prepared vegetables. Eating vegetables is a journey of discovery. Travellers will know that in most countries of the world, people present delicious vegetables. Back home, almost every time you go into the greengrocer's shop or local supermarket, you will be able to find some new vegetable or one you may have forgotten about. It's a never-ending delight and new varieties of vegetables are likely to continue appearing for some time to come.

Vegetables are so versatile they need never be boring. They can be baked, barbecued, microwaved, steamed or stir-fried. Many are even more delicious served with elegant sauces or dressings, and some form the basis of classic dishes from cuisines around the world. Without their colour, the dinner plate and buffet table would look pale and pathetic. Vegetables bring meals to life.

There are now many more nutritional reasons for eating vegies than just their vitamin C, vitamin A and dietary fibre. Recent research shows that vegetables contain literally thousands of phytochemicals (*phyto* means 'plant') that should be commanding more of our attention as they are vitally important for human health. Some of these are antioxidants, which prevent fats from damaging arteries and free radicals from destroying body tissue. Others have anti-cancer activity: more than 200 studies show that people who eat the most vegetables and fruits have the lowest incidence of cancer at almost every site in the body. This does not mean that people who eat their vegies will never get cancer, but it does mean that doing so will reduce the risk more than almost any other controllable factor, except perhaps giving up smoking. Even among smokers, there is clear evidence that those who eat the most vegetables have the lowest incidence of lung cancer.

Vegetables are also important in the fight against coronary heart disease. In both Greece and Japan, smoking rates are high and you would therefore expect the incidence of coronary heart disease to be comparable to that of other nations with high rates of smoking. But coronary heart disease rates are very low in both these countries. The explanation seems to be at least partly due to the high intake of vegetables.

We do not yet know why vegetables are so protective against disease. There is now, however, good evidence that the modern tendency to snack on junk and then try to make up for the inevitable imbalance by taking nutrient supplements is unlikely to give the same protection provided by eating vegetables. Some recent research shows the folly of such an approach.

A trial in Finland gave supplements of the vitamins found in vegetables, either alone or in combination, to 29 000 smokers over an eight-year period. There were no positive benefits and those taking beta carotene had a significantly higher incidence of lung cancer. The same thing occurred in a study of 18 000 smokers in the United States and the trial was abandoned for ethical reasons. Similar findings have occurred in several trials of people with bowel polyps, which can develop into bowel cancer (one of the most common cancers in the western world). In every case, those taking the beta carotene supplements had worse results than those on the placebo. These trials were a disappointment to those selling vitamin supplements, but the findings do not negate the many studies showing the value of eating more fruits and vegetables. Nature is more complicated than we have previously realised and we cannot duplicate the range and combinations of the thousands of protective phytochemicals that occur in vegetables: no supplement pill will ever be able to match what nature has provided. Some companies even sell a collection of vegetables condensed into a pill, but research found that each of these capsules contains the equivalent in antioxidant content of just 10 g of vegetables. The companies now boost their capsules with extra vitamins, but they haven't a hope of reaching the amazing variety found in the real thing.

There have been claims that vegetables no longer contain nutrients because our soils are devitalised. While there are important and urgent environmental reasons to take action to protect soil quality and minimise the use of fertilisers, tests of vegetables bought from regular supermarkets and suppliers show there is no loss of nutrients in our current crops. My personal preference is for organically grown produce because of the environmental wisdom of this practice. But although I would love to be able to say that organically grown produce has higher levels of vitamins than regular crops, laboratory surveys don't support such assumptions.

Dinner used to be 'meat and three veg' then we moved on to meals based on pasta, pizza or rice. We also became a nation of fast-food lovers, with 35 per cent of the average food budget now going on foods prepared outside the home, many of them from fast-food restaurants. Vegetables do not figure prominently in these meals, partly because they are bulky and don't re-heat well.

If we ate more vegies we'd eat less junk, simply because many vegetables are filling. Most people know that vegetables are good for them and almost everyone intends to eat them. But many people get through most evening meals without a decent helping of vegies. In homes where vegetables have always been boiled to an unappetising mush, with little texture, colour or flavour, no one complains about their absence.

We praise Mediterranean and Asian diets for their healthfulness, the quality of which stems from the fact that they are based largely on plant foods, with meat added almost as a condiment. Yet when dishes from Italy or Thailand or elsewhere are transported to other countries, the traditional balance is usually altered. Italians eat pasta with a sauce based on tomatoes or other vegetables; many Australians accompany it with bolognese or cream-based sauces. In Thailand, the meal is based on rice and vegetables with only a small quantity of fish, meat or chicken; many westerners choose their Thai dishes from those containing meat, chicken or seafood, usually cooked in coconut milk. It's the same with food from Japan, China, France or Greece. We draw inspiration from their cuisines but change the balance so that protein dominates, and vegetables are secondary. It's time for a change.

There are also social considerations. Eating vegetables usually means sitting down at a table and that, in turn, usually means some interaction with other people. Increasingly though, we eat on the run—usually fast finger foods, full of fat and lacking vegetables other than the ubiquitous French fry with its high content of saturated fat. What a terrible thing to do to a noble vegetable like the potato!

Vegetables make ecological sense too, being much further down the food chain than animal foods. Why feed animals vegetables and then eat the animals, when we could eat the vegetables ourselves? There is probably no need to take this to its ultimate conclusion and eliminate all animal products from our diets—humans have always been omnivorous—but eating more meat and animal foods and fewer vegetables does not make nutritional or environmental sense.

An incredible array of wonderful vegetables graces our supermarkets and greengrocery shelves. Most are quick and easy to prepare, as the recipes that follow show. The aim of this book is to give vegetables the attention they deserve. With their superb virtues, I think it's time we ate more of them.

Rosemary Stanton

Using this book

The recipes in this book have all been analysed in terms of the major nutrients—protein, fat, carbohydrate, dietary fibre and kilojoules (kJ)—and rated according to their content of some minerals and vitamins. An 'excellent source' of vitamin or mineral is where one serving will provide more than 80 per cent of the recommended dietary intake (RDI) for that nutrient. A 'good source' provides 50–80 per cent of the RDI. 'Also provides' means that a serving supplies 25–50 per cent of the RDI.

Most of the recipes have low to moderate fat content. Some fats are essential and, in the case of vegetables, some fat is needed for many of their important phytochemicals to be absorbed. My philosophy is to use as little saturated fat as possible and to be moderate with other fats, always in keeping with presenting foods that taste good. Occasionally, a recipe *needs* a little bit of butter. Where at least 75 per cent of the fat in a recipe is in the form of highly beneficial fats, I have used the term 'good' fat: good fats are the unsaturated fats that come with beneficial antioxidants and include the fats from olive oil and other vegetable oils that are cold-pressed (all olive oil is cold pressed except for olive pomace which is the oil extracted from the olive cake left after pressing), nuts, seeds and avocado.

All recipes in this book which include fish, chicken or meat have a vegetarian alternative.

Alfalfa (see **Sprouts**)

Amaranth

There are many types of amaranth grown throughout the world, often as a substitute for spinach, although some regard it as a weed. Some types of amaranth are grown for their seed, which can be ground for use as a cereal known as quinoa (pronounced kin-wah). Many varieties of amaranth are native to Central and South America; others come from India, South-east Asia and parts of Africa. It is widely used as a food in India, China, Japan, Thailand, Vietnam and the Philippines.

In Australia, green or red amaranth are sold in bunches with the roots attached, and are also known as *en choy* or Chinese spinach. The green leaves centred with a deep-red colour spreading over the leaf veins distinguishes red amaranth from Asian greens.

Amaranth is amazingly rich in nutrients, with high levels of many antioxidants. It is an excellent source of vitamin C and a good source of beta-carotene and folate, also providing iron, calcium, potassium and dietary fibre. A typical 50 g serving has no fat and 40 kJ.

CHOOSING AND STORING • It is available in spring, summer and autumn. Select bunches with firm roots and fresh leaves that have not wilted. Plants with many leaves usually have the sweetest flavour.

Keep refrigerated in a plastic bag for up to 3 or 4 days.

PREPARATION AND COOKING • Remove the roots and lower stems, then wash thoroughly. Use as you would spinach: steam, stir-fry or microwave, or include in soups or noodle dishes.

AMARANTH WITH HOKKIEN NOODLES

A quick and easy dish that takes less than 15 minutes to prepare. If you have fresh young kaffir lime leaves, add 3 or 4 shredded leaves just before serving (dried will do but the flavour is not as good).

You could add 300 g chicken breast, cut into strips, with the onion and stir-fry without a lid. Alternatively, just before serving add 300 g tofu cut into 2.5 cm cubes, and toss gently to combine. Use vegetable stock in place of chicken stock.

200 g fresh hokkien noodles
1 tbsp sesame oil
2 eggs, beaten
1 onion, sliced
1 clove garlic, crushed
1 red capsicum, seeded and sliced
1 bunch (about 350 g) amaranth
1 cup chicken stock
1 tbsp salt-reduced soy sauce
juice of 1 lime

SERVES 4

Place noodles into a saucepan or heat-proof bowl and pour boiling water over them. Leave for a minute, then drain and rinse.

Add 2 teaspoons of the sesame oil to a hot wok and pour in the eggs. Swirl to spread over the wok and allow to set, then slide omelette onto a plate. Cut into strips.

Pour remaining oil into wok, add onion, garlic and capsicum, cover with a lid and cook for about 3 minutes, stirring several times. Remove roots and coarse stems from amaranth and add to wok, stir-frying for a minute. Add drained noodles and chicken stock, and bring to the boil. Gently stir in the strips of egg and the soy sauce. Serve in bowls, squeezing a little lime juice into each.

NUTRITIONAL VALUE: 14 g protein, 9 g fat, 34 g carbohydrate, 5.5 g dietary fibre, 1140 kJ (275 Cals). An excellent source of vitamins A, C and niacin, and a good source of calcium, iron and dietary fibre.

Arrowhead (see **Other vegetables**)

Artichokes, Globe

The globe artichoke is a thistle-like plant belonging to the same family as daisies and chrysanthemums. It originated around the Mediterranean, especially in Italy and Greece, but was also found in North Africa where it still grows wild. Italy and Spain currently dominate world production.

The word 'artichoke' comes from an Arabic word meaning 'barbs of the earth',

referring to the sharp leaves or bracts that form around the central flower bud. Catherine de Medici introduced globe artichokes to the French in the sixteenth century and they are still sometimes called French artichokes.

Globe artichokes range in weight from about 80 g to more than 400 g. Each globe looks like an unopened flower bud, with tightly wrapped green leaves, often with a purplish tinge. The heart of the artichoke is tender, as are the smaller fleshy-based bracts that form around it, although the hairy 'choke' in the centre is inedible.

Artichokes contain an unusual organic acid called cynarin, a derivative of quinic acid. Some claim that extracts of artichoke can reduce cholesterol, but properly controlled studies do not support this. The leaves have a long folk history of use against diseases of the liver or gall bladder. In the early 1970s, scientists reported that about 60 per cent of people say that water tastes sweet if drunk after eating artichokes. This is presumably an effect of the cynarin, and it also alters the flavour of wine. Many wine buffs consider that no wine should be consumed when eating artichokes.

A 250 g globe artichoke provides about 100 g of edible flesh in the heart, the base of the bract and the top portion of stalk. Artichokes are a good source of folate and some other B complex vitamins. They have only very small amounts of carbohydrate and protein. A cooked globe artichoke has no fat, 1 g of dietary fibre and 90 kJ.

CHOOSING AND STORING • Artichokes are available from late winter to early summer, but the flavour is best in spring. Choose brightly coloured specimens with tight leaves and heavy for their size. Avoid those where the tips look dehydrated.

Keep in a plastic bag in the refrigerator until ready to use, preferably within five days after purchase.

PREPARATION AND COOKING • Prepare just before cooking. Cut stem to within about 3 cm of the base, remove the coarse outside leaves and use kitchen scissors to trim any pointed tips remaining. Cut off the top third of the artichoke and immediately rub a cut lemon over the surface and stem end to stop the cut surfaces turning an unattractive dark grey-green.

Cook artichokes whole or cut in half. Use a stainless-steel saucepan to cook them, as aluminium will cause them to discolour. Steam whole artichokes for about 20 minutes and halves for about 10 minutes, or until the stem end is tender when pierced with a skewer. Alternatively, cook in boiling water (with a tablespoon of lemon juice added) for 10 to 20 minutes.

When eating an artichoke, pull off the leaves one by one, and scrape them between the teeth to remove the fleshy base. Discard the rest of the leaf. When you come to the hairy 'choke' in the centre, scoop it out and discard, then eat the bottom (or 'heart') and stem. Do not store cooked artichokes for more than 24 hours, as they can develop a blue-green toxic mould.

CRUNCHY STUFFED ARTICHOKES

You need soft breadcrumbs for this recipe.

4 medium-sized artichokes
1 cup soft breadcrumbs
1/2 cup grated parmesan
1 tablespoon fresh thyme leaves
2 cloves garlic, chopped finely
1 small onion, chopped finely
1/4 cup lemon juice
1 tbsp olive oil

SERVES 4

Cut artichoke stem close to base. Remove coarse outside leaves and trim the rest, then place in a bowl of iced water with 3 or 4 slices of lemon. In a stainless-steel saucepan, steam artichokes for 20 minutes. When cool enough to handle, pull out the centre leaves and scoop out the choke.

Meanwhile, make the breadcrumbs by placing 2 slices of torn bread in a blender or food processor.

Preheat oven to 200°C. Combine breadcrumbs, parmesan, thyme, garlic, onion and lemon juice. Separate artichoke leaves and push crumb mixture between them. Place artichokes on a baking tray, sprinkle with olive oil and bake in preheated oven for 15 minutes, or until crumbs are brown.

Serve as a first course, or with roast rack of lamb.

NUTRITIONAL VALUE: 11 g protein, 11 g fat, 8 g carbohydrate, 2.5 g dietary fibre, 730 kJ (175 Cals). An excellent source of vitamin C and a good source of calcium.

ARTICHOKES AND CHICK PEAS

With some crusty bread, this makes a delightful lunch dish.

2 lemons
4 globe artichokes
1 tbsp olive oil
1 medium-sized onion, chopped finely
2 stalks celery, finely sliced
$^{1}/_{2}$ red capsicum, seeded and cut into strips
2 cloves garlic, crushed
1 tbsp finely chopped fresh rosemary
   (or use 1$^{1}/_{2}$ tsp dried)
2 cups cooked or canned chick peas
$^{1}/_{4}$ cup liquid from the chick peas
   (or use stock)
2 tbsp finely chopped parsley

SERVES 4

Slice one lemon and place in a bowl of water. Prepare artichokes by removing all coarse outer leaves until you have only pale soft leaves. Cut off the top third of the artichoke, halve it and scoop out choke, using a spoon or melon baller. Cut the remaining lemon in half and immediately rub one half over all cut surfaces.

Heat olive oil in a large pan or wok, add onion, cover and cook for 3–4 minutes, stirring several times. Add celery, capsicum, garlic and rosemary, and cook for another 3–4 minutes, tossing ingredients together.

Remove artichokes from water, slice and immediately add to the pan. Stir in chick peas and liquid, bring to the boil and simmer for 5 minutes. Top with parsley and serve with crusty bread and some good cheese.

NUTRITIONAL VALUE: 10 g protein, 7 g fat, 15 g carbohydrate, 6.5 g dietary fibre, 690 kJ (165 Cals). An excellent source of vitamin C and a good source of potassium and iron.

Artichokes, Jerusalem

This knobbly tuber is not an artichoke and does not come from Jerusalem. It belongs to the sunflower family and its name derives from the Italian word *gira-sole*, meaning 'turning to the sun', as sunflowers do. One of the few vegetables that originated in North America and Canada (where they still grow wild), Jerusalem artichokes were taken to Europe in the seventeenth century and became a food for livestock and the poor. These beginnings hindered their status and acceptance.

Jerusalem artichokes vary in size and may be yellow or cream in colour, sometimes tinged with pink. About 15 per cent of the artichoke consists of inulin, a form of soluble dietary fibre that passes to the large intestine where it is fermented by helpful bacteria. This gives rise to a lot of gas (and is responsible for the nickname 'fartichoke'), but also produces acids that may give protection against bowel cancer.

Jerusalem artichokes provide fibre as well as some potassium and small amounts of vitamin C and iron. A 125 g serving provides 4 g of dietary fibre, no fat and 125 kJ.

CHOOSING AND STORING • Available from late autumn until spring. Choose tubers that are crisp and firm, preferably without too many knobbly bits, as these can be difficult to clean or peel. Avoid those where the knobs have been broken off.

Store Jerusalem artichokes in a plastic bag in the refrigerator for up to two weeks. Some people maintain that colder temperatures increase their sweetness and prefer to keep them outside the fridge in a cool place for a maximum of 2 to 3 days.

PREPARATION AND COOKING • Scrub to remove any dirt. If desired, use a potato peeler to remove skin. Jerusalem artichokes are suitable to boil, steam, microwave, roast or barbecue.

ROASTED AND CARAMELISED JERUSALEM ARTICHOKES

A delightful accompaniment to roast meat and other roast vegetables. No need to peel the artichokes for this recipe.

1 tbsp olive oil
500 g Jerusalem artichokes, scrubbed
2 tsp brown sugar
2 tbsp lemon juice
1 tbsp salt-reduced soy sauce
1 tbsp sesame seeds

SERVES 4

Preheat oven to 200°C. Heat a baking dish for 3 minutes, then pour olive oil into the dish, add artichokes and shake well to coat. Roast for 20 minutes, turning once.

Combine sugar, lemon juice and soy sauce. Pour over artichokes, shake well and return to oven for another 10 minutes, turning artichokes once. Sprinkle with sesame seeds and serve piping hot.

NUTRITIONAL VALUE: 3.5 g protein, 6.5 g fat, 6.5 g carbohydrate, 4 g dietary fibre, 420 kJ (100 Cals). A good source of vitamin C and fibre, plus some iron.

JERUSALEM ARTICHOKE SOUP

A warming winter soup. It's worth peeling the artichokes, as otherwise the soup will be pale brown rather than creamy white. To prevent discolouration, drop the peeled pieces into a bowl of water with half a lemon added, while you are preparing the rest.

1 tbsp olive oil or butter
1 large onion, roughly chopped
1 clove garlic, crushed
1 kg Jerusalem artichokes, peeled
2 cups chicken stock
$\frac{1}{2}$ lemon
4 bay leaves
2 cups milk, fat-reduced or regular

SERVES 4

Place oil or butter in a large saucepan. Add onion and garlic, cover and allow to sweat for 3–4 minutes, stirring occasionally. Add artichokes, stock, lemon and bay leaves, bring to the boil, cover and simmer for 20 minutes. Remove lemon and bay leaves. Purée soup, adding the milk. Reheat before serving.

NUTRITIONAL VALUE: 11 g protein, 7 g fat, 18 g carbohydrate, 7.5 g dietary fibre, 760 kJ (180 Cals). An excellent source of vitamin C and fibre, and a good source of niacin, calcium and potassium, plus some iron.

Arugula (see **Rocket**)

Asian greens

There are many Asian greens available in supermarkets and an even greater number in Asian markets and groceries. Most can be used in similar ways. *Choy*, sometimes spelled '*choi*', means vegetable.

Asian greens are highly nutritious. They are all excellent sources of vitamin C and most are also very good sources of vitamin A and many antioxidants (the darker the colour, the higher the antioxidant levels). With the exception of Chinese cabbage, Asian greens are also good sources of iron. Unlike spinach, the English vegetable with the highest iron content, Asian greens do not contain oxalic acid which 'ties up' the iron in spinach, so that it is not available to the body. Chrysanthemum leaves, mustard cabbage, tatsoi and Chinese broccoli also provide calcium. All Asian greens supply folate, are low in fat, and a cup of most varieties, (cooked) supplies 2 g of dietary fibre and approximately 40 kJ.

VARIETIES • *Bok choy* (also called baak choy, pak choy, Chinese chard or Chinese white cabbage) has thick fleshy white stems and dark-green leaves. Native to China, it has been cultivated for thousands of years. Asian food shops generally distinguish between bok choy and pak choy, the bok choy having white stems and pak choy greenish stems. It is best steamed, braised or stir-fried. Baby bok choy is popular served whole, usually braised. Some cultivars of pak or bok choy grow are plants, halfway in size between lambs lettuce and tatsoi.

Choy sum (also called chye sim or flowering cabbage) has firm, fleshy green stems and green leaves with small yellow flowers emerging above the leaves. It is good in stir-fried dishes.

Chinese broccoli (also called gai larn, gai lum or Chinese kale) has strong stems, dark-green leaves and small white flowers. Unlike regular broccoli, where the flowering head is the main part used, with Chinese broccoli you use the stems and leaves. Often served stir-fried on its own, Chinese broccoli is also useful in mixed stir-fries.

Chinese cabbage (also called Peking cabbage or wong nga bak) comes in slightly different shapes. Some are similar to a cos lettuce, with pale-green crinkled leaves and a crisp but soft, white centre rib. Others are more squat, although not as much as a regular round cabbage. The whole cabbage (green leaves and white rib parts) can be eaten raw or cooked and has a very slight mustard flavour.

Chinese spinach and *en choy* are also known as amaranth (see page 1).

Chrysanthemum greens (also known as chong ho, thong ho and chop suey greens) are native to the Mediterranean area, but were taken to China and other parts of Asia and are now used more there. The leaves grow like a small, loose Asian cabbage, have blunt lobes, are mid-green in colour and feel slightly rough. They look like larger versions of the leaves of garden chrysanthemums. They have a somewhat floral flavour and are best used in stir-fried dishes: the young leaves are used, as older ones are bitter.

Mizuna is a Japanese vegetable, a member of the Brassica family with light-green, deeply serrated leaves and creamy stems. It can be used in salads, or cooked. The smaller and lighter the colour, the milder the flavour: these mild leaves are included in mixed salad greens. Darker leaves have a strong mustard flavour and are better used in stir-fried dishes.

Mustard cabbage (also known as gai choy) is a type of cabbage or rape (canola). Many varieties of mustard cabbage have been developed from the original ones that grew in India. Some are grown for their oil, others for their seeds (black, yellow or brown) and yet others for their highly nutritious, mustard-flavoured leaves. Bamboo mustard cabbage (chuk gai choy) has a slightly ribbed green stalk, the leaf blade extending almost to its base. Sow cabbage (jiu la choy) is a long mustard cabbage with smooth leaves that wrap around the base like a soft celery leaf. Swatow mustard cabbage (daai gaai choy), which looks like a coarse lettuce that is about to go to seed, has a pungent flavour. Most mustard cabbages are only found in Asian markets and food stores. Use them in stir-fries or soups.

Tatsoi (also called rosette bok choy or Chinese flat cabbage) is a pretty vegetable looking like a flat, dark-green rosette. The leaves in the centre are small, with those on the outside about 5–6 cm long. Tatsoi has a strong flavour and many people prefer it cooked rather than raw, but the young centre leaves are delicious in salads.

CHOOSING AND STORING • Most Asian greens are available all year, but are generally at their best in terms of both quality and price during the winter months. For all types, select those with fresh-looking leaves and firm stalks. Avoid any that are wilted.

Asian greens store in a plastic bag in the refrigerator for a day or two. Chrysanthemum greens wilt quickly, so wrap in paper towels and store in the refrigerator for no more than one day.

PREPARATION AND COOKING • Wash greens well and then slice or chop. Baby bok choy can be cooked whole and Chinese broccoli looks good with the stems trimmed but left whole. Most Asian greens are ideal to stir-fry; they do not steam well and lose their character if boiled.

STIR-FRIED FISH WITH CHINESE CABBAGE

A quick and very healthy dish. You can substitute other Asian greens, if you like.

1 tbsp peanut or light olive oil
1 clove garlic, crushed
2 tsp finely sliced fresh ginger
1 red capsicum, seeded and sliced
1 cup sliced green shallots (spring onions)
½ small Chinese cabbage, shredded
½ cup white wine
400 g boneless white fish, cut into strips
2 tbsp salt-reduced soy sauce
2 tbsp sweet chilli sauce

SERVES 4

Add the oil to a hot wok and cook garlic, ginger and capsicum for 3 minutes. Add onions and cabbage, and toss well to combine. Pour in the wine and place the fish pieces on top. Cover and simmer for 4–5 minutes, or until the fish flakes when pierced with a fork. Combine soy and chilli sauces, stir gently into the fish mixture and cook for 2 minutes. Serve with steamed rice.

NUTRITIONAL VALUE: 23 g protein, 8 g fat ('good' fat), 6.5 g carbohydrate, 2.5 g dietary fibre, 810 kJ (195 Cals). An excellent source of vitamin C, a good source of niacin and provides some potassium, magnesium, zinc, iron and vitamin A.

CHINESE BROCCOLI WITH SESAME SEEDS

Serve this as a vegetable with roast duck or with other Chinese dishes.

2 tbsp sesame seeds
2 tsp sesame oil
2 cloves garlic
2 tsp chopped fresh ginger
1 bunch Chinese broccoli (gai larn)
2 tbsp oyster sauce
1 tbsp mirin (or use water)
1 tsp cornflour
2 tbsp water

SERVES 4

Heat a wok over a moderate heat, add the sesame seeds and brown them, stirring often to prevent burning. Tip onto a plate.

Pour the sesame oil into the hot wok and add the garlic, ginger and broccoli. Stir-fry for 2 minutes, add the oyster sauce and mirin, then cover and cook for another 2 minutes, stirring once. Combine cornflour and water, and add to wok, stirring. Sprinkle with sesame seeds and serve at once.

NUTRITIONAL VALUE: 4.5 g protein, 6 g fat ('good' fat), 7 g carbohydrate, 3.5 g dietary fibre, 400 kJ (95 Cals). An excellent source of vitamin C, a good source of vitamin A and provides some iron.

ANTI-COLD SOUP

This is a spicy soup that I eat whenever I think I am getting a cold. The chilli makes your nose run and clears the sinuses and the greens provide plenty of vitamin C. For me, the cold never comes.

2 tsp sesame oil
1–2 chillies, chopped
1 tbsp chopped fresh ginger
1 tbsp finely sliced lemongrass
2 cloves garlic, crushed
6 cups chicken stock
2 lime leaves (preferably fresh), shredded finely
300 g chicken breast, cut into strips (optional)
2 bunches Asian greens (e.g. tatsoi, bok choy, mustard greens), sliced
1 red capsicum, seeded and finely sliced
2 tbsp lemon juice
2 tsp fish sauce
300 g silken tofu, cut into cubes

SERVES 4

In a large saucepan, heat the sesame oil and cook the chillies, ginger, lemongrass and garlic over a gentle heat for 1–2 minutes. Add stock and lime leaves, and bring to the boil. Add the chicken and cook for 3 minutes. Stir in the Asian greens and capsicum, and simmer for a further 2 minutes. Add lemon juice, fish sauce and tofu and serve at once.

NUTRITIONAL VALUE: 30 g protein, 8.5 fat (good fat), 13 g carbohydrate, 5.5 g dietary fibre, 1020 kJ (245 Cals). An excellent source of vitamins A and C, and a good source of niacin, folate, potassium, magnesium, calcium, iron and zinc.

Asparagus

Asparagus is native to the region between the eastern parts of the Mediterranean and the Caucasus mountains. It has been cultivated for more than 2000 years and is a member of the lily family. In spring, asparagus shoots (called spears) emerge from clusters of buds that issue from an underground crown of roots. If not picked, the spears produce a stem with feathery leaves, commonly known as asparagus fern. The development of the fern allows the underground crown to store carbohydrate ready for the next season's crop. White asparagus, particularly popular in Japan and parts of Europe, is produced by mounding earth around the developing buds so they are not exposed to light. Once they reach the light, the spears turn green, so the grower must know exactly when they are about to reach beyond their cover to harvest them without colour. Purple asparagus spears are a hybrid variety that turn green during cooking, unless the cooking time is very short.

After asparagus is eaten, one of the amino acids present (asparagine aminosuccinic acid monoamide) breaks down to form methyl mercaptan, a compound with a distinctive odour, which is excreted in urine. Everyone produces this compound after eating asparagus, but only some people have the genes which enable them to detect its odour.

One of the best natural sources of folate (with 175 mg per 100 g), asparagus is also a source of vitamin E and contributes small quantities of many other vitamins and minerals as well as dietary fibre. An average 80 g portion has no fat, 1.5 g of dietary fibre and 80 kJ.

CHOOSING AND STORING • Asparagus is best in spring, but is now also harvested through summer. Choose firm, brittle spears with tightly closed tips. Avoid bunches where the ends are dry or split or the tips are damaged. If the spears are bent sideways near the tip, it means the asparagus was stored horizontally instead of upright; this does not affect eating quality. Thicker spears are not necessarily more fibrous and often have more flavour.

Asparagus can be stored in the refrigerator for 3–4 days, either in a plastic bag or with the spears placed upright in a glass containing 1 cm of water and the whole lot covered with a plastic bag. The earlier you use asparagus the better, as its sugars are used up as it ages and the spears develop tougher fibres.

PREPARATION AND COOKING • Break off the bottom of each asparagus stem at a point where it snaps easily. If the stems bend, they are fibrous and unpalatable. The bottom half of the stems of white asparagus may need to be peeled (use a potato peeler), but green asparagus does not need peeling.

Whole bunches can be cooked upright in an asparagus cooker (or in a deep saucepan, the tips hooded with foil), or steamed. You can also cook asparagus in a frying pan of boiling water, or cut the spears into shorter lengths and stir-fry. Do not overcook (2–4 minutes is usually enough), and always drain thoroughly. If using asparagus in a salad, cook for 1 minute only, and drain immediately. If you do not mind a slight loss of flavour, plunge the cooked spears into cold water to retain their green colour and crisp texture. If adding lemon juice, do so at the table as it bleaches the attractive green colour and makes the stems wrinkle.

ASPARAGUS AND PRAWN STIR-FRY

An easy recipe that looks as good as it tastes. For a vegetarian alternative, omit the prawns and instead add 300 g silken tofu, cut into 2.5 cm cubes, with the green shallots.

1 tbsp sesame oil
1 medium-sized onion, cut into 8 wedges
2 cloves garlic, crushed or sliced
1 small red chilli, finely sliced
2 tsp finely chopped fresh ginger
1 red capsicum, seeded and sliced
500 g green prawns, shelled and deveined
1 bunch (about 200 g) asparagus, cut into
*   5 cm lengths*
1/2 bunch green shallots (spring onions), cut
*   into 5 cm lengths*
1 tbsp salt-reduced soy sauce
1/2 tsp sugar
1/4 cup vegetable stock or water
1/2 cup fresh coriander leaves

SERVES 4

Heat the oil in a wok, add the onion and cook over a medium heat for 2–3 minutes. Add garlic, chilli, ginger and capsicum, and stir-fry for another 2–3 minutes. Push mixture to one side of the wok, add the prawns and asparagus, and continue stir-frying for 3–4 minutes, or until prawns turn pink. Do not overcook. Add the green shallots, soy sauce, sugar and stock or water and heat until boiling. Serve at once with steamed rice and with coriander scattered on top.

NUTRITIONAL VALUE: 29 g protein, 6 g fat (good fat), 6 g carbohydrate, 3 g dietary fibre, 830 kJ (200 Cals). A good source of vitamins A, C, niacin and folate, plus iron, calcium and zinc.

ASPARAGUS SALAD

A fine lunch dish or first course at dinner.

2 bunches (about 400 g) asparagus
2 tbsp pine nuts
300 g salad greens (e.g. lettuces including
*   mizuna, rocket)*
2 tbsp extra-virgin olive oil
1 tbsp lemon juice
1 tsp Dijon-style mustard
coarsely ground black pepper
1 punnet cherry tomatoes
2 hard-boiled eggs, shelled and finely chopped

SERVES 4

Trim the ends of the asparagus and place spears in a frying pan of boiling water. Cook for 2 minutes, tip into a colander and run under cold water. Drain.

Heat a dry frying pan, add pine nuts and shake gently over moderate heat until they are golden-brown. Tip onto a plate to cool.

Place salad greens in a bowl. Combine olive oil, lemon juice, mustard and pepper in a screw-top jar and shake until combined. Pour dressing over salad leaves and toss well. Tip salad leaves onto serving plates, arrange asparagus and cherry tomatoes on top and scatter with egg and pine nuts.

NUTRITIONAL VALUE: 9 g protein, 17 g fat ('good' fat), 5 g carbohydrate, 5 g dietary fibre, 860 kJ (205 Cals). A good source of vitamins A, C, E and folate, plus potassium and iron.

BARBECUED ASPARAGUS

An ideal accompaniment for barbecued or grilled meats, chicken or fish, or vegetable kebabs. Or serve in grilled Turkish bread with a good home-made mayonnaise.

2 bunches (about 400 g) asparagus
1 tbsp olive oil
1 tbsp lemon juice
2 tsp honey
2 tsp Dijon-style mustard
black pepper

SERVES 4

Snap ends off asparagus. In a flat dish, combine the oil, lemon juice, honey, mustard and pepper. Add asparagus, toss to combine, then cover and refrigerate for at least 10 minutes. Cook on a hot barbecue plate for about 2 minutes, turning once.

NUTRITIONAL VALUE: 3.5 g protein, 2.5 g fat ('good' fat), 5 g carbohydrate, 2 g dietary fibre, 235 kJ (55 Cals). A good source of vitamin C and folate, plus some potassium and iron.

Aubergines (see **Eggplant**)

Bamboo shoots

There are many varieties of bamboo, and many types of bamboo shoots. The shoots have a rounded base that tapers towards the top. Only the inner part of small shoots are eaten. Most people are familiar with canned bamboo shoots and they are available fresh at many Asian market stalls and in Chinatown precincts. They are popular in Pekinese and Shanghai cooking, and are also used in other parts of Asia and in South America. Some varieties used in Japan have a pungent odour.

Bamboo shoots are a good source of potassium. Half a cup of cooked bamboo shoots has virtually no fat and 30 kJ.

CHOOSING AND STORING • In China, winter bamboo shoots available are considered to have a superior flavour to the paler varieties sold in spring. Choose smaller shoots with a pale-yellow colour for the sweetest flavour; greener shoots are bitter.

In a plastic bag in the refrigerator, bamboo shoots will keep for up to a week.

PREPARATION AND COOKING • Fresh bamboo shoots contain hydrocyanic acid, a poisonous substance that is destroyed when the shoots are parboiled. To prepare the shoots, remove the leaves, cut off the tough base at the stem, peel away the outer layer and slice the central portion crosswise. Place the slices in a saucepan of cold water, bring to the boil and cook for 5 minutes. Drain well, and repeat with fresh water. The bitter taste should now be gone. You can either use the shoots at this stage or refrigerate them for up to 3 or 4 days.

BAMBOO SHOOTS WITH PORK

A stir-fry dish that cooks in about the same time as the accompanying rice. For a vegetarian version, omit the pork and add cubes of tofu at the same time as the fish sauce.

1 tbsp peanut oil
400 g pork fillet, sliced
2 cloves garlic, crushed
1 tsp dried shrimp paste (blachan)
1 small red chilli, sliced
1 cup sliced and parboiled bamboo shoots
1 bunch bok choy, washed
½ cup chicken or vegetable stock
1 tbsp fish sauce
2 tbsp lime juice

SERVES 4

Heat the peanut oil in a hot wok and stir-fry the pork until it changes colour. Add garlic, shrimp paste and chilli, and stir-fry for 2 minutes. Add bamboo shoots, bok choy and stock and cook for a further 2 minutes. Stir in fish sauce and lime juice. Serve with steamed rice or cooked noodles.

NUTRITIONAL VALUE: 26 g protein, 6.5 g fat ('good' fat), 4.5 g carbohydrate, 2 g dietary fibre, 740 kJ (175 Cals). An excellent source of vitamin C, good source of niacin, with some calcium, iron and zinc.

Beans

More than 12 000 species of beans, collectively known as legumes, have been cultivated for more than 7000 years. Most beans originated in Mexico, the warmer regions of Guatemala, or in Peru, Ecuador and Bolivia. When dried, their highly nutritious seeds are called pulses (sometimes *gram* in Asia). They are not covered in this book, though I have included a couple that are usually bought dried but are now also available fresh.

VARIETIES • *Green beans* are also known as French, runner, snap or stringless beans. Runner beans (which come from a climbing bean plant native to the higher mountains of Mexico) are occasionally called butter beans, although this name is more commonly used for dried lima beans. Older varieties of beans with strings, not surprisingly, are called string beans. They tend to have darker seeds, which can turn greyish when cooked. Modern pale-yellow bean hybrids are sometimes called wax beans (and occasionally but incorrectly, butter beans). There is also a purple variety which turns green when cooked and has an excellent flavour. All the newer bean cultivars have little or no strings, and fewer and paler seeds than the original string beans. Stringing beans is no longer a kitchen chore.

Green beans, including flat beans, are a good source of dietary fibre, folate and vitamin C. They also supply small quantities of iron and beta carotene. A 100 g serving has 3 g of dietary fibre, virtually no fat, and 85 kJ.

Flat beans, also called Italian flat beans or Roman beans, are wider than regular green beans and have a wavy appearance along one edge because of their seeds. The flavour is almost buttery, though they do not contain any fat. As their name suggests, they are popular in parts of Italy.

Snake beans can range from 20–90 cm in length, but when sold fresh are commonly about 40 cm long. The longer varieties originated in China and are popular in South-east Asia, where they are called yard-long beans or occasionally asparagus beans or long-podded cow peas. In southern China the whole bean is eaten, preferably while it is young and tender. In the north, the beans are left to mature and the seeds, known as black-eyed peas or black-eyed beans, are then consumed. Another variety of snake bean was also cultivated in Ethiopia from 4000 to 3000 BC and was later grown in India.

Snake beans are a good source of folate, vitamin C, dietary fibre and selenium. They also contribute beta carotene, potassium and small quantities of many minerals. One cup of sliced, cooked snake beans has virtually no fat, 3.5 g of dietary fibre, and 90 kJ.

Winged beans are also known as wing, four-angled, Manila, Goa and asparagus beans (the last, confusingly, a term also used for the snake bean). They are commonly grown in Thailand, Myanmar, Malaysia, India, Sri Lanka and Papua New Guinea, although the plant probably originated along the east African coast. Their tuberous roots, and their shoots, leaves, flowers, stems, pods and seeds are edible but only the green seeded pods are usually available in markets. The pods have four sides, each with a ridged serrated edge, and the central enclosure contains 5–25 tiny seeds, usually white or black but occasionally brown. The starchy tuberous roots are the favoured part of the plant in Papua New Guinea and the plants are grown in the Philippines because their large flowers and twining habit are so decorative.

Winged beans provide vitamin C, folate, dietary fibre and some protein. One cup of sliced, cooked winged beans has no fat and 90 kJ.

Borlotti beans are also called cranberry beans. They are occasionally available when young and fresh, although most of the crop is dried. When fresh, the pods have attractive cream and pink stripes and the seeds are speckled with cream, pink and brown. Although popularly thought to have originated in Italy, they are native to Central and South America.

Fresh borlotti beans are an excellent source of dietary fibre and a good source of iron, protein, potassium, selenium and folate. A ½-cup serving has 7.5 g of protein, 25 g of starchy carbohydrate, 7 g of dietary fibre, virtually no fat, and 540 kJ.

Broad beans are native to the eastern Mediterranean region from Turkey to Iraq and Iran. They are delightful eaten fresh, provided they are young: older, larger broad beans are best dried and are then commonly called fava beans. Some people from Mediterranean countries who lack a particular enzyme can develop a serious form of anaemia from vicine and convicine, two substances found in broad beans. The problem is apparent within 24 hours of eating broad beans and, in severe cases, can result in jaundice, internal bleeding and blood in the urine. Contact with the pollen from the bean flowers can also induce a reaction. If this problem runs in your family, you should avoid broad beans. Long cooking may reduce the problem, but all broad beans should be avoided by those with a genetically determined reaction to them.

Broad beans are highly nutritious, an excellent source of vitamin C, dietary fibre and the B complex vitamins, folate, niacin, pantothenic acid and biotin. They also contribute some protein. Half a cup of fresh broad beans has no fat, 5.5 g of dietary fibre, and 150 kJ.

Lima beans, also known as butter beans, hail from South and Central America and take their name from the capital of Peru, where they have been cultivated for thousands of years. Like borlotti beans, most of the crop is dried, but fresh lima beans are also available and are deliciously sweet when young. Lima beans come in various colours, from green to light brown, sometimes splashed with red. These need to be soaked to remove poisonous cyanogenetic glucosides. Modern varieties with white or very pale green seeds, including those sold as fresh beans, do not contain these substances and so do not need to be soaked before use.

Fresh lima beans are a good source of dietary fibre, protein, starchy carbohydrate, magnesium, potassium, and contribute some folate and vitamins C and E. Half a cup of cooked beans has 6 g of protein, no fat, 20 g of starchy carbohydrate, 4.5 g of dietary fibre, and 435 kJ.

Fresh soy beans are new to many westerners, who are more familiar with the dried variety. Fresh green soy beans are available from Asian food stores, either fresh or as frozen green seeds. Apart from breast milk, soy beans come closer than any other food to providing a full complement of nutrients. They originated in China, where they have been cultivated for almost 5000 years, but are also popular in other Asian countries, either fresh or dried, or processed into soy drinks, tofu or tempeh. Fresh soy beans have three to six bright-green seeds enclosed in a greenish, slightly furry pod, which is inedible. Don't be tempted to eat fresh soy beans raw, because they contain a substance that inhibits the action of trypsin, an enzyme secreted by the pancreas and necessary for the digestion of protein. Eating a couple of raw soy beans will not cause problems, but boiling destroys the inhibitor.

Fresh soy beans are highly nutritious, providing an excellent source of folate, vitamin C and dietary fibre. They are also a good source of protein, iron, calcium,

potassium, various vitamins of the B complex, selenium, essential fatty acids, magnesium, zinc and phytoestrogens (52 mg per 100 g). Half a cup of the green seeds has 10 g protein, 5.5 g of fat (mostly essential unsaturated fat), 490 kJ and 3.5 g of dietary fibre.

CHOOSING AND STORING • *Green beans* are best in the summer months. Select pods that are crisp and bright in colour and snap easily and cleanly. Reject any that are limp, where the seeds are large enough to burst through the pods or where the ends are broken.

Flat beans are available in summer and autumn. Select those with small seeds, which will have only small swellings along the length of the bean.

Snake beans are available in autumn. Choose beans that look firm, without obvious signs of withering at the ends or any dehydration along the length.

Winged beans are available in spring. Look for crisp pods, preferably about 10 cm long. The alternative name 'asparagus bean' refers to the fact that these beans are delicious steamed and eaten in the fingers, like asparagus.

Fresh borlotti beans are available for a few weeks at the end of winter or in early spring. Make sure the beans are crisp and firm: if the pod is limp or the seeds have burst through, the beans will be tough. When shelled, 500 g of borlotti beans give about 1½ cups of beans.

Fresh broad beans are available in early spring. After that, they become tough and are less attractive. When shelled, 500 g of broad beans with small seeds give 1 cup of beans.

Fresh lima beans are sold only for a few weeks in autumn. Choose pods that are pale cream. If they have turned yellow, the seeds will have lost their sweetness and need to be dried. When shelled, 500 g of lima beans gives 1½ cups of beans.

Fresh soy beans appear briefly in late summer and early autumn. Choose beans that have intact firm pods. Until recently, many fresh soy beans have been frozen to service Asian food stores, but more fresh beans are beginning to reach the market. When removed from their pods, 500 g of soy beans gives 1½ cups of bright-green seeds.

Do not wash beans until ready to use. Refrigerate green or flat beans in a plastic bag for up to 5 days. Borlotti, broad, lima, soy and snake beans should also be kept in a plastic bag in the fridge, but are best eaten soon after purchase, preferably within 3 days. Winged beans need to be eaten within 2 days of purchase.

PREPARATION AND COOKING • Prepare *green or flat beans* just before cooking by removing tops and tails. They can be cooked whole or cut into pieces. Do not overcook, or they will become a greyish-green and lose many nutrients into the cooking water. If boiling, use a large amount of water and cook with the lid off for 3–5 minutes. This retains the best colour but will result in greater vitamin loss than steaming.

Snake beans have no strings and need no preparation apart from cutting them into shorter more manageable lengths before steaming or stir-frying. They need only a few minutes cooking or they lose some of their bright colour.

Winged beans should be cooked as they contain a substance that can prevent proper action of some protein-splitting enzymes within the body. They need no preparation and are usually sliced across the bean and stir-fried.

With fresh *borlotti and lima beans*, remove seeds from pods and boil or steam until just tender—usually 10 minutes.

Very young baby *broad beans* picked straight from the garden when less than 10 cm long can be eaten whole, pod and all. However, broad beans sold in shops will usually have passed this stage and the pods should be removed. It is also best to remove the slightly fibrous skin of the podded beans as this exposes the sweetness of the inner bean. It is a fiddly task, but easier if you first place the seeds into a pot of boiling water and cook for 3 minutes. Tip them into a colander and run under cold water: the skins will slip off easily and you can then reheat the bright-green, sweet-tasting beans.

Fresh soy beans are fiddly to pod, so drop them whole into boiling water and cook for 3 minutes. Use the bright-green seeds either as a vegetable or in salads or other dishes. In Taiwan, Hong Kong and Singapore, the lightly steamed green beans are sold as a snack to serve with drinks.

GREEN BEAN SALAD

This recipe uses both green and flat beans. You can use just one variety and double the quantity. Served with good bread, it makes an ideal dish for lunch or a summer supper. A variation is to drain the beans and toss them with the dressing while still hot: serve at once.

2 tbsp flaked almonds
500 g green beans
500 g flat beans
2 tbsp extra-virgin olive oil
finely grated peel of 1 lemon
2 tsp white-wine vinegar
freshly ground pepper
50 g shaved parmesan

SERVES 4

Toast almonds in a dry frying pan over medium heat until golden-brown. Tip onto a plate to cool.

Bring a large saucepan of water to the boil, add both types of beans and cook for 2–3 minutes. Tip immediately into a colander, run under cold water and drain well.

Combine olive oil, lemon peel, vinegar and pepper. Place beans in a serving dish and add dressing, tossing gently to coat beans. To serve, arrange beans on individual dishes and top with parmesan and almonds.

NUTRITIONAL VALUE: 11 g protein, 17 g fat (good fat), 6.5 g carbohydrate, 7.5 g dietary fibre, 930 kJ (220 Cals). A good source of vitamin C, iron, zinc, potassium and folate, and provides some vitamin E.

Soy-bean snacks

Serve these snacks with drinks. If concerned about salt, omit it.

2 tbsp sesame seeds
400 g fresh green soy beans (or use 300 g
*   frozen green soy beans)*
1 tsp ground Szechuan pepper
1 tsp sea salt
1 tsp chilli flakes

SERVES 8

Toast sesame seeds in a dry frying pan until golden-brown. Tip onto a plate and allow to cool.

Drop the whole beans into boiling water and cook for 3 minutes. When cool enough to handle, remove pods. (If using frozen soy beans, cook in boiling water for 3 minutes and then drain well.) Combine sesame seeds, pepper, salt and chilli flakes in a plastic bag. Add beans and shake to coat. Serve as a nibble.

NUTRITIONAL VALUE: 6 g protein, 4 g fat ('good' fat), 5 g carbohydrate, 2 g dietary fibre, 320 kJ (75 Cals). A good source of iron.

Green bean, tomato and mint omelette

A good summer dish.

2 medium-sized tomatoes
250 g green beans, topped, tailed and cut into
*   5 cm lengths*
2 tsp olive oil
4 eggs
¼ cup water
½ cup sliced green shallots (spring onions)
2 tbsp chopped fresh mint
freshly ground pepper

SERVES 2

Bring a saucepan of water to the boil. Remove cores from tomatoes and cut a shallow cross in the end. Slip the tomatoes into the boiling water and leave for 1 minute then remove using a slotted spoon. When cool enough to handle, remove the skins and dice the flesh.

Drop the beans into boiling water and cook for 3–4 minutes. Drain.

Heat oil in a heavy-based frying pan. Beat eggs and water, and pour mixture into pan. When it begins to set, add the beans, tomatoes and green onions. Continue cooking, lifting edges of the omelette mixture to allow any uncooked mixture to run underneath. When almost set, sprinkle with mint and pepper, and fold in half. Cut in half to serve.

NUTRITIONAL VALUE: 17 g protein, 15 g fat, 6.5 g carbohydrate, 5.5 g dietary fibre, 955 kJ (230 Cals). A good source of vitamins A, C and riboflavin, and also provides iron, zinc, potassium, calcium and magnesium.

BORLOTTI BEAN PURÉE

This purée can be served with grilled vegetables or as part of an antipasto plate. It is one of the few dishes that I think needs some salt.

1 head garlic, left whole
1 kg borlotti beans, shelled
1 tbsp extra-virgin olive oil
2 tbsp lemon juice
sea salt
freshly ground pepper

SERVES 4

Preheat oven to 190°C. Cut the garlic in half across the centre and roast for 30 minutes.

Meanwhile, cook the beans in a large saucepan of boiling water for 15 minutes, or until soft. Drain, reserving a little of the water.

Squeeze the roasted garlic to extract its soft flesh. Place garlic, beans, olive oil and lemon juice in a food processor and process until smooth. Add salt and pepper to taste. Serve warm.

NUTRITIONAL VALUE: 10 g protein, 5.5 g fat ('good' fat), 32 g carbohydrate, 10 g dietary fibre, 895 kJ (215 Cals). A good source of iron and potassium, and provides some vitamin E.

BROAD BEANS AND PEAS, WITH CRUSTY TOPPING

A simple dish, but always popular.

1.5 kg fresh broad beans, shelled
2 slices wholemeal bread
1/2 cup parsley sprigs
1 tbsp chopped walnuts
1 tbsp olive oil
1 medium-sized onion, chopped finely
2 cups (400 g) frozen peas

SERVES 4

Cook broad beans in boiling water for 3 minutes. Drain in a colander, run cold water over beans, then peel.

Place the bread and parsley in a food processor and process to fine crumbs. Stir in the walnuts and set aside.

Heat oil in frying pan and cook onion over a gentle heat, without browning, for 5 minutes. Add crumb mixture and stir well to combine.

Preheat griller. Meanwhile, cook peas in a small amount of boiling water until just tender (about 3 minutes). Add peeled beans and bring back to the boil. Drain beans and peas, and place in an ovenproof dish. Sprinkle crumb mixture on top and place under griller until crumbs are golden-brown. Serve at once.

NUTRITIONAL VALUE: 14 g protein, 7.5 g fat ('good' fat), 13 g carbohydrate, 12 g dietary fibre, 740 kJ (175 Cals). A good source of vitamins A, C, E, niacin and folate, and also of iron, zinc and potassium.

BROAD BEANS WITH TOMATOES

Delicious on a cold day, accompanied by thick slabs of wholemeal toast.

1 kg fresh broad beans, shelled
1 tbsp olive oil
1 medium-sized onion
2 cloves garlic, crushed
1 tbsp fresh lemon thyme (or 1 tsp dried)
4 large tomatoes
2 tbsp water
2 tbsp chopped parsley

SERVES 4

Cook broad beans in boiling water for 3 minutes. Drain in a colander, run cold water over, then peel.

Heat oil in a large saucepan and cook onion, garlic and thyme over a gentle heat for 5 minutes. Meanwhile, remove core from tomatoes and cut a shallow cross on the bottom end. Place tomatoes in a bowl and pour boiling water over them. Leave for 1 minute, then drain, remove skin and chop the flesh.

Add beans, tomatoes and water to onions, bring to the boil and simmer for 5 minutes. Add parsley and serve at once.

NUTRITIONAL VALUE: 6.5 g protein, 5.5 g fat ('good' fat), 5 g carbohydrate, 6.5 g dietary fibre, 400 kJ (95 Cals). A good source of potassium and vitamins A, C and folate, and also provides some iron and zinc.

LIMA BEAN AND CORN SALAD

Use fresh beans and canned or frozen corn for a salad with 'body'.

500g fresh lima beans, shelled
400 g canned corn kernels, drained
½ red capsicum, seeded and sliced
2 medium-sized tomatoes, diced
1 avocado, peeled, seeded and sliced
8 iceberg lettuce leaves

DRESSING
2 tbsp extra-virgin olive oil
1 tbsp white-wine vinegar
2 tsp Dijon-style mustard
1 tbsp chopped chives
freshly ground black pepper

SERVES 4

Cook lima beans in a saucepan of boiling water for 10 minutes, then drain. Combine beans, corn, capsicum, tomatoes and avocado.

To make the dressing, combine the oil, vinegar, mustard, chives and pepper. Add to the vegetables and toss carefully to combine.

To serve, spoon salad into the lettuce leaves.

NUTRITIONAL VALUE: 10 g protein, 19 g fat ('good' fat), 33 g carbohydrate, 10 g dietary fibre, 1435 kJ (345 Cals). A good source of vitamins A, C and folate, and also provides potassium, iron, magnesium and zinc.

WINGED BEANS IN COCONUT MILK

Delicious hot, but it can also be served cold as a salad. Coconut milk is high in saturated fat, so this dish is not suitable for those with high cholesterol levels.

2 tbsp crushed peanuts
4 cups winged beans, sliced thinly
2 tsp sesame oil
1 medium-sized onion, sliced
2 cloves garlic, sliced
1–2 tbsp Thai red curry paste
2 tbsp lime juice
1 tsp palm sugar or brown sugar
¾ cup coconut milk

SERVES 4

Toast nuts in a dry frying pan over medium heat, shaking frequently, until lightly browned. Tip onto a plate to cool.

Add sliced winged beans to a saucepan of boiling water. Cook for 2 minutes then drain.

Add oil to a hot wok and cook the onion and garlic for 5 minutes. Stir in the curry paste, lime juice, sugar and coconut milk, and bring to the boil. Add winged beans and cook for 1 minute. Serve topped with peanuts, accompanied by steamed rice.

NUTRITIONAL VALUE: 6.5 g protein, 18 g fat, 8 g carbohydrate, 2 g dietary fibre, 865 kJ (205 Cals). Provides iron and vitamin C.

SNAKE-BEAN, PEANUT AND CHICKEN STIR-FRY

A fast and easy recipe that children enjoy. Serve with steamed rice. If you are cooking for adults or teenagers, add a small sliced hot chilli with the chicken. For vegetarians, omit the chicken and double the quantity of peanuts.

2 tbsp unsalted peanuts
1 tbsp peanut oil
300 g chicken strips
1 medium-sized onion, cut into 8 wedges
2 cloves garlic, crushed
500 g snake beans, cut into 6 cm lengths
1 red capsicum, seeded and sliced
200 g button mushrooms, sliced
¼ cup oyster sauce
¼ cup water
juice of 1 lime or lemon
fresh coriander leaves

SERVES 4

Heat a dry wok and toss peanuts until they begin to brown. Tip onto a plate.

Add oil to wok and when it is hot add the chicken, onion and garlic. Stir-fry for about 5 minutes, or until chicken is brown. Add snake beans, capsicum and mushrooms, and continue stir-frying for another 2 minutes. Combine oyster sauce and water, and add to wok. Cover and cook for about 2 minutes, or until vegetables are tender-crisp. Add lime or lemon juice and serve at once, sprinkled with the peanuts and coriander leaves.

NUTRITIONAL VALUE: 27 g protein, 11 g fat ('good' fat), 12 g carbohydrate, 7.5 g dietary fibre, 1070 kJ (255 Cals). A good source of iron, zinc, potassium, magnesium, folate, niacin and vitamins A and C.

GADO GADO SALAD

A filling and delicious salad.

THE SALAD

400 g potatoes (Jersey royal, Desirée or
Nicola), steamed and sliced
300 g snake beans, cut into 10 cm lengths,
steamed
250 g mung-bean sprouts
½ small Chinese cabbage, shredded
1 medium-sized carrot, peeled and cut into
julienne strips
½ red capsicum, seeded and cut into strips
½ green capsicum, seeded and cut into strips
4 eggs, hard boiled

PEANUT SAUCE

2 tsp sesame oil
1 small onion, chopped finely
1 clove garlic, crushed
1 tsp chopped chilli
2 tsp dried shrimp paste (blachan)
1 tbsp tomato paste
½ cup (75 g) crushed peanuts
1 tbsp peanut butter
½ cup coconut milk
½ cup water
2 tbsp salt-reduced soy sauce
2 tbsp lime or lemon juice

SERVES 4

First make the sauce. Heat the sesame oil in a saucepan and add onion, garlic, chilli, and shrimp paste. Cover and cook over a medium heat for 4–5 minutes, stirring once or twice. Add tomato paste, peanuts, peanut butter, coconut milk and water, and stir over a low heat for 5 minutes. Add soy sauce and lime or lemon juice.

To serve the salad arrange vegetables and eggs on a large platter. Drizzle sauce over the top.

NUTRITIONAL VALUE: 18 g protein, 15 g fat ('good' fat), 24 g carbohydrate, 12 g dietary fibre, 1270 kJ (305 Cals). Provides a good source of iron, magnesium, potassium, calcium and vitamins A, B, C and E.

FLAT BEANS WITH OLIVES AND ANCHOVIES

Delicious served in split toasted pita bread with hummus.

500 g flat beans, left whole
2 tsp olive oil
12 black olives
2 large or 4 small anchovy fillets, chopped
1 lemon, sliced

SERVES 4

Steam or boil the beans for about 8 minutes, or until tender. Place in a heated serving bowl and add the oil, olives, anchovies and lemon slices. Toss gently to combine. Serve hot or warm.

NUTRITIONAL VALUE: 4 g protein, 4 g fat (good fat), 3.5 g carbohydrate, 4.5 g dietary fibre, 290 kJ (70 Cals). A good source of vitamin C and provides some vitamin A, folate, iron and zinc.

Bean sprouts (see **Sprouts**)

Beetroot

In many parts of the world, beetroot are referred to as 'beets'. Originally native to the Mediterranean region, including North Africa, beetroot also grew as far away as the United Kingdom and India. The leaves were once considered more important as a food source than the root, which does not seem to have been eaten to any extent until about the sixteenth century. The wild roots were long, thin and white. Cultivated varieties are the familiar deep red-purple colour, but white beets are also grown in many areas as a source of processed white sugar—hence the term 'sugarbeet'. The beetroot we eat as a vegetable has about 7 per cent sugar, while the sugarbeet varieties contain about 20 per cent sugar. The colder the growing temperature, the deeper the red-purple colour of the beetroot. Orange-fleshed beetroot, quaintly called mangel worzels, and looking like large turnips, are grown as animal feed in parts of England. Some can reach 4–5 kg in weight.

Beetroot's major nutritional contribution is its high folate content. It also provides some dietary fibre, some iron (it is not a rich source, as is popularly believed) and a small quantity of vitamin C. Beetroot also contain some valuable antioxidants belonging to the cyanine and xanthin families. These are missing from sugarbeet. A medium-sized beetroot (around 130 g) has virtually no fat, 11 g of carbohydrate, 4 g of dietary fibre and 225 kJ. The leaves are rich in beta carotene, which the body converts to vitamin A, and also supply vitamin C, calcium, potassium, magnesium and iron. A cup of raw leaves has no fat, 1.5 g of dietary fibre and 30 kJ.

CHOOSING AND STORING • Beetroot are available all year round, but their flavour is best during winter and spring. Choose well-shaped specimens with a deep-purple colour. Any leaves still attached should look fresh, not wilted.

Remove any leaves, leaving about 2.5 cm of stems attached. Store in a plastic bag in the refrigerator for a week or more: do not wash beforehand, as wet beetroot tend to rot easily.

PREPARATION AND COOKING • Before using beetroot, wash well but try not to break the skin or the colour will bleed. If serving raw, remove skin using a potato peeler and grate the flesh or cut into fine julienne sticks. If cooking the bulbs, do not peel or trim the stems. Boil or steam for 30–60 minutes, depending on the size: they should pierce easily with a fine skewer when cooked. Leave until cool enough to handle, put on rubber gloves (to prevent staining) and slip the skins off by rubbing gently.

Adding a couple of cloves to the cooking water gives beetroot a delightful flavour. Medium-sized beetroot are also delicious wrapped individually in foil and baked in a moderate oven for about 45 minutes; they develop an earthy flavour and are slightly drier than when boiled or steamed. You can also microwave beetroot with about $\frac{1}{4}$ cup of water for about 10 minutes. Beetroot goes well with strongly flavoured meats and is also good with citrus flavours and caraway seeds.

Young beetroot leaves can be steamed or stir-fried. Mature beetroot leaves, such as those attached to fully grown beetroot, can be used like spinach but are bitter. They are highly nutritious, but like some other leaves contain oxalic acid which can interfere with absorption of minerals such as calcium, iron and zinc. This is only likely to be a problem where large quantities are consumed on a daily basis: an occasional meal containing beetroot leaves will not cause any problems.

BEETROOT RELISH

Serve with duck, kangaroo, lamb or beef. It is also delicious with steamed Jersey royal, Nicola, kipfler or nadine potatoes or as part of a meal with hummus and grilled Turkish bread.

1 tsp cumin seeds
2 tsp sesame seeds
2 medium-sized beetroot, peeled
2 tsp olive oil
1 small onion, finely chopped
1 clove garlic, crushed
1/2 cup red wine

SERVES 4

Heat a frying pan and add the cumin and sesame seeds. Cook for 1–2 minutes, stirring constantly, until sesame seeds are golden-brown. Remove from the pan and set aside. Grate the raw beetroot coarsely (a food processor makes this easy).

Add the olive oil to a hot frying pan and cook onion and garlic for about 3 minutes, without allowing onion to brown. Add the beetroot and continue cooking, stirring, for 3–4 minutes. Add the red wine and simmer for 3 minutes, stirring occasionally, then stir in the cumin and sesame seeds.

NUTRITIONAL VALUE: 2 g protein, 3.5 g fat, 7.5 g carbohydrate, 3 g dietary fibre, 280 kJ (65 Cals). Provides some iron and folate.

BEETROOT AND POTATO SALAD

Looks pretty, tastes good and is filling enough to appeal to those who consider salads 'rabbit food'.

4 medium-sized beetroot, washed
4 cloves
400 g potatoes (Jersey royal, bintje, kipfler
    or sebago)
200 g natural yoghurt
2 tsp finely grated orange peel
2 tbsp orange juice
2 tsp grainy mustard
1/2 cup shredded fresh mint

SERVES 4

Trim beetroot stalks to 2 cm. Place beetroot in saucepan, cover with water and add cloves. Bring to the boil, cover, and simmer for 30 minutes or until just tender. Drain and when cool enough to handle, slip off skins. Cut into 1.5 cm dice.

Steam the potatoes, peel and cut into 1.5 cm dice.

Mix together the yoghurt, orange peel and juice, and mustard.

Gently combine with the beetroot, potatoes and mint. Serve warm or chilled.

NUTRITIONAL VALUE: 8.5 g protein, 2.5 g fat, 29 g carbohydrate, 6.5 g dietary fibre, 660 kJ (155 Cals). If using fat-reduced yoghurt, fat content is 0.5 g per serving. Also a good source of folate, vitamin C, potassium, iron and zinc, and provides some calcium.

BEETROOT SOUP

This soup is equally good hot or cold. Use low-fat yoghurt if you prefer, but the texture will not be as good. For a vegetarian version, omit the bacon and use 1 tbsp olive oil to cook the onion and caraway.

2 rashers bacon, diced
1 tsp caraway seeds
1 medium-sized onion, chopped
1 carrot, diced
1 parsnip, diced
1 stalk celery, sliced
4 medium-sized beetroot, peeled, washed
*   and diced*
800 g canned tomatoes
2 cups water
2 cups shredded Chinese cabbage
another medium-sized beetroot, peeled and
*   coarsely grated*
2 tbsp wine vinegar
freshly ground pepper
200 g thick yoghurt

SERVES 4

In a large saucepan, sauté the bacon, caraway seeds and onion for 3 minutes, stirring occasionally. Add carrot, parsnip and celery, and cook for a further 2 minutes. Add the diced beetroot, the tomatoes and the water, bring to the boil, cover and simmer for 15 minutes or until vegetables are tender.

Purée in batches and return soup to saucepan. Bring to the boil, add cabbage and grated beetroot, and simmer for 5 minutes.

If serving soup chilled, cool and refrigerate at this stage. Just before serving (hot or cold), add wine vinegar and pepper. Serve in deep bowls, topped with a dollop of yoghurt, swirled through the soup with a fork.

NUTRITIONAL VALUE: 13 g protein, 5 g fat, 30 g carbohydrate, 11 g dietary fibre, 905 kJ (215 Cals). A good source of vitamins A, C, niacin and folate, and also of potassium, iron, zinc, magnesium and calcium.

Bitter melon (see **Other vegetables**)

Bok choy (see **Asian greens**)

Breadfruit

Native to Malaysia and now popular throughout the islands of Polynesia, bread-fruit gets its name from its texture and taste. It has achieved some historical significance because the *HMS Bounty* was sent by the British government to take breadfruit trees from Otaheite to the West Indies in 1788. Captain Bligh was nicknamed 'Breadfruit Bligh'.

The breadfruit tree grows quickly and mature trees can produce 700 fruit, ranging from 1–4 kg in weight, in a season. The massive breadfruit has a knobbly green skin which ripens to a dirty yellow colour. When ripe, the flesh is creamy-yellow. The skin is not eaten, but the seeds (dark and about the size of a watermelon seed) can be roasted or boiled. In New Guinea, the flesh is discarded and only the seeds are eaten. In most other areas, the flesh is prepared as a savoury dish—with chilli, spices and coconut in parts of Asia and on some Pacific Islands, cooked in a ground oven in a similar way to yams or potatoes. The flesh has a slight banana flavour.

Breadfruit is a starchy vegetable with little protein or fat, but it is a good source of fibre, vitamin C and potassium, and supplies small quantities of iron. A 200 g portion has 54 g of carbohydrate, 10 g of fibre and 860 kJ. Breadfruit seeds provide some protein and are a good source of iron, potassium, magnesium, vitamin C, niacin, pantothenic acid and vitamin B_6. A 50 g serving of seeds has less than 1 g of fat and provides 770 kJ.

CHOOSING AND STORING • Breadfruit is usually available during summer. Choose one that is firm and has an unbroken skin. To see how close the flesh is to being ripe, press gently near the stalk end, which should give slightly. You can tell if the fruit is ripe by making a small cut near the stem: the flesh should be a creamy yellow.

Store breadfruit whole in the refrigerator for up to a week. To ripen, remove from the fridge and leave at room temperature for a day or so.

PREPARATION AND COOKING • Breadfruit can be eaten ripe as a fruit, or picked under-ripe while still starchy and then boiled or roasted to use as a vegetable. It is often cored and stuffed with coconut before roasting.

Like many starchy foods, breadfruit can be bland so it may need spices, chilli or onion to add flavour. Usually it is peeled with a sharp knife and cut into wedges which are steamed, rolled in spices and baked or fried, or made into thin crisps. Or halve the breadfruit, leave its skin on but scoop out most of the flesh to leave a shell about 2 cm thick: stuff with a spicy minced-meat mixture and bake for about 1½ hours, or until tender.

These recipes come from my brother-in-law Henk de Jong, an excellent cook who lived for some years in Fiji.

CHILLED BREADFRUIT SOUP

Serve on its own as a lunch dish.

1 tbsp macadamia oil
1 large onion, diced
4 cloves garlic, chopped
2 litres chicken stock
1 medium-sized breadfruit (1.5–2 kg) peeled,
    cored and chopped
1 cup light coconut milk
2 cups fat-reduced milk
salt to taste
$^1\!/_2$ tsp black pepper
freshly grated nutmeg

SERVES 6

Heat the oil in a large heavy saucepan and cook the onion and garlic for 5 minutes. Add the chicken stock, bring to the boil then add the breadfruit and simmer for 20–30 minutes, or until breadfruit is tender. Purée in batches in a blender. Stir in the coconut milk, milk, salt and pepper, and chill for about 3 hours. Scatter with fresh grated nutmeg before serving.

NUTRITIONAL VALUE: 8.5 g protein, 9 g fat, 53 g carbohydrate, 9.5 g dietary fibre, 1335 kJ (320 Cals). An excellent source of vitamin C, a good source of niacin, potassium, magnesium, calcium and iron.

BREADFRUIT SALAD

In Fiji this dish is served as part of a meal, usually with fish. If preferred, de-seed the chilli to reduce its heat, then chop finely.

1 unripe breadfruit
3 cloves garlic, chopped finely
1 medium-sized red onion, chopped finely
1 medium-sized green cucumber, peeled and
    thinly sliced
$^1\!/_4$ red capsicum, finely chopped
$^1\!/_4$ green capsicum, finely chopped
1 tbsp finely chopped parsley
1 fresh red chilli
$1^1\!/_2$ cups fresh lime juice
1 cup water
freshly ground pepper
extra parsley

SERVES 6

Peel the breadfruit thickly. Quarter it, remove the core, cut flesh into cubes and place in cold salted water to prevent discolouration. Drain, add to a pot of boiling water and cook for 20–25 minutes or until fork-tender (the cubes will float initially but then sink in the water as they cook). Remove the breadfruit, drain and place in salad bowl.

Combine garlic, onion, cucumber, capsicums, parsley, chilli, lime juice and water. Pour over the breadfruit, cover and refrigerate for 3–5 hours or overnight. Drain off liquid before serving chilled.

NUTRITIONAL VALUE: 3.5 g protein, 0.5 g fat, 45 g carbohydrate, 9.5 g dietary fibre, 810 kJ (195 Cals). An excellent source of vitamin C, a good source of potassium and provides some vitamin A, magnesium and iron.

ROASTED BREADFRUIT

One of the most popular ways to enjoy bread-fruit in Fiji.

1 medium-sized breadfruit, about 1.5–2 kg

SERVES 4

Roast the breadfruit whole over charcoal (the best method), or on a barbecue or directly over a gas burner. Turn the fruit as it begins to char and continue cooking for 1 hour: when steam starts to escape from the stem end, the breadfruit is done. Cut a circle at the stem end, scoop out the core and discard it. Scoop out the flesh, or cut off the charred outer skin and then slice the flesh. Serve hot.

NUTRITIONAL VALUE: 3.5 g protein, 1 g fat, 61 g carbohydrate, 13 g dietary fibre, 1070 kJ (255 Cals). An excellent source of vitamin C, a good source of potassium and provides some niacin, magnesium and iron.

Broccoli

Native to the eastern shores of the Mediterranean, broccoli is a member of the Brassica family and developed at some stage from a wild cabbage. It was known to the Romans in the second century and was cultivated in Italy from the seventeenth century (it was then known as Italian asparagus). A number of varieties are now available. They include the familiar green heads, sprouting broccoli with smaller heads on individual stems (often sold tied in bunches), purple-tinged broccoli which matures in summer and also known as calabrese, and broccolini, a new hybrid of broccoli and Chinese kale.

Broccoli, like all Brassicas, is a source of sulphur-containing compounds called isothiocyanates. These produce the characteristic odour during cooking, which becomes stronger the longer broccoli is cooked. To make broccoli more attractive to reluctant eaters, cook it briefly and serve while still crisp and bright-green.

Broccoli is one of the most nutritious of all vegetables. It is an excellent source of antioxidants, vitamin C, dietary fibre and folate and also supplies iron, calcium, vitamin E and beta carotene (which is converted to vitamin A in the body). As a bonus, many of the sulphur-containing compounds in broccoli, including sulphoraphane and other isothiocyanates, appear to have anti-cancer properties. A 100 g serving of cooked broccoli has virtually no fat or carbohydrate, but provides several days' supply of vitamin C, 4 g of dietary fibre and 100 kJ. Purple or sprouting broccoli has even more vitamin C, is very high in folate (195 mg per 100 g), has almost twice as much iron and three times as much calcium. It has more kilojoules, but like all vegetables, a 100 g serving has only a moderate 150 kJ. Broccolini has similar nutritional virtues to regular broccoli. Because the stems are consumed, the levels of some nutrients may be slightly higher.

CHOOSING AND STORING • Broccoli is available year-round, but the best supplies occur in winter and spring. Choose closely bunched, firm heads of bright-green or green-blue broccoli with firm stems. Avoid any florets that are yellowing, limp or developing brownish patches. Also avoid woody stalks with a hollow at the cut end, as they will be tough and bitter. Broccolini looks like a cross between slender broccoli and asparagus. It is sold in neat bunches: the stalks are the best indicator of freshness—they should be crisp.

Broccoli leaves are rich in vitamins and antioxidants. Slice and stir-fry or use as you would spinach.

Store broccoli in a plastic bag in the refrigerator for up to 5 days.

PREPARATION AND COOKING • Broccoli needs no preparation other than trimming the stalks and breaking or cutting the florets into evenly sized portions. Suitable cooking methods include steaming, boiling, microwaving and stir-frying; the stalks can be removed and stir-fried separately, if desired. Broccoli can be eaten raw, but it loses its rather bitter flavour if it is first cooked for up to a minute in boiling water: drain, then run under cold water to preserve a slight crispness that will make it ideal to use with dips or as a crudité. Many small children enjoy the appearance of broccoli 'trees'.

BROCCOLI AND WALNUT PASTA

A quick meal that's handy to serve unexpected guests. If you like, you could use broccolini cut into 5 cm pieces instead of regular broccoli.

2 tbsp walnut pieces
375 g pasta bows, shells or spirals
1 tbsp olive oil
2 cloves garlic, crushed
1 cup sliced green shallots (spring onions)
500 g broccoli, broken into florets
2 tsp finely grated lemon peel
2 tbsp lemon juice
freshly grated black pepper
freshly grated parmesan

SERVES 4

Brown walnuts in a dry frying pan, stirring and taking care they do not burn. Set aside.

Cook the pasta in a large quantity of boiling salted water until just tender. Meanwhile, add olive oil to a hot wok and sauté the garlic and green shallots over a gentle heat for 2 minutes. When the pasta is almost tender, add the broccoli to the saucepan and cook for 2–3 minutes. Drain, then add pasta and broccoli to the wok with lemon peel and juice, pepper and walnuts. Toss gently to combine. Serve topped with parmesan.

NUTRITIONAL VALUE: 22 g protein, 14 g fat ('good' fat), 68 g carbohydrate, 11 g dietary fibre, 2065 kJ (495 Cals). It is an excellent source of vitamin C and a good source of folate, vitamin A, calcium, potassium, magnesium, iron and zinc.

STIR-FRIED BROCCOLINI

Serve with rice, or as an accompaniment to grilled fish, chicken or steak.

1 bunch broccolini
2 tsp sesame oil
1 medium-sized onion, sliced
2 tbsp hoisin sauce
2 tbsp mirin or dry sherry
1 tsp honey
2 tbsp water

SERVES 4

Steam broccolini until barely tender (about 3 minutes).

Add sesame oil and onion to a hot frying pan, cover and allow to sweat over a gentle heat for 3–4 minutes.

Combine hoisin sauce, mirin or sherry, honey and water. Add this mixture and the broccolini to the frying pan and cook for 1 minute, stirring to coat the broccolini with the sauce. Serve at once.

NUTRITIONAL VALUE: 6.5 g protein, 3.5 g fat ('good' fat), 7 g carbohydrate, 6.5 g dietary fibre, 360 kJ (85 Cals). An excellent source of vitamin C, a good source of folate and provides some vitamin A, potassium, iron and zinc.

BROCCOLI SOUP

A small amount of cream gives texture to this soup, but if you must restrict your intake of saturated fat, omit the cream and use fat-reduced milk.

1 tbsp olive oil
1 large onion, chopped roughly
2 cloves garlic, chopped
750 g broccoli, chopped roughly
3 cups chicken stock
3 or 4 large sprigs fresh mint
1 cup milk
2 tbsp cream
a pinch of nutmeg
freshly ground black pepper

SERVES 4

Heat the olive oil in a large saucepan, add the onion and garlic, cover and allow them to sweat for 5 minutes, stirring occasionally. Add broccoli, stock and mint, bring to the boil, cover and simmer for 15 minutes. Remove mint and purée soup in batches. Return to saucepan, add milk and reheat. Stir in cream, nutmeg and pepper just before serving.

NUTRITIONAL VALUE: 13 g protein, 13 g fat, 8 g carbohydrate, 8.5 g dietary fibre, 815 kJ (195 Cals). If you omit cream and use fat-reduced milk, fat is 6 g and energy 595 kJ (140 Cals). An excellent source of vitamins A and C, and a good source of folate, riboflavin, potassium, magnesium, calcium, iron and zinc.

Brussels sprouts

A member of the Brassica family, this vegetable looks like a miniature version of the wild cabbage from which it is descended. Although cabbages first grew around the Mediterranean, the earliest records show that brussels sprouts were apparently cultivated in 1587 in Belgium, whence comes their name. Brussels sprouts were popular in France by the nineteenth century, and soon after in England.

It is a pity so few people see brussels sprouts growing, as they look like something a child might draw, each little sprout growing directly out of the major stem of the parent plant.

Brussels sprouts are known for their high content of sulphur compounds with anti-cancer properties. They are especially rich in sulphoraphane and other isothiocyanates. They have higher levels of vitamins although lower levels of minerals than broccoli and are an excellent source of vitamin C, dietary fibre and folate, and a good source of vitamin B_6, pantothenic acid and vitamin E. A 100 g serving of cooked sprouts has no fat, 3.5 g of dietary fibre and 100 kJ.

CHOOSING AND STORING • Choose tight compact sprouts no larger than a ping-pong ball. Avoid strong-smelling sprouts.

Refrigerate unwashed for up to 5 days. The sooner they are used, the sweeter they will be.

PREPARATION AND COOKING • Brussels sprouts are one of the least popular vegetables and this is almost certainly because of the way they are often prepared. The longer they are cooked, the more their sulphur compounds break down to give a bitter flavour and unpleasant aroma. The younger and fresher the sprouts, the sweeter their flavour: even keeping them in the fridge for 5 days is enough for them to lose some of their sweetness.

The secret to getting more people to like brussels sprouts may be to avoid boiling them. I also dislike their flavour if they are microwaved. Many people who are reluctant to eat brussels sprouts accept them quite happily if they are sliced lengthwise and stir-fried. For those who like brussels sprouts, steaming is an excellent cooking medium. However, if they are steamed whole until they are cooked right through, they will lose their bright colour and look less appetising. Cutting them in half means they are still green when cooked. If you do cook them whole, cut a cross in the stem to allow it to cook as quickly as the leafy parts.

STIR-FRIED BRUSSELS SPROUTS WITH CHICKEN AND SESAME

Even those who don't like brussels sprouts never object to them this way. For a vegetarian version, substitute 1½ cups drained canned chickpeas for the chicken.

2 tbsp sesame seeds
2 tsp sesame oil
1 clove garlic, crushed
1 small red chilli, sliced finely
2 tsp finely chopped fresh ginger
400 g chicken strips
400 g brussels sprouts
½ cup orange juice
2 tbsp salt-reduced soy sauce

SERVES 4

Toast sesame seeds in a dry frying pan over a gentle heat, shaking frequently, until they are golden-brown. Tip out and reserve.

Pour sesame oil into a hot wok or frying pan and add the garlic, chilli, ginger and chicken. Stir-fry over a moderate heat for 5 minutes, turning chicken so that it browns. Trim the base of each sprout and slice each head lengthwise into 4. Add to wok and continue stir-frying for 2–3 minutes. Add orange juice and soy sauce, and cook for a further 1–2 minutes. Toss sesame seeds through, then serve with steamed rice.

NUTRITIONAL VALUE: 29 g protein, 8.5 g fat ('good' fat), 6.5 g carbohydrate, 4.5 g dietary fibre, 910 kJ (245 Cals). An excellent source of vitamin C and a good source of iron, zinc, potassium, niacin and folate.

BRUSSELS SPROUTS, BROWN RICE AND CASHEWS

I first made this dish 30 years ago when we were on holidays. I offered to go back to the house we were staying in and prepare dinner: the only ingredients to hand were brussels sprouts, brown rice, cheese, onions and cashews. We've been enjoying it ever since.

2 cups brown rice
4 cups vegetable stock or water
1 tbsp olive oil
2 medium-sized onions, sliced into fine rings
500 g brussels sprouts
1 cup grated cheddar
¾ cup cashews

SERVES 4

Place rice and stock (or water) into a saucepan, bring to the boil, cover and simmer for 30 minutes. Meanwhile, heat the olive oil in another saucepan and add the onions. Cover and allow to sweat for 20 minutes, stirring occasionally.

Preheat oven to 200°C. Halve and steam the brussels sprouts for 5 minutes. Place the cooked rice into a greased shallow oven dish. Top with brussels sprouts, onions, cheese and cashews, and bake for 15 minutes.

NUTRITIONAL VALUE: 21 g protein, 23 g fat (some of it 'good' fat), 67 g carbohydrate, 9.5 g dietary fibre, 2340 kJ (560 Cals). An excellent source of vitamin C and a good source of vitamin A, riboflavin and niacin, potassium, iron, zinc, magnesium and calcium.

BRUSSELS SPROUT PURÉE

Delicious with roasted pork loin, roasted potatoes and red cabbage shredded and then cooked slowly with a little oil and sliced onion.

500 g brussels sprouts, quartered
¼ cup hot milk
1 tbsp butter
2 tbsp light sour cream
a good pinch of nutmeg
freshly ground black pepper

SERVES 4

Preheat oven to 190°C. Steam brussels sprouts until tender (6–8 minutes). Mash with a potato masher, adding milk, butter, sour cream, nutmeg and pepper: the mixture should be smashed but not smooth. Pile into a buttered ovenproof dish and reheat until piping hot.

NUTRITIONAL VALUE: 5.5 g protein, 6.5 g fat, 4 g carbohydrate, 4.5 g dietary fibre, 415 kJ (100 Cals). An excellent source of vitamin C and provides some vitamin A, and riboflavin and iron.

Burdock (see **Other vegetables**)

Cabbage

Wild cabbages originally grew around the Mediterranean, and almost certainly also in southern England, France and Spain. The word cabbage comes from the French *caboche*, a colloquial term for 'head'. Various forms of cabbage may also be native to North Africa. Cabbages like the firm-headed ones we now consume were first cultivated in Germany in the twelfth century, while the crinkled varieties were almost certainly developed in Italy in the sixteenth century. Greek mythology has it that the first cabbage came from the tears of a prince, who was sad at being punished for trampling on the grapes of the Greek god of wine, Dionysus.

VARIETIES • The many varieties now available include some with round or oval heads of tightly wrapped, firm waxy leaves and others with softer leaves, sometimes loosely collected from the stem rather than forming a firm head. Cabbages also come in various colours from dark to light bright green, white or red. The differing colours represent their content of carotenoids, chlorophyll and anthocyanins. Many of these colourants are valuable antioxidants, so it makes sense to choose cabbages of different colours at various times. The content of carotenoids and many antioxidants is higher in green parts than white.

Some of the cabbage varieties available include:
- savoy, a sweet green cabbage (the outside leaves are bluish) with loose crinkled leaves. Originally grown in Belgium and France.
- sugarloaf, a pointy-headed green cabbage with strong waxy leaves.
- white cabbage, with a firm oval head of strong waxy leaves ranging from white to pale green on the outside.
- spring greens, loose-leafed varieties grown in the United Kingdom.
- Chinese cabbages (see **Asian greens**).
- red cabbage, particularly popular in Germany and Scandinavia, with a firm, round head of strong waxy leaves, usually crinkled.
- mustard cabbage, a spicy variety from India and China (see **Asian greens**).

All cabbages are excellent sources of vitamin C, good sources of dietary fibre and provide folate. Savoy cabbages have more than twice as much folate as any other variety, and savoy and mustard cabbages also have the highest levels of beta carotene, vitamin C, potassium and iron. A 100 g serving of cabbage has about 4 g of fibre, virtually no fat and averages 55 kJ.

CHOOSING AND STORING • Cabbages are generally available all year, but most are at their best (and cheapest) in spring, summer and autumn. Whatever the variety, choose one that is solid and feels heavy for its size. The leaves should be crisp and unbroken, without brown or wilted edges.

Keep cabbages in a plastic bag in the refrigerator. Most will keep for at least a week and whole red cabbage will keep for 2 weeks.

PREPARATION AND COOKING • Cabbage contains sulphur compounds, some of which are given off during cooking. The longer the cooking period, the greater the release of these compounds and the stronger the flavour and aroma. When cooking cabbage, the production of hydrogen sulphide (rotten-egg gas) doubles between the fifth and seventh minute of cooking. To avoid it, eat cabbage raw or cook for less than five minutes (red cabbage can be cooked for longer).

If starting with a whole cabbage, cut out a wedge sufficient for immediate use. Remove any tough outer leaves and the heavy rib along the centre, and wash well. Before you use the next portion, trim off and discard the cut surface. Red cabbage tends to turn purple when cooked: to preserve its red colour, add a little lemon juice or vinegar while cooking.

Cabbage can be steamed, microwaved, cooked in a pan with a small amount of olive oil, or added to stir-fries. Red cabbage can also be used in pickles and relishes.

RED CABBAGE ROLLS

These look pretty and may appeal to those who do not like 'vegies'.

8 red cabbage leaves
1 cup water
1 cup apple juice
2 tbsp wine vinegar
2 tsp honey

FILLING
1 cup cooked rice
1 carrot, grated
1 Lebanese cucumber, cut into thin strips
½ cup chopped fresh mint
2 tbsp salt-reduced soy sauce
2 tbsp sunflower seeds

SERVES 4

Remove the coarse centre rib from each cabbage leaf. In a large saucepan, combine the water, apple juice, vinegar and honey, and bring to the boil. Add 2 cabbage leaves and allow them to cook for 1–2 minutes. Remove, then repeat with remaining leaves.

Combine all the filling ingredients and mix well. Place a spoonful of this mixture on each cabbage leaf and roll up to form a firm parcel, tucking in edges as you go. Serve cold. Or place the rolls in an oiled shallow ovenproof dish, cover and heat in a moderate oven for 10 minutes.

NUTRITIONAL VALUE: 5 g protein, 3.5 g fat ('good' fat), 19 g carbohydrate, 5.5 g dietary fibre, 545 kJ (130 Cals). An excellent source of vitamins A and C, a good source of potassium and provides some vitamin B_1, iron and zinc.

cabbage

COLESLAW

Coleslaw is too often drowned in a fatty, salty dressing. Try this fresher tasting version.

2 tbsp walnuts
1 large apple, cored and finely sliced
2 tbsp lemon juice
4 cups finely shredded green, white or red
    cabbage
1 cup sliced celery
1/2 cup finely sliced green shallots (spring
    onions)
3/4 cup natural yoghurt
1 tbsp cider vinegar
1 tsp Dijon-style mustard

SERVES 6

Brown walnuts in a dry frying pan, shaking frequently to prevent them burning. Tip onto a plate and allow to cool.

Toss apple slices with lemon juice, add cabbage, celery and green onions, and mix gently. Combine the yoghurt, vinegar and mustard. Add to cabbage mixture and stir well. Top with walnuts and serve at once.

NUTRITIONAL VALUE: 5 g protein, 6 g fat ('good' fat), 10 g carbohydrate, 5 g dietary fibre, 475 kJ (115 Cals). An excellent source of vitamin C and provides some potassium and calcium.

RED CABBAGE WITH CARAWAY AND APPLE

Delicious with roast chicken, kangaroo, veal or pork.

2 tsp olive oil
1 small onion, sliced finely
4 cups shredded red cabbage
2 tbsp raisins
2 tbsp orange juice
1 cinnamon stick
1 granny smith apple, peeled and cored
2 tsp caraway seeds

SERVES 4

Heat olive oil in a medium-sized saucepan and cook onion, without browning, for 3 minutes. Add cabbage, raisins, orange juice, cinnamon, apple and caraway. Cover and cook over a low heat for 15 minutes, stirring occasionally.

NUTRITIONAL VALUE: 3 g protein, 3 g fat ('good' fat), 14 g carbohydrate, 5.5 g dietary fibre, 390 kJ (95 Cals). An excellent source of vitamin C and provides some potassium and iron.

41

GREEN CABBAGE WITH POPPY SEEDS

Cabbage is particularly popular if prepared this way. White cabbage would be just as successful as green.

2 tsp olive oil
6 cups shredded savoy or sugarloaf cabbage
¼ cup apple juice
2 tsp finely grated lemon peel
3 tsp poppy seeds

SERVES 4

Heat olive oil in a medium-sized saucepan. Add cabbage, apple juice and lemon peel, cover and cook over medium heat for 4 minutes, stirring once or twice. Add poppy seeds and toss well to combine.

NUTRITIONAL VALUE: 3 g protein, 3.5 g fat ('good' fat), 5.5 g carbohydrate, 5 g dietary fibre, 280 kJ (65 Cals). An excellent source of vitamin C and provides some iron and calcium.

Capsicums

Capsicums are also known as bell peppers or sweet peppers, but capsicum is the correct term for these members of the Solanaceae family, which also embraces chillies, potatoes, tomatoes, tobacco and deadly nightshade. Native to tropical America, capsicum seeds have been found in caves in Mexico and at Peruvian burial sites that existed as far back as 5000 BC. Spanish raiders took them back to Europe, where they have been cultivated for more than 400 years.

Capsicums come in a variety of colours—unripe green, ripe red, and modern hybrids that may be yellow, pale green–yellow, orange, brown or purple. Red capsicums have more than twice as much sugar as the unripe green ones and so taste milder and sweeter.

All capsicums are highly nutritious and are rich natural sources of vitamin C. Red capsicums have twice as much vitamin C as green ones, and are also an excellent source of beta carotene. All varieties contribute small quantities of other vitamins and minerals, and have virtually no fat. Half an average red capsicum has 2 g of fibre and 115 kJ: half an average green capsicum has 1.5 g of fibre and 70 kJ.

CHOOSING AND STORING • Available all year round, capsicums are at their best in summer. As with most vegetables, when they are cheaper than usual is a good time to buy. Select firm capsicums with shiny skins and no wrinkling or soft spots. If you are going to roast and peel capsicums, choose those that are bright red and have the fewest deep grooves or fissures.

Store capsicums in the crisper section of the fridge, but not in a plastic bag as they tend to sweat when wrapped. They should keep for a week.

PREPARATION AND COOKING • Remove stem, cut capsicum in half and scrape out the seeds. Remove the membranes.

Capsicum skin contains some bitter substances and may also make some people burp. The easiest way to skin capsicums is to preheat the oven to 250°C and place capsicums directly onto oven shelf (put a baking tray on the shelf below to catch any drips). Reduce oven heat to 220°C and cook capsicums for 35 minutes, by which time the skin will have blackened and blistered. Transfer capsicums to a bowl, place it inside a plastic bag and leave until cool enough to handle. Peel away fine skin, making sure you do so over the bowl to catch the juices and seeds (do not wash the capsicums at this stage, as it reduces their flavour). Strain the juices and use later in sauces. An alternative method is to hold the capsicum on a long fork over a flame to char the skin: this gives a better flavour, but in practice it can be difficult to blacken all surfaces and the peeling can take a long time. Cutting capsicums in half and blackening under the griller is not recommended, as the delicious juices are lost.

RED CAPSICUM SAUCE

This is a delicious sauce that is amazingly healthy. Serve it with grilled chicken, fish or lamb, or roasted or barbecued vegetables.

1 medium-sized onion
2 red capsicums
½ head garlic
1 tsp olive oil
1 tbsp balsamic or sherry vinegar

SERVES 4

Preheat oven to 250°C. Peel onion and cut in half through the centre. Place onion and garlic on one side of an oven tray and drizzle with olive oil. Place the capsicums directly on an oven shelf and position the oven tray on the shelf below so that the capsicums sit over the empty part of the tray. Reduce oven heat to 220°C and cook the vegetables for 35 minutes.

Transfer capsicums to a bowl, place the bowl inside a plastic bag and leave until cool enough to handle. Peel fine skin from the capsicums, over a bowl to collect the juices, then strain out the seeds. Squeeze softened garlic flesh into a food processor with the peeled capsicums, the onion and vinegar. Process, adding enough of the capsicum juices to produce a sauce consistency. Reheat to serve.

NUTRITIONAL VALUE: 2.5 g protein, 1.5 g fat ('good' fat), 6.5 g carbohydrate, 2.5 g dietary fibre, 210 kJ (50 Cals). A good source of vitamins A and C.

CAPSICUM AND RICOTTA DIP

A healthy dip which looks as good as it tastes.

2 red capsicums, roasted and skinned
  (see page 43)
1 clove garlic, crushed
200 g ricotta
1 tbsp tomato paste
freshly ground black pepper

SERVES 4

Place capsicums, garlic, ricotta, tomato paste and pepper in a blender and process until smooth.

Serve with blanched broccoli, raw carrot and celery sticks, and raw button mushrooms or with chargrilled vegetables (see page 188).

NUTRITIONAL VALUE: 7 g protein, 4.5 g fat, 6 g carbohydrate, 1.5 g dietary fibre, 390 kJ (95 Cals). A good source of vitamins A and C, and also supplies some calcium.

CAPSICUMS STUFFED WITH TUNA

Choose capsicums with even bases, so they will stand upright. You could substitute 1 cup of chopped cooked chicken, lamb or chick peas for the tuna.

4 capsicums, any colour
1 tbsp olive oil
1 medium-sized onion, chopped finely
1 clove garlic, chopped
1 tsp dried thyme leaves
1$\frac{1}{2}$ cups cooked rice
$\frac{1}{2}$ cup chopped parsley
200 g cottage cheese
2 tbsp tomato purée or tomato-based
  pasta sauce
1 egg, beaten
200 g canned tuna, drained
2 tbsp fresh breadcrumbs

SERVES 4

Slice tops off whole capsicums, then remove seeds and membranes. Heat a large saucepan of boiling water, add capsicums and cook for 2 minutes. Remove and drain well.

Heat olive oil in a heavy-based saucepan and cook onion, garlic and thyme over a gentle heat for 5 minutes. Add rice, parsley, cottage cheese, tomato purée and egg, and stir well. Carefully stir in the tuna.

Preheat oven to 180°C. Place capsicum shells in an ovenproof dish so that they fit snugly. Spoon in the stuffing mixture and top with breadcrumbs. Carefully pour about $\frac{3}{4}$ cup of water around the base of the capsicums, and bake for 20 minutes.

NUTRITIONAL VALUE: 28 g protein, 8.5 g fat ('good' fat), 32 g carbohydrate, 4 g dietary fibre, 1330 kJ (315 Cals). An excellent source of vitamin C, a good source of vitamin A, niacin, potassium, magnesium, iron and zinc.

CAPSICUM SALAD

Quick, easy and colourful. Goes well with lamb, or pile it into split toasted pide bread spread with tahini.

1 cup snow peas
1 red capsicum
1 green capsicum
1 yellow capsicum
16 black olives

DRESSING
1 tbsp extra-virgin olive oil
1 tbsp balsamic vinegar
½ cup fresh mint leaves
ground black pepper

SERVES 4

Place snow peas in a saucepan of boiling water for 1 minute. Drain, and run under cold water.

Cut capsicums in half, remove seeds and membranes, and slice. Place in salad bowl with the olives and drained snow peas.

To make the dressing, process oil, vinegar, mint and pepper in a blender. Pour over salad and toss thoroughly.

NUTRITIONAL VALUE: 4.5 g protein, 6 g fat ('good' fat), 7.5 g carbohydrate, 3.5 g dietary fibre, 420 kJ (100 Cals). An excellent source of vitamins A and C, and also provides some iron and zinc.

Cardoon (see **Other vegetables**)

Carrots

Carrots are native to Afghanistan, where the early varieties were red, black or purple. Wild carrots also grow in the eastern Mediterranean regions. Carrots were cultivated from the tenth century but our familiar orange-coloured variety did not appear until the seventeenth century when it was developed in the Netherlands. By that time, carrots were already used in India, China and Japan, although the cultivars grown in Asia have never been as sweet or crisp as those preferred in Europe.

The carrot is a member of the Umbelliferae family, which includes more than 3000 species including coriander, parsley, dill, fennel and caraway. The length of a carrot depends to a large extent on the temperature in which it was grown. Those grown in warmer climates tend to be short and stubby, whereas cool-climate carrots are long and slender. New varieties of small, round 'golfball' carrots are now available.

45

Carrots are an excellent source of alpha carotene and beta carotene ('carotene' comes from the word carrots) and also contain many other compounds that form the carotenoid family. Carrots tinged with red contain some lycopene, a carotenoid that may reduce the risk of prostate cancer. Older carrots have a deeper colour and higher levels of sugar and nutrients than younger ones. Cooking carrots also makes some of their carotenoids more available, although raw carrots are so high in these nutrients that they are an excellent source. One medium-sized older carrot has enough beta carotene for the body to make two days' supply of vitamin A. Carrots also supply vitamin C and small amounts of other vitamins and minerals. They have much less iron than green vegetables and, like other vegetables, almost no fat. One medium carrot has 4 g of dietary fibre and 110 kJ.

Carrot juice is a potent source of carotenoids. Drinking it regularly, or eating lots of carrots (two or three a day), will cause the skin to turn a yellowish colour, especially on the palms of the hands. This condition is called carotenaemia and is generally considered harmless. If it continues over a long period or carotene intake is really excessive, the whites of the eyes will also turn yellow and some people develop nausea.

Carrots have been damned by some people because early reports suggested they had a high glycaemic index (GI), a measure of the rate at which carbohydrates in a food are converted to blood glucose. A low GI indicates that a food is beneficial for those with diabetes and some people believe low GI foods are useful for those needing to lose weight, although this has not been proven. By definition, the GI refers to a portion of the food containing 50 g of carbohydrate. To get 50 g of carbohydrate from carrots would mean eating 1 kg of carrots in a single sitting. More recent data shows that a normal serving of carrots does not have a high GI, so you can ignore the diet books that tell you not to eat carrots. It would not be possible to gain weight by eating carrots.

CHOOSING AND STORING • Choose firm, brightly coloured carrots. If buying by the bunch, the state of the green tops is a good indication of their freshness (and the greens can be eaten). Avoid limp, damaged or split carrots. If you find carrots in the bottom of your fridge that are sprouting new shoots, throw them out as they will be dry and woody.

Kept in a plastic bag in the refrigerator, carrots will keep for many weeks. Do not store them near apples, bananas or melon as the ethylene gas those fruits produce will increase bitter-tasting compounds in carrots called isocoumarins. Remove green tops from bunches of baby carrots, as the carrots will otherwise soon wilt.

PREPARATION AND COOKING • Wash and scrub carrots with a brush. Carrots, like many vegetables, are best left unpeeled, not because all the goodness lies just *under* the skin but because much of the goodness (at least in terms of their antioxidants) is *in* the skin.

Carrot, cardamom and pistachio pilaf

Delicious on its own, or serve with grilled or barbecued chicken.

1 tbsp olive oil or butter
1 medium-sized onion, finely chopped
2 cups long grain rice
2 cups coarsely grated carrot
8 cardamom pods
3 cups chicken or vegetable stock
1 cup white wine
2 tbsp shelled pistachio nuts
freshly ground pepper

SERVES 4

Heat oil or butter in a heavy-based saucepan and add the onion. Cover and sweat for 3 minutes, stirring occasionally. Add rice and stir well to coat rice with oil. Add carrot, cardamom, stock and wine, bring to the boil, cover and cook over low heat for 20 minutes, or until rice is tender. Add nuts and pepper, and stir well.

NUTRITIONAL VALUE: 9.5 g protein, 8.5 g fat ('good' fat), 88 g carbohydrate, 5.5 g dietary fibre, 1780 kJ (475 Cals). An excellent source of vitamin A, a good source of vitamin C and niacin, and provides some iron and zinc.

Carrot and orange soup

A warming winter soup with protective properties from its rich supply of vitamins.

2 tsp olive oil
1 leek, washed and sliced
1 clove garlic, crushed
$1/2$ tsp dried sage
800 g carrots, scrubbed and chopped
$1 1/2$ cups orange juice
$2 1/2$ cups chicken or vegetable stock
3 bay leaves
$1/2$ cup natural yoghurt
1 tbsp chopped chives

SERVES 4

Heat oil in a large saucepan and add the leek, garlic and sage. Cover and allow to sweat over a gentle heat for 5 minutes. Add carrots, orange juice, stock and bay leaves, bring to the boil, cover and simmer for 15 minutes or until carrots are tender. Purée soup in batches. Reheat, and serve topped with a dollop of yoghurt and a sprinkle of chives.

NUTRITIONAL VALUE: 5 g protein, 4 g fat ('good' fat), 23 g carbohydrate, 7 g dietary fibre, 630 kJ (150 Cals). An excellent source of vitamins A and C, a good source of niacin and potassium, and also provides some iron, zinc and calcium.

CARROT AND RAISIN SANDWICH SPREAD

This spread may not look attractive, but was a regular request when my children were growing up. A food processor makes grating the carrot very easy.

2 tbsp raisins
1/2 cup orange juice
1 large carrot, grated (use food processor)
3 tbsp peanut butter
2 slices lavash or mountain bread

SERVES 2

Soak raisins in orange juice overnight. Add carrot and peanut butter, and mix well. Spread over lavash bread, roll up and wrap in plastic wrap.

NUTRITIONAL VALUE: 14 g protein, 17 g fat, 46 g carbohydrate, 7.5 g dietary fibre, 1630 kJ (390 Cals). An excellent source of vitamins A and C and niacin, and a good source of potassium, magnesium, iron and zinc.

PECAN CARROT CAKE

A healthy cake which tastes delicious. Make sure you grate the carrots finely (a food processor does this well).

125 g pecan nuts
5 eggs, separated
1 1/4 cups castor sugar
2 tsp cinnamon
1 tsp vanilla
2 cups finely grated carrots
1/2 cup plain flour, sifted
1 tsp baking powder
1 tsp icing sugar

SERVES 10

Preheat oven to 190°C. Grease a 23 cm non-stick cake tin. In food processor, grind pecan nuts.

Beat egg yolks with 1 cup of the castor sugar until thick and creamy. Gently stir in the ground pecans, cinnamon, vanilla, carrot, flour and baking powder. Beat egg whites to soft peaks, add remaining sugar and continue beating until firm. Fold egg whites into carrot mixture.

Pour mixture into prepared tin and bake for 45 minutes, or until a skewer inserted into the cake comes out clean. Cool, remove cake from tin and sprinkle with icing sugar.

NUTRITIONAL VALUE: 5.5 g protein, 12 g fat ('good' fat), 33 g carbohydrate, 2 g dietary fibre, 1045 kJ (250 Cals). A good source of vitamin A and provides some zinc, iron and vitamin E.

HONEYED CARROTS

These carrots delight everyone, including children. You can also add finely chopped fresh ginger.

500 g carrots, scrubbed
2 tsp honey
2 tsp butter
2 tbsp orange juice
2 tsp finely grated orange peel

SERVES 4

Slice carrots diagonally or into thick matchstick pieces. Steam for 5 minutes.

Combine honey, butter, orange juice and peel, and stir over a low heat for 1 minute. Add carrots and toss well to combine. Allow to stand over gentle heat for 2 minutes before serving.

NUTRITIONAL VALUE: 1 g protein, 2 g fat, 10 g carbohydrate, 3.5 g dietary fibre, 260 kJ (60 Cals). An excellent source of vitamins A and C.

Cassava (see **Other vegetables**)

Cauliflower

A member of the cabbage family, cauliflowers first grew in Cyprus, Crete, Turkey and Syria. The oldest records of cauliflower date to the sixth century BC and it was also mentioned by Pliny in the second century AD. Cauliflowers were cultivated in Italy in the late fifteenth century, arriving in England about a hundred years later.

Commercial cauliflower varieties are usually white, but there are also cultivars available that are pale-green, pink or purple. Romanesco, a pointed pale-green variety, could be included under cauliflower or broccoli as it has characteristics of both. Miniature cauliflowers are now available to serve whole. They look attractive and retain their firm texture well when cooked.

Cauliflower is an excellent source of vitamin C, supplies vitamin K, folate, biotin (one of the B complex vitamins) and small quantities of other vitamins and minerals. An average serving has no fat, 2 g of dietary fibre and 90 kJ.

CHOOSING AND STORING • Although cauliflowers are available all year round, their flavour is best from late autumn to early spring. The romanesco is best in winter. For all types of cauliflower look for firm florets pressed tightly together. Avoid those with opening flowers or a yellowish tinge, as they have a stronger flavour. The leaves should be crisp.

49

Keep cauliflower in a plastic bag in the refrigerator for 3 or 4 days. The sooner they are consumed after picking, the sweeter their flavour.

PREPARATION AND COOKING • Discard the leaves and, if cooking whole, remove the centre core. Otherwise, break off florets. Cauliflower can be steamed, microwaved, boiled or sliced and stir-fried. To keep it white, add a squeeze of lemon juice to the water when boiling or steaming. It is delicious in curries and is widely used in India. Romanesco looks delightful served whole: trim the stalk flat and steam the head for 10–15 minutes, or until just tender.

CAULIFLOWER CHEESE

When I mentioned to anyone I was writing a vegetable book, they all said they hoped I would not forget to include a healthy cauliflower cheese. This is the best healthy version I can come up with that still tastes good.

about 500 g cauliflower
1 tbsp butter
1 tbsp plain flour
¼ tsp dry mustard
300 mL skim milk
1 egg, beaten
1 tbsp finely grated parmesan
½ cup grated gruyère
1 slice bread, made into crumbs
2 tbsp chopped parsley

SERVES 4

Steam cauliflower until tender. Place in a shallow ovenproof dish. Preheat oven to 190°C.

In a saucepan, place butter, flour and mustard. Cook, stirring constantly, for 2 minutes. Add milk gradually and stir until sauce boils and thickens. Remove from heat and add beaten egg and parmesan, stirring constantly. Pour sauce over cauliflower. Combine gruyère, breadcrumbs and parsley, and sprinkle over cauliflower. Bake for 10 minutes, or until cheese has melted and crumbs are crisp.

NUTRITIONAL VALUE: 13 g protein, 11 g fat, 12 g carbohydrate, 2.5 g dietary fibre, 835 kJ (200 Cals). An excellent source of vitamin C, a good source of vitamin A, riboflavin, calcium and potassium, and provides some iron and zinc.

SPICY CHICK PEAS AND CAULIFLOWER

A deliciously simple way to use legumes.

1 tbsp macadamia nut oil (or use olive oil)
1 medium-sized onion, finely chopped
2 cloves garlic, crushed
1 tsp chopped fresh chilli
2 tsp chopped fresh ginger
2 tsp ground coriander
2 tsp garam masala
500 g cauliflower, sliced
400 g canned chick peas
2 tbsp lime or lemon juice

SERVES 4

Place oil in a hot wok and add the onion, garlic, chilli, ginger and coriander. Cook over low–medium heat for 5 minutes, stirring so the mixture does not burn. Add garam masala, cauliflower and chick peas (with their liquid). Cook, stirring occasionally, for 5 minutes. Add lime or lemon juice.

NUTRITIONAL VALUE: 8.5 g protein, 7 g fat ('good' fat), 16 g carbohydrate, 7 g dietary fibre, 675 kJ (160 Cals). An excellent source of vitamin C and a good source of potassium, magnesium, zinc and iron.

CURRIED CAULIFLOWER

This is a 'dry' curry, delicious served on its own with steamed rice, or as part of a meal that also includes meat, fish or chicken curries. Cook pappadums in the microwave: two pappadums take 40–60 seconds on High, but watch carefully to avoid burning them.

1 tbsp mustard oil (or use olive oil)
1 tsp black mustard seeds
1 tsp cumin seeds
1 medium-sized onion, finely chopped
1 tbsp Indian curry paste
1 clove garlic, crushed
2 tsp finely chopped fresh ginger
1 small red chilli, seeded and sliced
1/2 cauliflower, broken into florets
2 tbsp water

SERVES 4

Heat oil in a saucepan, add cumin and mustard seeds, and stir until the mustard seeds burst. Add onion, cover and sweat for 3 minutes. Stir in curry paste, garlic, ginger and cauliflower. Add water, cover and cook for 10 minutes, shaking saucepan several times. Serve with steamed rice, pappadums and a lime chutney.

NUTRITIONAL VALUE: 4 g protein, 6.5 g fat ('good' fat), 5.5 g carbohydrate, 3.5 g dietary fibre, 415 kJ (100 Cals). An excellent source of vitamin C and provides some vitamin A, potassium and iron.

CRUNCHY CRUSTED CAULIFLOWER

An alternative to cauliflower cheese. A food processor can convert bread to crumbs and chop parsley at the same time.

1 small whole cauliflower
1 lemon, sliced
1 tbsp walnut oil (or use olive oil)
2 tbsp rolled oats
1 tbsp sunflower seeds
2 slices wholemeal bread, made into crumbs
½ cup chopped parsley

SERVES 4

Trim away leaves and core of cauliflower and place whole in steamer. Add lemon slices to water in steamer base, and steam cauliflower for about 12 minutes (it should not be soggy). Transfer cauliflower to an ovenproof dish.

Preheat oven to 200°C. Combine oil, oats, seeds, crumbs and parsley. Press onto cauliflower and bake for 10 minutes, or until crumbs are brown and crunchy. Serve from the dish.

NUTRITIONAL VALUE: 7 g protein, 7.5 g fat ('good' fat), 11 g carbohydrate, 5 g dietary fibre, 575 kJ (140 Cals). An excellent source of vitamin C and potassium, and provides some iron and magnesium.

Celeriac

Also known as knob or root celery, celeriac is popular in Asian and Mediterranean regions where it is used more commonly than regular celery. It is also widely used in northern and eastern Europe and was introduced to England in about 1720. Celeriac is the ugly sister of the celery family, although the white flesh inside the brownish bulbous knobbly swollen stem (it is not a root and you can see the real roots straggling from it) is delicious, with the flavour of celery in a smooth, string-free texture.

Celeriac, with no apparent stringiness, has more than three times as much fibre as regular celery and some is valuable soluble fibre. It is also a good source of vitamin C and folate, and provides some potassium and small quantities of iron and calcium. Celeriac has virtually no fat, and a typical serving provides 4 g of dietary fibre and 80 kJ.

CHOOSING AND STORING • Celeriac is available in autumn and winter. Choose those about the size of a grapefruit, which are firm, feel heavy for their size and have a greenish colour where the leaves join. The leaves usually attached to celeriac look a bit like skinny celery, but have a strong flavour. They never stand as crisply upright as regular celery, but they should not be too wilted. Avoid celeriac with splits or soft sections.

Refrigerate celeriac in the vegetable crisper for up to a week.

PREPARATION AND COOKING • Remove the leaves and peel celeriac (unfortunately, it is impossible to peel some knobbly ones without creating a lot of waste). If you scrub the skin first, you can add celeriac to vegetable stock for a delightful mild celery flavour. Like artichokes, celeriac goes brown when cut, so after peeling or cutting it, put it straight into a bowl of water with a few slices of lemon or a tablespoon of lemon juice, or rub the cut surfaces with a cut lemon half. Celeriac is delicious cooked and mashed: to prevent discolouration, boil rather than steam it, and it is a good idea to add a couple of lemon slices to the water. Celeriac can also be fried into chips, or brushed with olive oil and baked.

CELERIAC SALAD

Celeriac keeps its texture in a salad and this one improves if made an hour or two before serving.

3 tbsp lemon juice
3 tbsp cider vinegar
2 medium-sized celeriac
2 tbsp extra-virgin olive oil
1 tbsp Dijon-style mustard
2 tbsp light sour cream
1/2 cup finely chopped fresh mint

SERVES 4

Add 2 tablespoons of the lemon juice and vinegar to a bowl of water. Peel celeriac, dropping the pieces into the water as you go. Slice each piece of celeriac into fine julienne strips and put back in the water while you slice the remainder.

Combine the remaining lemon juice and vinegar with the olive oil, mustard, sour cream and mint, and mix well. Drain the celeriac and combine with the dressing. Cover and refrigerate for an hour before serving.

NUTRITIONAL VALUE: 2.5 g protein, 12 g fat (mostly 'good' fat), 6.5 g carbohydrate, 5.5 g dietary fibre, 605 kJ (145 Cals). A good source of vitamin C.

CELERIAC MASH

A warming winter accompaniment to roast chicken.

1 lemon, sliced
1 celeriac
2 medium-sized parsnips, peeled and cut into
*   large chunks*
3 medium-sized potatoes, peeled and cut into
*   large chunks*
3 sprigs fresh thyme
approximately ½ cup hot milk
2 tsp butter
freshly ground pepper

SERVES 4

Place lemon slices in a saucepan of water. Peel the celeriac, cut into large chunks and drop into the water. Add parsnips, potatoes and thyme, bring to the boil and simmer until vegetables are soft. Drain thoroughly, discarding lemon and thyme. Mash vegetables, adding enough hot milk to produce a creamy mash. Add butter and serve with ground pepper.

NUTRITIONAL VALUE: 5 g protein, 3.5 g fat, 21 g carbohydrate, 4.5 g dietary fibre, 565 kJ (135 Cals). An excellent source of vitamin C and a good source of potassium.

Celery

Wild forms of celery originally grew in marshes in Mediterranean areas and western parts of Asia. It still grows wild in wet areas of Europe, around the Mediterranean, east to the Caucasus mountains and in the Himalayas. Homer's *Odyssey*, dating from about 850 BC, referred to 'celinon' which was almost certainly celery, a somewhat bitter plant at that time and used mainly for medicinal purposes. Its first use as a food was recorded in France in the early part of the seventeenth century.

Celery is still recommended for many diseases, and there is some evidence that limonene (also found in lemons) and phthalides in celery (they produce its distinctive odour) have anti-cancer effects, at least for animals and in the test tube. Concentrated celery extracts also have anti-inflammatory properties and may be useful for many conditions, including rheumatic complaints. Celery seeds also contain an oil which prevents the development of experimental tumours in animals. Celery-seed oil is used to flavour celery salt. At this stage, we know that concentrated celery products contain valuable components but we do not have evidence that eating extra celery as a vegetable (or even as celery juice) can cure various ailments (reliable medical trials have not yet been done). However, celery is a member of the same family as carrots, parsley and ginseng, and there is a wealth of evidence supporting some medicinal effects of ginseng.

54

celery

Farmers and those who handle celery in markets can develop an intense allergic sunburn due to a reaction between compounds called psoralens in celery and sunlight or tanning lamps. This may also occur from celeriac, but there are few records of any reaction from *eating* either vegetable.

For many years celery was blanched, first by piling soil around it and later by covering the stalks with opaque material to prevent light getting to them. The process kept the inner stalks tender and more succulent. Modern cultivars stay tender without blanching, although the inner stalks are always paler than the dark-green outer ones, which are exposed to more sunlight. Chinese celery is small and leafy and is used more as a flavouring.

Celery contributes some vitamin C and potassium, and small amounts of many vitamins and minerals. An average serving of 3–4 stalks has about 1.5 g of fibre and 40 kJ.

CHOOSING AND STORING • Celery is available throughout the year, but is at its peak from mid-summer until late winter. Select crisp, pale-green stalks with bright-green leaves. Avoid bunches where the outside stalks are split.

Ideally, remove the green leaves from celery before refrigerating, as otherwise the stems go limp. Celery should keep for at least a week in the refrigerator.

PREPARATION AND COOKING • Many people discard the base of the celery bunch, but you can make a delicious dish from this 'heart'—the bottom 6–10 cm. Cut it off in one piece, wash well, then split into four portions and cook over a low heat in a tightly lidded saucepan for 20 minutes with a tablespoon each of olive oil and water.

When preparing celery, remove the leaves and use a sharp knife to strip off the strings from the outside stalks. No other preparation is needed. Celery can be sliced finely for use in sandwiches or salads. Celery sticks filled with crunchy peanut butter are a children's snack that many of us love for ever after. Celery is also good in stir-fries and can be used in soups, although if you purée cooked celery for a soup you need to sieve it as well to remove small pieces of 'string'.

To make celery curls, cut the stalks into 10 cm lengths and holding the celery so it curls towards you, make one to three straight cuts across the stalk and then one at the middle. Place into ice-cold water for 10 minutes.

CELERY, APPLE AND PECAN SALAD

A true Waldorf salad uses mayonnaise. This version is lighter, but still good.

3 red apples (Jonathon, sundowner or pink lady), cored and diced (skin left on)
2 tbsp lemon juice
2 tbsp raisins
4 cups sliced celery
200 g natural yoghurt
1 tsp finely grated lemon peel
1 tbsp lemon juice
¹/₂ cup toasted pecan or walnut pieces

SERVES 4

Toss apple pieces with lemon juice, then add the raisins and celery. Combine yoghurt, lemon peel and juice, then pour over celery and apple mixture. Just before serving, add the pecans or walnuts.

NUTRITIONAL VALUE: 5.5 g protein, 11 g fat (mostly 'good' fat), 27 g carbohydrate, 6 g dietary fibre, 945 kJ (225 Cals). An excellent source of vitamin C, a good source of potassium and calcium, and also provides some iron and zinc.

CHILLED CELERY AND AVOCADO SOUP

A chilled soup is refreshing on a hot day. With some crusty bread, this makes a complete summer meal.

1 ripe avocado
1 green-skinned cucumber, peeled and seeded
1 clove garlic
¹/₄ cup lemon juice
1 tsp finely grated lemon peel
3 cups chicken stock
200 g low-fat natural yoghurt
1¹/₂ cups finely sliced celery
freshly ground pepper
¹/₂ cup fresh coriander leaves

SERVES 4

In food processor or blender, combine the avocado flesh, cucumber, garlic, lemon juice and peel, chicken stock and yoghurt. Purée until very smooth. Add celery and stir well to combine. Refrigerate for at least an hour, or overnight. Serve in chilled bowls, topped with pepper and coriander.

NUTRITIONAL VALUE: 5.5 g protein, 18 g fat ('good' fat), 7.5 g carbohydrate, 2.5 g dietary fibre, 890 kJ (215 Cals). A good source of vitamin C, folate, potassium, magnesium and calcium, and also provides some vitamin A, niacin, iron and zinc.

Chicory (see **Endive and chicory**)

Chillies

Chillies and capsicums belong to the same family as tomatoes, potatoes and egg-plants. They originated in Mexico and Central America, from where they spread to India and Asia and eventually North Africa and Spain. In the United States, chilli is spelled 'chili' and is often called a hot pepper. The confusing name of 'pepper' started with Columbus, who thought he had found a relative of pepper-corns which were highly prized at the time. This may have led to the habit of drying chillies and grinding them to a powder to use instead of pepper.

The heat or burning qualities of chillies comes from capsaicin, a chemical found in their membranes and, to a lesser extent, in the seeds. Chillies make cap-saicin to discourage insects from attacking them while they're ripening; the quantities of capsaicin increase in chillies grown in hot conditions or a hot cli-mate. There is some evidence that capsaicins increase the body's metabolic rate, but it is unlikely that most people would eat enough to burn up significantly more kilojoules and cause weight loss. Not all chillies are hot but, with only a few exceptions, most of the several hundred varieties have some degree of pungency for the palate. Only a few are as mild as their sweet cousins, the capsicums.

Chillies can be red, green, orange or almost the colour of chocolate. They can be pointy, round, small, club-like, long, thin, globular, tapered, or shaped like a granny's bonnet. Their skin may be shiny, smooth or crinkled, and their walls may be thick or thin. The colour of chillies is no guide to the intensity of their flavour, nor is their size. All chillies begin life green and turn yellow or red as they ripen. There is no rule that either green or red ones have more heat.

Eating hot chillies causes the body to produce endorphins, the same chemi-cals produced during an athlete's 'high'. Whether this makes chillies addictive is debatable, but many people who eat them regularly find it difficult to do without them.

Chillies are rich in vitamins A and C—one small red chilli has a whole day's supply of vitamin C. A small chilli has 25 kJ.

CHOOSING AND STORING • Chillies are available all year round. Choose firm ones with no wrinkles. Many supermarkets and greengrocers now label chillies according to whether they are mild, medium, hot or very hot. Some of the very hot chillies include bird's eye (small, pointed, red or green), serrano (small, red or green), inferno (yellow to red), habanero (a Mexican chilli with folded appear-ance, light green to orange colour, and exceptionally hot) and jalapeno (dark green to red, medium size). Banana chillies, pimiento and longish red chillies tend to be mild and are often labelled as sweet chillies.

Chillies will keep in a paper bag in a cool dark place for 3–4 days. For longer storage, keep in a glass jar in the refrigerator.

PREPARATION AND COOKING • The capsaicins that give chillies their heat can damage eyes. When preparing chillies, wear disposable gloves and thoroughly wash all knives, cutting boards and anything else that comes in contact with a cut chilli. Above all, don't rub your eyes after preparing any kind of chilli and do not allow chilli to come in contact with a cut or graze as it can burn the skin. The seeds are particularly damaging to the eyes, so discard them carefully if you're not eating them. Most of their heat is in the seeds and the membrane, so to reduce the heat, discard some of the membranes and seeds.

GUACAMOLE

The coolness of avocado goes well with the heat of chillies. Guacamole is traditionally served with corn chips, but it is also delicious as a dip for prawns or dolloped on top of a potato baked in its jacket.

1 large ripe avocado
1 small red or green chilli, chopped finely
2 tbsp lime or lemon juice
2 tomatoes, skinned and diced
2 tbsp torn coriander leaves

SERVES 4

Mash avocado flesh and add the chilli, lime juice, tomatoes and coriander. If not serving at once, cover closely with plastic wrap and refrigerate.

NUTRITIONAL VALUE: 2 g protein, 11 g fat ('good' fat), 3 g carbohydrate, 2 g dietary fibre, 510 kJ (120 Cals). A good source of vitamin C and provides some vitamin A and potassium.

CHILLI JAM

This is very good with game or fish, or served with mashed potatoes or noodles.

1 cup small red chillies
1 medium-sized onion, finely chopped
500 g tomatoes, skinned and diced
½ cup malt vinegar
2 tbsp balsamic vinegar
½ cup brown sugar

MAKES ABOUT 1½ CUPS

Remove stems and cut chillies in halves. Discard seeds. Place chillies, onion, tomatoes, vinegars and sugar into a saucepan, bring to the boil, turn heat low and simmer until thick (about 20 minutes). Store in the refrigerator.

NUTRITIONAL VALUE: 1 tablespoon has 0.5 g protein, no fat, 0.5 g carbohydrate, 0.5 g dietary fibre, 70 kJ (15 Cals). A good source of vitamin C and provides some vitamin A.

VIETNAMESE CHILLI DRESSING

Use as a dipping sauce for spring rolls or chicken pieces. If palm sugar is not available, use castor sugar.

1 small red chilli, sliced finely
1 clove garlic, crushed
1 tsp palm sugar or castor sugar
2 tbsp lime juice
1 tbsp fish sauce
1 tbsp water

SERVES 4

Combine all ingredients, stirring until sugar dissolves. Serve in small bowls for dipping.

NUTRITIONAL VALUE: 1 tablespoon has 0.5 g protein, no fat, 2.5 g carbohydrate, 0.5 g dietary fibre, 55 kJ (13 Cals). A good source of vitamin C and provides some vitamin A

HARISSA

There are many recipes for this fiery Moroccan sauce. If desired, dilute with water before using.

10 small red chillies, seeds removed
6 cloves garlic, peeled
2 tbsp ground coriander
1 tsp ground cumin
1 tbsp ground caraway seeds
2 tsp dried mint
2 tbsp olive oil

MAKES ABOUT ½ CUP

Place all ingredients in food processor and blend until smooth. Store in refrigerator for up to several weeks.

NUTRITIONAL VALUE: 1 teaspoon has no protein, 0.5 g fat, 0.5 g carbohydrate, 0.5 g dietary fibre, 30 kJ (7 Cals).

Chokos

Variously known outside Australia as chayote, vegetable pear or mango squash, the choko comes from the gourd family and is native to Central America and Mexico. It is also grown in the West Indies and is popular in Algeria. In Australia, choko vines once grew in almost every backyard. The ready availability of chokos, their connotations as a food for the poor, and past habits of boiling them until soggy and then coating them with white sauce, meant they are not always popular. However, if eaten when young, and sliced and stir-fried, they are delicious and have a wider appeal.

Those who do not like chokos are usually delighted to discover that, apart from a medium level of vitamin C, chokos are not rich in any particular nutrient. Half a smallish choko has 1 g of dietary fibre and 85 kJ.

CHOOSING AND STORING • Chokos are available from late summer through to spring, with peak season being autumn to late winter. Select small firm chokos about the size of a pear, which show no signs of sprouting.

Store in a cool dry place or refrigerate for a week.

PREPARATION AND COOKING • Wash, cut off the broad folded end and cut the choko in half lengthwise. Remove the core, and peel. Chokos produce a type of sap, so wash your hands and the choko thoroughly after peeling.

S T I R - F R I E D   C H O K O   A N D   P U M P K I N

Serve as an accompaniment to grilled meat, fish or chicken.

4 chokos, peeled
½ small butternut pumpkin, peeled
    and seeded
1 tbsp sesame oil
2 cloves garlic, crushed
1 tbsp salt-reduced soy sauce
2 tbsp mirin (or use sherry)
2 tbsp fresh coriander leaves

SERVES 4

Slice chokos and pumpkin about 5 mm thick. Heat a wok and add oil, garlic, chokos and pumpkin. Stir-fry for 4–5 minutes, or until vegetables are tender-crisp. Add soy sauce, mirin and coriander leaves, and serve.

NUTRITIONAL VALUE: 2.5 g protein, 5.5 g fat ('good' fat), 10 g carbohydrate, 3.5 g dietary fibre, 400 kJ (95 Cals).

Courgette (see **Zucchini**)

Cucumbers

Members of the melon family, cucumbers are native to northern India although various other members of its family are native to Africa. Almost three-quarters of the world's cucumbers are produced in Asia. Cucumbers have been cultivated for over 4000 years in India and were also grown in ancient Egypt, Greece and Rome. They fell from favour during the eighteenth century, when they were considered indigestible. In the 1950s, I remember my grandmother insisting that cucumbers must be scraped with a fork to 'let the poisons out'.

The first cucumbers were the small, rather bitter type known as gherkin cucumbers. Gherkins sold as pickles are made from small gherkins pickled in brine. Round white apple cucumbers are a recent type: they are usually about 9 cm in diameter and 12 cm long and the skin is creamy-white. Gherkin cucumbers have a dull green skin and are usually picked when they are 5–8 cm long. The common green cucumber is usually about 20 cm long and has a greater diameter than the more slender, green-skinned Lebanese cucumber. Telegraph cucumbers are like a longer version of the Lebanese or continental cucumber and may be 40–50 cm long; their crisp flesh is pale green.

Most cucumbers are about 97 per cent water. The familiar phrase 'as cool as a cucumber' may refer to their high water content or to their cooling effect in the mouth.

Cucumbers provide some vitamin C and small quantities of other vitamins and minerals. Lebanese cucumbers have about twice the vitamin C content of other varieties. Half a cup of cucumber provides 0.5 g of dietary fibre and 25 kJ.

CHOOSING AND STORING • Select firm cucumbers and avoid those that are beginning to soften. With green-skinned cucumbers, also avoid any where the skin is beginning to yellow. With apple cucumbers, a slight yellow colour on the skin is normal.

Store in the refrigerator, but not in plastic. Avoid storing cucumbers with fruit, as the gas given off by fruit causes cucumbers to soften.

PREPARATION AND COOKING • Cucumbers are usually eaten raw, but they can also be cooked or pickled. Apple cucumbers need to be peeled, but the skin of other varieties can be eaten.

CUCUMBER SALAD

Deliciously cooling as a side dish with curries. You can use low-fat yoghurt if you prefer.

2 green-skinned cucumbers or 1 telegraph cucumber
salt
3 green shallots (spring onions), sliced finely
1 cup natural yoghurt
1 tbsp lemon juice
1/4 tsp ground cumin
2 tbsp chopped fresh dill

SERVES 4

Peel cucumbers, slice in half lengthwise and scoop out seeds. Slice flesh, place in a strainer, sprinkle with salt and leave for 15 minutes. Rinse thoroughly to remove salt and pat dry in a clean tea-towel. Combine cucumber with yoghurt, lemon juice, cumin and dill, and place in serving dish.

NUTRITIONAL VALUE: 4.5 g protein, 2.5 g fat, 7.5 g carbohydrate, 1 g dietary fibre, 315 kJ (75 Cals). A good source of vitamin C and contributes some calcium.

LEBANESE CUCUMBER SALAD

Serve with Turkish bread as a healthy lunch.

6 Lebanese cucumbers, sliced
1 punnet cherry tomatoes, halved
150 g button mushrooms, halved
125 g fetta cheese, cubed
16 black olives
2 tbsp olive oil
2 tbsp lemon juice
2 tbsp chopped fresh mint
freshly ground black pepper
1 tbsp chopped hazelnuts

SERVES 4

Combine cucumbers, tomatoes, mushrooms, cheese and olives in a bowl. Place olive oil, lemon juice, mint and pepper into a jar and shake to combine. Pour over salad and toss gently. Just before serving, sprinkle hazelnuts on top.

NUTRITIONAL VALUE: 11 g protein, 18 g fat, 6.5 g carbohydrate, 5 g dietary fibre, 985 kJ (235 Cals). An excellent source of vitamin C, a good source of calcium and also provides some vitamin A, riboflavin, iron and zinc.

PICKLED GHERKINS

This pickle is delicious made with small gherkin cucumbers, but can also be made with large cucumbers cut into strips.

1 kg cucumbers
3 cups white vinegar
1 tbsp salt
½ cup sugar
2 small red chillies
6 cloves garlic, halved
1 tbsp dill seeds
1 tbsp whole black peppercorns
12 allspice berries
8 bay leaves

MAKES ABOUT 4 JARS

If you have small gherkin cucumbers, leave them whole. If using larger cucumbers, cut into quarters lengthwise and then into 7 cm lengths (or an appropriate length to fit upright in your jars).

To sterilise jars, place in a large saucepan, fill jars and saucepan with boiling water and boil for 5 minutes. Lift jars out and drain upside down on a clean paper towel.

Bring a large saucepan of water to the boil, add cucumbers and cook for 1 minute. Drain immediately and pack into sterilised jars. Place vinegar, salt, sugar, chillies, garlic, dill seeds, peppercorns, allspice and bay leaves into a large saucepan, bring to the boil, reduce heat and simmer uncovered for 5 minutes. Pour this spiced vinegar over the cucumbers, filling jars to the brim. (It is hard to be exact about the amount of vinegar needed as it depends on the size of the jars. If you do not have enough spiced vinegar, top each jar with a little extra vinegar.)

Leave for at least 2 weeks and consume within 6 months. As this recipe uses less salt than most recipes, the gherkins are best stored in the refrigerator.

NUTRITIONAL VALUE: Each gherkin will have about 80 kJ (20 Cals).

Daikon (see Radishes)

Eggplant

Known by their French name, *aubergine*, in England and Europe, eggplants are available in various forms: the largish purple globular type, the shorter slender baby variety, and the small, round, green 'pea' or Thai eggplant. They can also be either white or white striped with purple, yellow, bright orange or pale-green.

The eggplant is native to India, where it remains popular. (There, as in Africa, it is called 'brinjal'.) It is also widely used in many other countries. The earliest records of its cultivation are from China in the fifth century BC. It was introduced to Spain by the Arabs about 1500 years ago, to Italy about a thousand years later and to France in the eighteenth century.

Eggplants belong to the same solanum family as potatoes, tomatoes and capsicums. Technically a giant berry, eggplants have varying degrees of bitterness (modern cultivars are less bitter). You can sometimes get an indication of potential bitterness in purple eggplants by looking for sharp spines around the calyx at the stem end: those without spines tend to be less bitter. The tiny pea-shaped eggplant are quite bitter and this is important in the Thai recipes that specify them. Much of the bitterness of eggplant is in the seeds and cutting the seeds, as can occur if cooked eggplant is puréed, enhances the bitterness.

Eggplant is not rich in any particular nutrient, but supplies small amounts of a range of vitamins and minerals. A typical serving has 0.5 g of fat, 2.5 g of dietary fibre and 80 kJ—but a serving of eggplant fried in plenty of oil could have 40–50 g of fat. The skin contains high levels of antioxidants called anthocyanins.

CHOOSING AND STORING • Available throughout the year, but best in summer and early autumn. Look for a firm shiny skin and choose those that feel heavy for their size. Avoid any with brown spots or where the skin is beginning to soften and wrinkle.

Do not store eggplants in plastic. Refrigerate for up to a week.

PREPARATION AND COOKING • Remove the stem, taking care if it has prickles. Eggplant does not need to be peeled. To reduce bitterness, slice or cube the eggplant and sprinkle thickly with salt. Leave for about 15 minutes, then rinse off the beads of bitter juice that develop and pat or squeeze dry.

Eggplant is not suitable to eat raw and does not take well to boiling or steaming. It is best fried, grilled or barbecued, baked, used in composite dishes such as moussaka, or added to casseroles. It is also wonderful charred over a flame, peeled and chopped finely. Because of its spongy texture, eggplant can absorb a lot of oil: to reduce the amount it absorbs, salt, rinse and squeeze it before cooking on a hot heavy-based pan with just a smear of oil, or grilling. Baby eggplant does not need to be salted and it absorbs less oil.

To grill eggplant, use a pastry brush to coat slices with olive oil. If you can find a good olive oil in a spray pack, it will also be suitable.

EASY TUNA EGGPLANT BAKE

A good dish to make for unexpected visitors, as you're likely to have all the ingredients in your kitchen. For a vegetarian version, replace the tuna with 2 cups of cooked drained kidney or white beans.

2 large eggplants, cut into 1.5 cm slices
1 tbsp olive oil
½ cup sliced green shallots (spring onions)
750 g jar good quality tomato-based
*   pasta sauce*
425 g canned tuna (no added salt), drained
2 cups skim milk
2 tbsp plain flour
2 tbsp grated parmesan
2 eggs, beaten
a pinch of nutmeg
½ cup grated cheddar
½ tsp ground paprika

SERVES 6

Preheat oven to 180°C.

Sprinkle eggplant with salt, leave for 15 minutes, rinse thoroughly and squeeze dry. Brush eggplant with olive oil and grill until lightly browned on both sides.

Combine green onions, tomato sauce and tuna. Line a shallow ovenproof casserole dish with one third of the eggplant slices. Cover with half the tuna mixture, another third of the eggplant, the remaining tuna mixture and the rest of the eggplant.

Blend milk and flour in food processor. Pour into a saucepan over a low heat and stir constantly until mixture boils and thickens. Add parmesan, then allow to cool a little. Stir in eggs and nutmeg. Pour sauce over eggplant, sprinkle with grated cheddar and the paprika, and bake for 30 minutes.

NUTRITIONAL VALUE: 29 g protein, 12 g fat, 23 g carbohydrate, 6 g dietary fibre, 1320 kJ (315 Cals). A good source of potassium, iron, zinc and calcium and provides some vitamin C and riboflavin.

OVEN-BAKED RATATOUILLE

This is delicious served hot or cold. I sometimes make double to ensure some leftovers for the next day's lunch.

1 tbsp olive oil
2 cloves garlic, crushed
12 baby eggplants, halved lengthwise
1 red capsicum, seeded and sliced
400 g zucchini, sliced
4 large tomatoes, sliced
½ cup fresh basil

SERVES 4

Combine oil and garlic, and leave to stand. Preheat oven to 190°C.

Score cut surfaces of eggplants in a diamond pattern and grill until brown. (Alternatively, cook on a hot, non-stick frying pan until cut surface is lightly browned.) In a casserole dish, place half the halved eggplants, skin-side down. Cover with capsicum, zucchini and tomatoes, and sprinkle with basil. Top with remaining eggplant, skin-side up. Remove garlic from oil and drizzle oil over vegetables. Cover tightly and bake for 30 minutes.

NUTRITIONAL VALUE: 5.5 g protein, 2.5 g fat ('good' fat), 12 g carbohydrate, 8.5 g dietary fibre, 385 kJ (90 Cals). An excellent source of vitamin C, a good source of vitamin A and potassium and also provides some niacin and iron.

BABA GHANNOUJ

This is delicious with Turkish or Lebanese bread plus felafel and salad. Alternatively, omit the tahini and use the purée as a sauce with grilled mushrooms and grilled lamb. If you don't have a gas stove or barbecue, you can bake the eggplant in a moderate oven for 30 minutes, but you will miss the smoky flavour. It is one of the few recipes that I think needs a pinch of salt.

1 medium-sized eggplant
2 cloves garlic, crushed
2 tbsp lemon juice
1–2 tbsp tahini
pinch of sea salt

SERVES 4

Hold eggplant on a long fork over a gas flame, turning often, until the skin goes black and blisters. Wrap eggplant in foil and leave for 10–15 minutes, then peel away the charred skin. Chop flesh finely, adding garlic, lemon juice and tahini to taste. (Don't use a food processor, as it will crush eggplant seeds and produce a bitter taste.) Add salt to taste, and serve with pita or Turkish bread.

NUTRITIONAL VALUE: 2.5 g protein, 6 g fat ('good' fat), 2 g carbohydrate, 3 g dietary fibre, 300 kJ (75 Cals). Provides some vitamin C.

EGGPLANT STACKS

One of my favourite lunchtime dishes. For an easy, healthy meal, serve it with some good bread, a good ricotta cheese and a green salad.

2 medium-sized eggplants, cut into 2 cm slices
1 tsp olive oil
4 large tomatoes, sliced thickly
2 roasted yellow capsicums (see page 43)
½ cup parsley pesto (see page 122)

SERVES 4

Sprinkle eggplant slices with salt, leave for 15 minutes, then rinse well and squeeze dry. Heat a heavy-based pan, add oil and cook eggplant until brown on both sides. Cut capsicums into strips.

On individual serving dishes, place a slice of eggplant, a slice of tomato and some capsicum strips. Repeat layers and top with pesto.

NUTRITIONAL VALUE: 7 g protein, 21 g fat ('good' fat), 11 g carbohydrate, 7.5 g dietary fibre, 1075 kJ (255 Cals). An excellent source of vitamin C, a good source of vitamin A and provides some potassium, magnesium, calcium, iron, zinc and niacin.

Endive and chicory

Endive is sometimes known as chicory, although the two are different. Endive has hairless curly leaves while chicory's leaves have hairs. To complicate matters, in France, the names are reversed.

There are two varieties of endive. One is available as curly endive (*chicorée frisée* in France), with dark-green deeply frilled outer leaves and pale-green curly inside leaves. The other is witlof (also called Belgian endive and French endive), for which see page 181. Radicchio (see **Lettuces**), which is more commonly used as a salad vegetable, is another member of the chicory family. The darker the green of curly endive and chicory leaves, the stronger and more bitter their flavour. To produce sweeter leaves, the plants are often blanched for a few weeks before picking. The inside leaves, protected from the light, are sweeter and more tender, and curly endive is often sold with the bunch turned inside out so you can see these leaves.

Endive is native to the Mediterranean region, and both chicory and endive were grown as salad vegetables by the Greeks and Romans. It is thought that endive was grown even earlier in Egypt and was the bitter herb used at the Passover. Some types of chicory have a strong root which can be roasted and used as a coffee substitute, although it has none of the flavour of coffee and is a poor substitute for the real thing. Chicory grown for its root usually has very bitter leaves, which are not eaten. Inulin, a form of soluble fibre also found in Jerusalem artichokes, is also extracted from chicory root and is used in some fat-reduced foods to provide 'body'. As consumers of Jerusalem artichokes are aware, inulin passes to the bowel where good bacteria ferment it, producing copious quantities of gas in the process—this feature is not mentioned in food products to which inulin is added! Chicory root can also be used for fuel alcohol production.

Chicory is an excellent source of vitamins C and A, carotenoids and folate and also supplies calcium. A cup of raw chicory has 2 g of dietary fibre and 50 kJ.

Curly endive has more folate than chicory and is a good source of iron. It also supplies vitamins C and A, but a smaller quantity of calcium. A cup of curly endive has 1.5 g of dietary fibre and 40 kJ.

CHOOSING AND STORING • Curly endive and chicory are available all year, but the peak seasons are during summer and autumn. Choose endive or chicory with crisp leaves. Avoid bunches where the inside portion shows any signs of becoming brown or slimy.

Endive and chicory can be refrigerated in a plastic bag for up to 4 days. If curly endive is kept for too long, the inside leaves begin to rot and turn brown.

PREPARATION AND COOKING • Endive and chicory can be cooked, but are more often served raw in salads. Wash well before using as the outer leaves often harbour grit.

CURLY ENDIVE WITH CHICK PEAS

In this dish, the bitterness of the endive marries well with the sweetness of the capsicum and chick peas.

1 tbsp olive oil
1 medium-sized onion, sliced
1 clove garlic, crushed
1 red capsicum, halved, seeded and sliced
1/2 bunch curly endive
2 cups cooked or canned chick peas
1/2 cup chopped parsley
freshly ground pepper

SERVES 4

Heat a wok and add the oil, onion, garlic and capsicum. Stir-fry for 4–5 minutes, or until onion is wilted. Add endive and chick peas, and toss well to heat through. Stir in parsley and pepper before serving.

NUTRITIONAL VALUE: 10 g protein, 7 g fat ('good' fat), 20 g carbohydrate, 7.5 g dietary fibre, 750 kJ (180 Cals). An excellent source of vitamin C and a good source of folate, vitamin A, potassium, iron and zinc.

Fennel

Grown for its seeds, its feathery dark-green leaves and its bulbous root, fennel contains some volatile oils that give a mild flavour of aniseed. It is a member of the carrot family and is native to the Mediterranean region. The bulb (also called Florence fennel, finocchio or sweet anise) looks a bit like slightly squashed celery and is delicious raw or cooked. It goes especially well with fish and is excellent raw, roasted, stir-fried or added to soups. The feathery leaves can be used as a substitute for dill and the stalks are excellent in small quantities in salads.

Wild fennel, also called common fennel, grows along roadsides and has been declared a noxious weed in some areas. Its feathery leaves can be used as a substitute for dill, but it does not develop the bulb of cultivated fennel.

Fennel seeds are used as a spice in some curries. As their flavour is like aniseed, they are usually used in small quantities.

Fennel provides vitamin C and some folate, but is not especially rich in any particular nutrient. It contributes small amounts of many vitamins and minerals. It has no fat and $\frac{1}{2}$ cup of sliced fennel has 2 g of dietary fibre and 45 kJ.

CHOOSING AND STORING • Fennel is best during the winter months, although it is also available in autumn and spring. Choose firm crisp fennel with feathery leaves. Avoid those that look dehydrated or where the outside stalk leaves are damaged or the feathery leaves are slimy. Whole baby fennel are sometimes available in spring and are sweet and delicious.

Store fennel in a plastic bag in the refrigerator for up to a week.

PREPARATION AND COOKING • Remove the outer leaves and trim the base of the fennel. Either cut it in halves or quarters lengthwise, or slice thinly across. If using the fennel in a salad, soak in iced water for 15 minutes to crisp. If you can find the baby fennel, use whole or halved.

fennel

FENNEL WITH PASTA

An ideal dish for those nights when you want a very simple meal.

500 g tagliatelle or other pasta
1 tbsp extra-virgin olive oil
2 small to medium-sized fennel bulbs, sliced thinly
1 medium-sized onion, finely sliced
2 cloves garlic
2 tsp finely grated lemon peel
1/2 cup white wine
1/2 cup finely chopped flat-leaf parsley
freshly ground black pepper
freshly grated parmesan

SERVES 4

Bring a large saucepan of water to the boil. When water is boiling, add pasta and cook until al dente. Drain and return to saucepan.

Meanwhile, heat oil in wok or frying pan, add fennel, onion and garlic, cover and allow to sweat for 10 minutes, stirring several times. Add lemon peel and wine, bring to the boil and simmer for 2 minutes. Add parsley and plenty of pepper.

Serve pasta in heated bowls, topped with fennel and parmesan.

NUTRITIONAL VALUE: 18 g protein, 8 g fat ('good' fat), 94 g carbohydrate, 11 g dietary fibre, 2195 kJ (525 Cals). An excellent source of vitamin C and provides some potassium, calcium, iron and zinc.

FENNEL AND ORANGE SALAD

One of the most simple salads. The slight aniseed flavour goes well with barbecued lamb, fish or chicken.

1 medium-sized fennel bulb
2 oranges
2 tsp finely grated orange peel
2 tbsp olive oil
freshly ground black pepper
about 20 black olives

SERVES 4

Trim base and long stalks from fennel, reserving a few of the feathery leaves. Slice bulb very thinly. Grate peel from 1 orange, then remove all peel and pith and slice the orange flesh. Squeeze 2 tablespoons of juice from the remaining orange, combine with the olive oil, peel and pepper, and pour over fennel. Toss well to combine. Pile fennel onto a serving plate and arrange oranges and olives on top. Snip off some of the reserved fennel leaves and sprinkle over the top.

NUTRITIONAL VALUE: 1 g protein, 10 g fat ('good' fat), 6 g carbohydrate, 3 g dietary fibre, 515 kJ (120 Cals). An excellent source of vitamin C.

ROASTED FENNEL

A delicious accompaniment to roast potatoes and rack of lamb.

1 tbsp extra-virgin olive oil
2 small fennel bulbs, about 250 g each
2 cloves garlic, crushed
2 lemons, sliced
2 tsp brown sugar

SERVES 4

Preheat oven to 190°C. Remove any loose outer leaves from the fennel, trim the stalks about 5 cm above where they meet the bulb and cut a thin slice from the base. Halve fennel lengthwise.

Place olive oil into a shallow ovenproof dish large enough to hold the fennel halves and heat in oven for 2 minutes. Add fennel and turn to coat with the oil. Place a few slices of lemon under each fennel half, turning the cut surface down. Sprinkle garlic over fennel and arrange remaining lemon slices on top. Cook in oven for 20 minutes.

Turn fennel, sprinkle cut surface with brown sugar and return to oven for a further 10 minutes. Serve hot. (I serve the lemon slices, but you can discard them if preferred.)

NUTRITIONAL VALUE: 1.5 g protein, 5 g fat ('good' fat), 7 g carbohydrate, 5 g dietary fibre, 355 kJ (85 Cals). A good source of vitamin C and provides some potassium.

Garlic

A member of the lily family and related to onions and leeks, garlic is native to central Asia, but has spread around the world. The Egyptians have used it for 3000 years and garlic was supposed to give strength and disease resistance to the slaves who built the pyramids. It has also been a regular element of the diet in India and China for over 1000 years. Anglo-Saxons took a little longer to get used to garlic and used to refer to it as the 'stinking rose'. The English word 'garlic' comes from an old Anglo-Saxon word meaning 'spear plant'.

More than 80 per cent of the world's garlic is produced in Asia, especially in China. Korea has the highest per-capita consumption of garlic.

The garlic bulb, or head, consists of a cluster of 8–10 individual cloves (sometimes more), each wrapped in a parchment-like skin. Single cloves can be broken off for use or the entire head can be roasted as a delicious vegetable. When garlic cloves are cooked whole and unpeeled, their flavour is mild. Fresh green garlic with its long green leaves attached is occasionally available in spring. It has a mild flavour and can be sliced like a spring onion, which it resembles. Most garlic is left in the ground until summer, when it is harvested and hung to dry, allowing it to develop greater pungency and to last many months.

Many claims are made for garlic's health-giving properties and it is supposed to have anticoagulant, antibacterial and cholesterol-lowering effects. Some of these claims may be true, although there is continuing debate over garlic's ability to lower blood cholesterol. Some researchers dispute whether most people are likely to eat enough garlic as a food for it to be effective. However, most medical scientists now accept that the antioxidants and sulphur compounds in garlic do have valuable roles. With most vegetable products, the whole food usually has the edge over extracts or supplements when it comes to medicinal benefits.

There are many tales about the best way to get rid of the smell of garlic from the breath. Chewing parsley is popular, while others claim you need to chew fennel or caraway seeds. None of these methods works after a good meal of garlic. The best solution is to make sure everyone around you has been eating garlic it too, as when you have been eating it, you do not notice the aroma on others. Odour-free garlic compounds are popular but you soon discover that their odour-free status is a myth. In any case, some of garlic's most valuable properties—both culinary and medicinal—occur in the very sulphur compounds that produce the mouth odour.

When garlic is crushed, an enzyme is released which causes an odourless sulphur compound called alliin (s-allylcysteine sulphoxide) to be converted to allicin (diallyl disulphide), producing the familiar aroma. Some people claim that to derive benefits from garlic you must eat whole cloves (with alliin), while others swear by the beneficial effects of crushed garlic (with allicin). In Mediterranean and Asian cuisines, both whole and crushed garlic are used, probably providing maximum benefits.

Apart from its sulphur compounds and valuable antioxidants, the quantity of garlic most people eat provides only small quantities of minerals and vitamins. An average-sized clove has 1 g of fibre and 25 kJ.

CHOOSING AND STORING • Garlic is available all year round. Choose a head with firm fat cloves. Avoid any that are softening or shooting, or dried out.

Store garlic in a cool airy place, not in the refrigerator. It should last for some months. Discard any cloves that darken or go soft.

PREPARATION AND COOKING • To peel a clove of garlic, place it on a cutting board, hold a kitchen knife flat over it and give the flat part of the knife a good thump: this splits the papery skin, which can then be removed easily. If slicing garlic, remove any green parts in the centre.

A head of garlic can be included in some rice dishes. Simply place the head, skin on, in the centre of a pilaf or paella. A delicate garlic flavour will pervade the rice and you can also squeeze out the soft creamy garlic when the dish is cooked.

To make bruschetta, toast bread, rub it with a cut clove of garlic and drizzle with olive oil. Finely diced tomato mixed with torn basil leaves makes a simple but good topping.

SKORDALIA

This delicious garlic sauce is served frequently in Greece. It is excellent served with fish, or simply as a spread for good bread or a dip with toast. For many people, the addition of sea salt will improve the flavour.

3 thick slices of Italian-style bread,
   crusts removed
½ cup mashed potato
4–6 cloves garlic, peeled
2 tbsp walnut pieces
¼ cup lemon juice
½ cup olive oil
a little sea salt (optional)

SERVES 6

Soak bread in water for 5 minutes, then squeeze to remove water. Place bread, potato, garlic, walnuts and lemon juice into food processor and process until smooth. Add a little portion of the olive oil and blend thoroughly. Continue adding olive oil until it is all incorporated. Add sea salt to taste.

NUTRITIONAL VALUE: 2.5 g protein, 23 g fat ('good' fat), 9.5 g carbohydrate, 1.5 g dietary fibre, 1065 kJ (255 Cals). A good source of essential fatty acids and provides some vitamin C.

ROASTED WHOLE GARLIC

This is delicious on its own, or you can squeeze out the softened flesh and add it to rice dishes or puréed eggplant, tomato, avocado, chick peas or white beans.

2 heads garlic
2 tsp olive oil

SERVES 4

Preheat oven to 180°C. Halve each unpeeled garlic head crosswise (or use them whole if you prefer). Place on a small baking tray and drizzle with oil. Bake for 30 minutes, after which the soft flesh paste can be squeezed out of each half head.

NUTRITIONAL VALUE: 2.5 g protein, 3.5 g fat ('good' fat), 4 g carbohydrate, 7 g dietary fibre, 245 kJ (60 Cals).

Globe artichokes (see **Artichokes, globe**)

Gourds (see **Other vegetables**)

Jicama

Also known as the Mexican potato or yam bean, there is nothing about the jicama (pronounced *hikarma*) that resembles a bean. Its Mexican name reflects its origins (Mexico to the northern parts of South America), while the English term 'yam bean' comes from the fact that the vine on which it grows (a member of the morning glory family) produces bean-like pods and yam-like tubers. The pods are poisonous, but the squat, light-brown tubers with their lobed bottoms are delicious. The crisp white flesh can be eaten raw and is a bit like a water chestnut.

In Mexico, jicama is eaten as a snack food, often sprinkled with lime juice and chilli powder. It is also used in fruit salads.

Jicama was taken to the Philippines and south China in the seventeenth century, grew prolifically and became popular to use in stir-fried dishes, often as a substitute for water chestnuts. It is now available in supermarkets in many other parts of the world.

Jicama is a good source of vitamin C and fibre, and also provides some potassium and a small amount of carbohydrate. Half a cup of sliced jicama has no fat, 5 g of carbohydrate, 3 g of dietary fibre and 85 kJ.

CHOOSING AND STORING • Available in winter and spring. Select tubers that are no more than 10–15 cm in diameter. Larger tubers tend to be more fibrous and less sweet.

Store in the refrigerator for up to a week.

PREPARATION AND COOKING • To peel jicama, insert a knife under the top and pull off the skin and the layer of fibrous white flesh just beneath it. It peels easily and the flesh does not darken on exposure to the air. To eat jicama raw, cut into sticks to use with dips. It can also be treated like a potato and steamed, baked, boiled or made into chips. It is also good to stir-fry. Even after cooking, it retains its crisp texture. Whether cooked or raw, combined in a fruit salad with pineapple, orange and mango, it adds a delightful crunchy element.

THAI-STYLE JICAMA AND BEEF SALAD

A substantial salad that is especially good on a warm summer evening. For a vegetarian version, omit the beef and substitute 300 g silken tofu, cut into cubes.

400 g beef fillet or rump in one piece
1 clove garlic, crushed
1 bunch coriander
1 tbsp finely sliced lemongrass (white part only)
1 tsp palm sugar or use brown sugar
2 tbsp lime juice
1 tbsp fish sauce
1 red chilli, sliced finely
1 medium-sized jicama
3 Lebanese cucumbers
1 red capsicum
1 tbsp Vietnamese mint leaves
1 tbsp purple basil leaves

SERVES 4

Grill beef until medium-rare. Cool and slice thinly. Use a mortar and pestle (if you have them—otherwise use a blender) to pound the garlic, the sliced roots and stems of the coriander, and the lemongrass and palm sugar. Add lime juice, fish sauce and chilli.

Peel jicama and cut into matchstick pieces. Slice cucumbers lengthwise. Seed and slice capsicum. Combine jicama, cucumber and capsicum with the mint, basil and coriander leaves. Arrange on a serving plate, top with the beef and sprinkle dressing over the top.

NUTRITIONAL VALUE: 26 g protein, 3 g fat, 15 g carbohydrate, 7.5 g dietary fibre, 790 kJ (190 Cals). An excellent source of vitamin C, a good source of iron, zinc, vitamin A, niacin and potassium, and also provides some magnesium and the B vitamins riboflavin and thiamin.

Kale

This open, frill-edged, dark-green cabbage is popular in northern Europe, partly because it survives cold growing conditions, even surviving under snow. A cultivar with smoother leaves, known as collards, is popular in the southern United States. Although it is one of the most nutritious of all green, leafy vegetables kale is often grown as an ornamental plant, and the purple and blue-green frilly varieties are sometimes used as a border in parks and gardens. It is also grown as animal fodder.

Seakale, a hardy plant with bright-green leaves curled at the edges, has small leafy folded shoots which can be eaten. It is a rich source of vitamin C and was used by sailors in times past to prevent scurvy.

Kale is very rich in vitamin C and antioxidants, has high levels of folate and vitamin A, and provides vitamin E, iron and manganese. An average serving of cooked kale has 1.5 g of fat, 3 g of dietary fibre and 100 kJ.

CHOOSING AND STORING • Available in winter. Select dark-green leaves that are firm and crisp. Avoid any that have wilted or are beginning to yellow.

Keep kale in a plastic bag in the refrigerator for 3–4 days. The longer it is stored, the stronger its flavour, so it is best used soon after purchase. Unlike most leafy vegetables, kale can also be frozen.

PREPARATION AND COOKING • Kale needs to be washed thoroughly, as small insects hide in its curly leaves. Although its leaves are strong, it is tender yet crisp after even a minute or two of cooking. It is ideal to stir-fry and can also be steamed and boiled (for no longer than one minute), and is ideal to add to soups. Use kale in any recipes calling for cabbage.

KALE SOUP

A nourishing winter soup that is a complete meal. For a vegetarian alternative, omit the meat, use 1.5 litres of vegetable stock in place of the lamb broth, and use 2 cans of chick peas or lima beans.

2 lamb shanks
1 medium-sized onion, chopped finely
2 large carrots, sliced
4 bay leaves
10 peppercorns
a few parsley stalks
2 L water
2 medium-sized zucchini, sliced
300 g canned chick peas or lima beans
400 g canned tomatoes
1 cup frozen peas
1 bunch kale (about 400 g)

SERVES 4

In a large saucepan, place lamb shanks, onion, one of the carrots, and the bay leaves, peppercorns, parsley stalks and water. Bring to the boil, cover and simmer for $1\frac{1}{2}$ hours or until meat falls from the bones. Strain, reserving the liquid, remove meat from shanks and cut into pieces.

Reheat strained broth, add carrot and simmer for 5 minutes. Add zucchini, chick peas, tomatoes and their liquid, frozen peas and meat. Simmer for 3 minutes. Separate stalks and leaves of kale, shred leaves coarsely, add to soup and cook for 1–2 minutes. Serve piping-hot.

NUTRITIONAL VALUE: 26 g protein, 4.5 g fat, 17 g carbohydrate, 11 g dietary fibre, 900 kJ (215 Cals). An excellent source of vitamins A and C, and a good source of iron, zinc, potassium, calcium, magnesium and niacin.

Kohlrabi

Looking a little like a child's drawing of a spaceship, kohlrabi has leaves emerging in a spiral pattern from a white and purple globular bulb. Some varieties are pale green rather than white. Contrary to popular belief, kohlrabi is not a root vegetable, but grows above the ground. It is a member of the cabbage family, a cross between a cabbage (*kohl* is the German word for cabbage) and a turnip (*rabi*). Its leaves (but not the tough stems) can be eaten by those who like strong cabbage flavour but the bulb is more popular, with flavour elements of radish, mild turnip, cabbage and artichoke.

Kohlrabi originated in northern Europe in the fifteenth century, although Pliny described a similar vegetable in his writings in 70 AD.

Kohlrabi is an excellent source of vitamin C and a good source of folate. It has no fat and an average serving has 3.5 g of dietary fibre and 80 kJ.

CHOOSING AND STORING • Available from autumn to spring, with the best flavour in autumn. Choose smaller bulbs (less than about 70 cm in diameter),

with leaves that look fresh. Avoid those that have been damaged or have wilted or yellowing leaves.

To store, remove leaves and their stems, place in plastic bag and refrigerate for 3–4 days.

PREPARATION AND COOKING • Remove stems, as they are tough and inedible, but use leaves if desired. The skin of kohlrabi is not usually eaten, but if you are steaming the vegetable it is best to remove the skin after cooking to retain flavour and nutrients. If peeling before cooking, cut a slice from the top and pull off the skin and underlying fibrous layer.

Kohlrabi can be eaten raw, or grated or cut into fine strips and added to salads. You can steam, boil, microwave or stir-fry it to tender-crisp, and it is also good in soups and casseroles. Or braise peeled and diced kohlrabi with some chopped onion in a little olive oil and chicken stock.

CHICKEN, KOHLRABI AND BARLEY SOUP

A warming soup ideal for chilly days and good to take to work, either in a thermos or to be reheated in a microwave. For a vegetarian version, replace the chicken with 1 cup black-eyed beans (no need to soak them first).

1 whole chicken
¾ cup pearl barley
4 bay leaves
1 lemon, cut in half
6 cups water
2 medium-sized kohlrabi, peeled and diced
2 medium-sized potatoes, scrubbed and diced
½ medium-sized butternut pumpkin, peeled, seeded and diced
1 leek, washed and sliced
2 tbsp chopped parsley

SERVES 4

Remove fatty pads from under chicken skin. Place chicken, pearl barley, bay leaves, lemon and water in a large saucepan, bring to the boil, cover and simmer for 1 hour. Remove and discard bay leaves and lemon. Lift out chicken, remove and discard skin and bones, and cut flesh into pieces.

Reheat chicken stock and add kohlrabi, potatoes, pumpkin and leek. Simmer for 10–15 minutes, or until vegetables are cooked. Return chicken to soup and simmer for another minute or two. Serve in deep bowls, sprinkled with chopped parsley.

NUTRITIONAL VALUE: 37 g protein, 8 g fat, 39 g carbohydrate, 8.5 g dietary fibre, 1600 kJ (380 Cals). An excellent source of vitamin C, a very good source of iron, zinc, potassium and thiamin, and also provides vitamin A, riboflavin and niacin.

Kumara (see **Sweet potatoes**)

Leeks

Leeks are a member of the lily family and have probably been cultivated since biblical times. Some close relatives grow from Portugal across to Turkey, so it is reasonable to assume this is their region of origin. The Romans grew leeks all over Europe and when the Welsh defeated the Anglo-Saxons in 640 AD, they are said to have worn leeks in their hats to help distinguish themselves from the enemy. Other writers maintain that this did not occur until the twelfth century, but whatever the date, the leek has become the national symbol of Wales and is still worn with pride on St David's Day.

Leeks are very popular because of their mild onion-like flavour and their versatility. The edible portion of the stem consists of the thick white part and the next pale-green section. To achieve a longer white section, many growers heap earth up the stems, but this makes leeks gritty. In my home garden, I don't do this, and although the stems turn pale green, they remain tender up to the part where the thick dark-green strappy leaves begin.

Leeks are a good source of vitamin C, provide folate and also some vitamin A and iron. The edible portion of a medium-sized leek has 0.5 g of fat, 3.5 g of dietary fibre and 100 kJ.

CHOOSING AND STORING • Available all year, but the flavour is best in late spring, summer and early autumn. Choose leeks that are firm and undamaged, with crisp green tops. Large leeks tend to have less flavour than the thinner ones.

Refrigerate unwashed in a plastic bag for up to a week.

PREPARATION AND COOKING • Removing the dirt caught inside the many layers of leeks can be a problem. Start by cutting off the dark green leaves where they join the lighter green area, then peel away a couple of outside layers, removing them right to the base. Cut the leek in half lengthwise and hold it under the tap, fanning the layers slightly to let any grit out. If you need the leeks left whole, cut a slit into the leaf end and stand this end down in a jug of water for 15 minutes. Wash well in a sink of cold water.

Younger, thinner leeks can be cooked whole or halved lengthwise. Older leeks are best cut into rings.

LEEK AND SUN-DRIED TOMATO RISOTTO

A good meal to eat by the fire on a cold night. Sun-dried tomatoes are now available in the fruit and vegetable section of the supermarket.

8 sun-dried tomatoes
1 cup boiling water
1 tbsp olive oil
3 leeks, washed and sliced
2 cloves garlic, finely chopped
120 g sliced button mushrooms
½ tsp saffron threads
2 cups arborio rice (short, round grains)
½ cup white wine
5 cups chicken stock
2 tbsp freshly grated parmesan
freshly ground pepper

SERVES 4

Cut each sun-dried tomato into several pieces. Place in a small bowl, pour boiling water over, cover and leave to stand for 15 minutes.

Heat olive oil in saucepan and add leeks, garlic, mushrooms and saffron. Cover and allow to sweat for about 4 minutes, stirring several times. Add rice and wine, and stir well to combine. Bring stock to the boil and leave it simmering with a lid on. Add a ladleful of stock to rice, stirring constantly until stock is absorbed. Continue adding stock by the ladleful, waiting until it has been absorbed by the rice before adding another. When all the stock has been absorbed, add the sun-dried tomatoes and their soaking liquid. When the liquid has been absorbed, the rice should be cooked. Stir in the parmesan and pepper, cover and leave to stand for 3 minutes. Serve in deep bowls.

NUTRITIONAL VALUE: 14 g protein, 8 g fat, 86 g carbohydrate, 7.5 g dietary fibre, 2000 kJ (475 Cals). An excellent source of vitamin C, a good source of magnesium, iron, zinc and niacin and also provides some vitamin A, riboflavin, calcium and potassium.

BRAISED LEEKS WITH A CRUNCHY CRUST

A simple dish that is good for lunch or for a first course at dinner. Also goes well with roast chicken or duck, or roast lamb. Try to use a concentrated, home-made chicken stock.

4 medium-sized leeks
1 tbsp olive oil
½ cup chicken stock
½ cup white wine
2 slices wholemeal bread made into crumbs
2 tsp finely grated lemon peel
2 tbsp freshly grated parmesan

SERVES 4

Preheat oven to 190°C. Cut off the dark-green leaves and slice leeks in half lengthwise. Wash well and pat dry.

Choose a shallow ovenproof casserole dish that will hold the 8 leek halves snugly. Place olive oil in the dish and warm in oven for a couple of minutes. Add leeks and shake to coat with the oil. Combine stock and wine, pour over leeks and bake uncovered for 15 minutes. Combine fresh breadcrumbs, lemon peel and parmesan, sprinkle over leeks and bake for a further 10 minutes.

NUTRITIONAL VALUE: 5.5 g protein, 7.5 g fat ('good' fat), 10 g carbohydrate, 4 g dietary fibre, 530 kJ (125 Cals). An excellent source of vitamin C and provides some calcium.

Lettuce

There are thousands of different varieties of lettuce, all developed from the original wild lettuces that grow in northern Europe, Asia, North Africa and parts of North America. Wild lettuces, with their lanky stalks and sparse, bitter and often prickly leaves, do not resemble our modern cultivated lettuces.

The name lettuce comes from the Latin *lactuca* and was used because the stem of lettuce gives out a milky sap when cut. This is supposed to induce sleepiness and was mentioned by the Greek physician Hippocrates, who was born in Cos in 456 BC. Lettuces were first cultivated by the Egyptians around 4500 BC. They were also popular with the Romans, who believed that Emperor Augustus was cured of illness by eating lettuce. Writings from the year 1597 mention eight different varieties of lettuce.

Most lettuces are used mainly as salad greens, although some of the older varieties which have been in existence for hundreds of years can be cooked.

The darker the leaves of a lettuce, the higher the content of various carotenoids including beta carotene: a green cos or mignonette lettuce can have six times as much beta carotene as the paler leaves on an iceberg. Iceberg lettuce also has less vitamin C than other varieties. All lettuces contribute fibre and folate. A typical serving has no fat, 2 g of dietary fibre and averages 55 kJ.

VARIETIES • *Butter* lettuce is a soft-leaved, bright-green 'head' lettuce and is often called butterhead. It has a mild flavour.

Coral lettuce (lollo rosso) has small, tightly curled, finely frilled loose leaves with a reddish tinge at the edges. The flavour is mild, but slightly grassy. There is also a pale-green variety (lollo verde) with no reddish edges.

Cos, also known as romaine, is a crisp pale-green lettuce with elongated leaves that overlap but do not really form a head. The leaves are crisp and the inner, paler green leaves are sweet.

Iceberg, also known as common lettuce, was the main variety used in North America and Australia for some years. It has coarse crisp leaves and a tight head. The inside leaves are paler in colour than the outside ones. Some varieties have fringed or frilled leaves.

Lamb's lettuce, also known as corn salad or *mâche*, has just a few small, mid-green leaves per plant. It is soft and has a delightful flavour, less grassy than some and almost slightly nutty.

Mesclun is a mix of leaves which may include any of the various lettuces, plus chicory, dandelion leaves, chervil, rocket and mustard. The plants are planted densely, the leaves are cut and the field left to grow back for the next picking.

Mignonette lettuce has a small soft leaf which may be curly or slightly frilly. The edges of the leaves are usually dark reddish: the centre leaves are pale green fading to cream, but still tinged with the darker colour. Mignonette lettuce with no reddish tinges are also available.

Mizuna (see **Asian greens**) is a Japanese vegetable with a slight mustard flavour that marries well with milder-flavoured salad greens. The younger, softly frilled leaves are preferred for use in salads.

Oakleaf is a loose-leafed lettuce that comes in light green or in reddish varieties. Not surprisingly, given its name, it has leaves shaped like an oak leaf.

Radicchio comes in different colours and shapes. Some varieties are dark red, while others have streaks of dark red on the leaves. It has a bitter flavour and is delicious shredded and combined with finely sliced fennel and a few black olives, dressed with a little olive oil and lemon juice. It can be cooked.

CHOOSING AND STORING • Lettuces are available all year round but the best supplies are from late spring, through summer and into early autumn. Select lettuces with bright crisp leaves and avoid any that look wilted. Iceberg lettuces should be heavy for their size.

Store lettuce in a plastic bag in the refrigerator for 3–4 days.

PREPARATION AND COOKING • Always remove the centre core and wash lettuce thoroughly, as small slugs and spiders can hide between the leaves. A salad spinner is an excellent investment and a simple plastic one costs very little. After washing the lettuce, all you do is put the leaves into the spinner, pull the cord or turn the handle (depending on the model chosen) and the moisture flies off the leaves. Leaves that have been dried after washing are best to use in a salad.

For cooking lettuce as a separate vegetable, cut off the base of the stem and cut small lettuce into quarters. Braise in a little olive oil and stock for about 5 minutes.

San choy bau

These are messy to eat, but worth every dribble down the chin. As a vegetarian alternative, substitute 1 cup tempeh cubes and 1 cup tofu cubes for the meat.

1 tsp sesame oil
400 g minced chicken or pork
½ cup sliced green shallots (spring onions)
100 g can water chestnuts, drained and
*   finely chopped*
100 g mushrooms, finely chopped
1 tbsp dry sherry
1 tbsp oyster sauce
1 tbsp salt-reduced soy sauce
1 iceberg lettuce, washed

SERVES 4

Heat sesame oil in wok and add minced chicken or pork. Stir over a high heat until meat is brown and starting to go crispy. Add green shallots, water chestnuts and mushrooms, and continue cooking for another 5 minutes. Combine sherry, oyster and soy sauces, and add to wok.

Trim lettuce leaves (use scissors) to form cups. At the table, encourage each person to spoon some of the meat mixture into the lettuce cups.

NUTRITIONAL VALUE: 25 g protein, 6 g fat, 6.5 g carbohydrate, 4.5 g dietary fibre, 760 kJ (180 Cals). A good source of iron and zinc, and also provides vitamin C, potassium and the B complex vitamins thiamin, riboflavin, niacin and folate.

GREEN SALAD

A green salad takes only minutes to make, but many people use too much dressing or a poor-quality commercial dressing. A well-dressed salad should have no dressing left in the bottom of the bowl.

about 10 cups green leaves (a variety of
lettuces including mizuna plus witlof,
curly endive or watercress, if desired)

DRESSING
2 tbsp good extra-virgin olive oil
1 tbsp lemon juice
½ tsp Dijon-style mustard
freshly ground black pepper

SERVES 6

If lettuce leaves are large, tear them gently (do not cut with a knife). Make sure all leaves are thoroughly washed and dried, preferably in a salad spinner. Place in salad bowl.

To make dressing, place olive oil, lemon juice, mustard and pepper in a screwtop jar and shake vigorously. In place of the lemon juice, you can use different types of vinegar: sherry vinegar, cider vinegar, raspberry vinegar or any herb-infused vinegars are excellent.

NUTRITIONAL VALUE: 1.5 g protein, 6.5 g fat ('good' fat), 1 g carbohydrate, 2.5 g dietary fibre, 290 kJ (70 Cals). A good source of vitamins A, C and folate.

Lotus root (see **Other vegetables**)

Luffa (see Gourds under **Other vegetables**)

Mange tout (see Snow peas under **Peas**)

Marrow (see **Squash**)

Mizuna (see **Asian Greens**)

Mushrooms

Mushrooms are not vegetables, but fungi. There are more than 2000 edible mushrooms, but only about 25 are cultivated for human food and some of these are mainly available dried. The first cultivation of mushrooms occurred in quarry tunnels near Paris at the end of the seventeenth century.

Fresh mushrooms now commonly available for sale include cèpes, chanterelles, cultivated, enoki, field, Jew's ear, morels, oyster, pine, shimeji, shiitake, slippery jacks, straw, Swiss brown, white coral and wood-ear. Truffles also fit into the general class of fungi. Cultivated mushrooms, *Agaricus bisporus*, available at different stages of growth as buttons, caps and flats, make up the majority of mushroom sales. There are varieties of mushrooms that produce toxic substances, some hallucinogenic and some so deadly that gathering wild mushrooms without a good knowledge of what you are collecting is not recommended.

We eat the fruiting body of the mushrooms that the roots (the mycelium) put out to produce and spread the spores. With truffles, the fruiting body does not come above ground and the truffle must be extracted from the roots of oak, hazelnut and linden trees. Specially trained pigs or dogs are used to sniff out their whereabouts. Truffles have traditionally been collected mainly from France and Italy, but cultivation began in the late 1970s and they are now being grown in Tasmania.

The cell walls of mushrooms are not made of cellulose, as occurs in vegetables, but of chitin, a similar substance to the outer skeleton of insects and crustaceans. The strong flavour of mushrooms, and their ability to highlight the flavours of other foods in the same dish, is due to a high content of glutamic acid, related to monosodium glutamate (MSG). A few people who are very sensitive to MSG may also react adversely to mushrooms.

The nutritional contribution of mushrooms is different to that of most other vegetables. They do not contain vitamins A and C, but are significant sources of many B complex vitamins, especially niacin, riboflavin, biotin, pantothenic acid and folate. Some cultivated mushrooms also contain a form of vitamin B_{12}, a

91

vitamin usually only found in animal foods. It comes from the compost in which mushrooms are grown and is more likely to be present in the stems than the caps. Not all forms of this vitamin are biologically active for humans and it is not yet clear how much of the B_{12} in mushrooms is useful. The kilojoules in mushrooms vary a little, but on average 100 g of mushroom have 0.5 g of fat, 3 g of dietary fibre and between 35 kJ (for oyster) and 100 kJ (for most cultivated types).

VARIETIES • *Cèpes* (known as *porcini* in Italy) are members of the *Boletus edulis* species. Their colour is a light, bright brown and they have a smooth texture and earthy flavour. They can reach 25 cm in diameter and are delicious sliced and cooked in butter. Cèpes are available dried and can be reconstituted for use in cooked dishes.

Chanterelles appear in autumn, winter and spring. They vary in shape from trumpet to funnel and in colour from bright yellow to orange. The texture is slightly chewy and they have a faint aroma of apricot. Chanterelles are best cooked for only a short time or added to dishes for the last minutes of cooking. They are also available dried.

Cultivated mushrooms are widely available and come as buttons (tight and white), caps (slightly opened, with the pink gills showing) and flats (fully opened with brown gills). The buttons and caps can be used raw and all varieties can be cooked whole, sliced or chopped.

Enoki (also called enokitake) grow on the stumps of the Chinese hackberry or enoki tree. They are now widely available and the cultivated variety has a long (about 8 cm) slender stem with a small white cap. Their slightly crunchy texture and delicate appearance make them ideal to use in clear, Asian-style soups. Just before using, cut away the base of the stem which holds the clump together.

Field mushrooms (*Agaricus campestris*) are often seen in paddocks where horses have been grazing. When young they have creamy-coloured tops and deep-pink gills. As they age, they become thick and the gills become darker, cooking to an inky blackness. Field mushrooms have excellent flavour, stronger than cultivated varieties, and they are delicious in soups or casseroles, or simply cooked in a little butter and served on toast.

Jew's ear is related to wood-ear. It has a folded, almost translucent appearance and a rubbery texture, and is mainly used in Chinese dishes. It is usually available dried.

Morels are a wild mushroom belonging to the same species as truffles. They are now cultivated in some areas. Their colour is usually light to dark brown, but sometimes white or black. They are hollow and cone-shaped, appear in spring and are dearly loved by mushroom enthusiasts because of their wonderful flavour. They range in size from that of a walnut to a small kiwi fruit, the hollow cone being about 5 cm high. The best way to prepare them is to sauté in a little butter for a few minutes.

Oyster mushrooms, also known as abalone mushrooms, are fan-shaped and vary in colour from pale grey to beige or even salmon-pink. They are now cultivated and so are widely available. Their flavour has a slight peppery quality, but is mild. They go well with many Asian dishes and are good grilled or cooked in a little olive oil.

Pine mushrooms, also known as saffron milkcap, are a meaty variety that springs up in autumn in pine forests or under pine trees along golf courses and other areas. The gills, cap and stem are orange and when cut, an orange juice emerges which turns green on exposure to the air. Make sure you have an expert with you, because these mushrooms look like some poisonous varieties. They are excellent sliced and fried in butter, or added to soups.

Shimeji mushrooms are now cultivated and widely available. They are sold in small clumps, with the white stalks joined at the base. The caps are grey, beige or brown and have a dint in the top where the stem is attached. Their delicate flavour and texture go well in Japanese soups and dishes.

Shiitake mushrooms, also known as Japanese, Chinese black, black forest or golden oak, are now widely cultivated. They grow on wood, especially on oak logs which may continue to produce the fungi for some years. The gills are cream-coloured and the caps are dark brown. The stems can be used to flavour stock or soups, but are too tough to eat. Many Japanese cooks prefer to use dried shiitake mushrooms because their earthy flavour is more intense.

Slippery jacks are sometimes called Blue Mountain cèpes, although they are not true cèpes. These wild mushrooms have a spongy area under the cap, rather than gills, and are a bright brownish colour. They appear in autumn, often in pine forests.

Straw mushrooms, also known as paddy or Chinese mushrooms, grow in tropical countries and are small, round and brown. Away from their origins, they are usually available dried or canned. As they closely resemble some very poisonous mushrooms, buy only from a trusted supplier. Straw mushrooms are one of the most popular mushrooms in Asian cooking and are especially good in many Chinese dishes.

Swiss brown mushrooms are cultivated and look like browner versions of cultivated button mushrooms. They have a stronger texture and more flavour than other cultivated mushrooms and are excellent in dishes where you want the mushroom to stay firm.

White coral fungus is more a pale cream than white and looks like a crinkled sea sponge. It has a chewy texture and is excellent sliced and used in soups or stir-fried dishes.

Wood-ear, also known as black fungus, cloud-ear or jelly mushroom, has dark-brown to black ruffled edges and looks like a piece of frilly black rubber. It has a silky texture and a slightly earthy flavour, and is excellent in stir-fried dishes, casseroles or simply cooked in butter or peanut oil. Add it to Chinese dishes only for the last few minutes of cooking, to retain its slightly crunchy texture.

CHOOSING AND STORING • Cultivated mushrooms are available all year round, but some others only in particular seasons. Pine mushrooms and slippery jacks appear in autumn, morels are gathered in spring. Choose mushrooms that are firm and avoid any that are slimy, wrinkled or broken.

Never store mushrooms in a plastic bag: keep them in paper or cloth bags in the refrigerator for up to 5 days. If you buy them on a tray, leave them on this but use soon after purchase. Enoki, oyster and pine mushrooms, slippery jacks and morels should be kept in a single layer. Discard any that are slimy.

DRYING MUSHROOMS • All types of mushrooms can be dried, most of them as whole mushrooms. To dry pine mushrooms or morels, slice them and place on a tray lined with several thicknesses of paper towels. Leave in a sunny dry position each day (bring them in at night), protected from flies and any animals. Turn each day and leave until thoroughly dry, which may take several days depending on the weather and the thickness of the mushrooms. Dried mushrooms should be stored in a jar or airtight container: if they develop any sign of mould, throw them out.

PREPARATION AND COOKING • Cultivated mushrooms do not need to be peeled and should not be washed or the flesh will go slimy. If necessary, they can be wiped with a damp cloth, but most are ready for use without. Field mushrooms picked from paddocks should always be cleaned. Brush away any obvious dirt and wipe with a damp cloth. If field mushrooms are very large (plate-sized), you may need to peel the coarse skin from the cap.

Only slice mushrooms when ready to use, as the cut surfaces of some varieties will darken on exposure to air. Except for shiitake mushrooms, the stem of mushrooms can usually be sliced and used.

Mushrooms can be grilled or barbecued, baked, stir-fried or added to soups and casseroles. Button mushrooms are delicious raw.

Simply divine mushrooms

This recipe is extremely simple, but the aroma when you open the foil is not to be missed.

250 g button mushrooms
150 g Swiss brown mushrooms
100 g oyster mushrooms
2 tbsp fresh thyme
2 tsp finely grated lemon peel
4 bay leaves

SERVES 4

Preheat oven to 180°C. Spread a large piece of foil on a flat baking tray. Place mushrooms, left whole, in the centre. Strew thyme, lemon peel and bay leaves over mushrooms, pick up opposite sides of the foil and fold together. Fold in ends and twist to seal then bake for 15 minutes. Open the foil at the table.

NUTRITIONAL VALUE: 4 g protein, 0.5 g fat, 1.5 g carbohydrate, 3.5 g dietary fibre, 110 kJ (25 Cals). A good source of riboflavin and provides some niacin.

Mushroom salad

Make this salad at least 30 minutes before you want to eat, so the mushrooms can absorb some of the flavours. It goes well with grilled meats, chicken or fish.

2 tbsp lemon juice
2 tbsp olive oil
1 tbsp balsamic vinegar (or use wine vinegar)
1 tbsp dry sherry
1 tbsp grainy mustard
freshly ground pepper
400 g button mushrooms, sliced
1 cup green shallots (spring onions), sliced
2 tbsp chopped chives

SERVES 4

Combine lemon juice, oil, vinegar, sherry, mustard and pepper. Place mushrooms, green shallots and chives into a bowl, pour lemon mixture over and toss lightly but thoroughly. Cover with plastic wrap and refrigerate for at least 30 minutes.

NUTRITIONAL VALUE: 4.5 g protein, 10 g fat ('good' fat), 3.5 g carbohydrate, 3.5 g dietary fibre, 540 kJ (130 Cals). A good source of vitamin C and the B complex vitamins riboflavin and niacin.

MUSHROOM FILO TRIANGLES

Serve these with drinks or as a simple lunch dish. You can use button mushrooms, mushroom cups or caps, or a mixture of mushroom varieties.

2 tsp olive oil
1 medium-sized onion, sliced
2 cloves garlic, chopped
500 g mushrooms, sliced
1 tbsp balsamic vinegar
250 g ricotta cheese
½ cup chopped fresh basil leaves
16 sheets filo pastry
olive-oil spray

MAKES 16

Heat olive oil in a saucepan, add onion then cover and allow to sweat for 3 minutes. Add garlic, mushrooms and vinegar, and cook, stirring occasionally, for 5 minutes. Cool slightly.

Beat ricotta and basil together. Fold in mushroom mixture.

Preheat oven to 190°C. Place 2 sheets of pastry flat on bench (keep remaining pastry covered to prevent it drying out). Spray the sheets with olive oil spray and top with another 2 sheets of pastry. Cut into 4 strips, each approximately 10 cm × 30 cm. Place a spoonful of filling on the bottom edge of each strip, fold pastry over to form a triangle and continue folding. Spray with olive oil spray and place on baking tray. Repeat with remaining pastry and filling, making 16 triangles. Bake for 15 minutes or until golden-brown. Serve hot.

NUTRITIONAL VALUE: of each mushroom triangle: 4.5 g protein, 3.5 g fat, 9 g carbohydrate, 1.5 g dietary fibre, 360 kJ (85 Cals). Provides some riboflavin.

Mustard cabbage (see **Asian greens**)

Nettles (see **Other vegetables**)

New Zealand spinach (see Warrigal greens under **Other vegetables**)

Okra

Commonly known also as lady's fingers, okra is a member of the Hibiscus family. In southern American states it is called gumbo which is also the name given to the New Orleans stew of okra, tomatoes, chilli and chicken or seafood. There is some dispute about whether okra originated in Ethiopia or India. Most writers assume that okra seeds were taken to the United States by African slaves.

Okra pods have five sides and may be smooth or ridged. They vary in colour from pale green to a dark purple-red. Most pods sold commercially are 5–10 cm long and have a smooth green skin (this skin can cause an allergic dermatitis in some people). Okra contains some mucilaginous gums which make it popular as a thickening agent in stews, casseroles and soups. The slimy juice is actually a valuable form of soluble dietary fibre, but that has not been enough to redeem this vegetable in some people's eyes.

Okra are a good source of dietary fibre, vitamin C and folate. They also supply some vitamin B_6, iron and riboflavin. A serving of 4 medium pods has virtually no fat, 3.5 g of dietary fibre (more than half of this in the form of soluble fibre), and 70 kJ.

In some parts of Africa, okra seeds are roasted and ground to a powder for use as a hot beverage. While the flesh has little fat and protein, the seeds are high in both these nutrients.

CHOOSING AND STORING • Available from spring to autumn, the best okra appears in the heat of summer. Select pods that are small and firm. The end of the pod should snap easily. Avoid those where the pod will bend, the ridges are damaged or the skin has become discoloured near the stem.

Keep in a plastic bag in the refrigerator for 2–3 days. Do not wash before storage or they will become very slimy. Okra can be blanched in boiling water for 3–4 minutes and then frozen for later use.

PREPARATION AND COOKING • Okra can be fried or steamed but is probably best in casseroles, curries or soups where it will thicken the liquid. When fried, its protein takes on a web-like appearance which does not appeal to some people. Okra goes well with tomatoes, capsicum and eggplant, but cannot be puréed as it forms a thick, unappetising glue. Okra pods are often cooked whole, especially when being served as a vegetable. In stews and casseroles, it is usually sliced.

OKRA AND CHICKEN CURRY

The okra will thicken the sauce for this curry. For vegetarians, omit the chicken and cook for an extra 5 minutes after adding onion. Add 2 cups cooked drained lima beans with the okra.

1 tsp fennel seeds
1 tsp mustard seeds
1 tsp fenugreek seeds
1 tsp cumin seeds
1 tbsp ground coriander
1 tbsp peanut or macadamia nut oil
1 red chilli, chopped finely
1 tsp finely chopped fresh ginger
400 g chicken thigh, trimmed and cut
    into strips
1 large onion, sliced
500 g okra, cut into chunks
1 cup water
3 medium-sized tomatoes, skinned and
    cut into 8 sections
2 tbsp lemon juice

SERVES 4

Heat a large frying pan and add fennel, mustard, fenugreek and cumin seeds, and the coriander. Cook over a gentle heat, stirring, until mustard seeds begin to pop. Add oil, chilli, ginger, chicken and onion, and stir well to combine with the spices. Stir-fry for 10 minutes, or until chicken begins to brown. Add okra and water, bring to the boil, cover and simmer for 10 minutes. Add tomatoes and continue cooking for another 2 minutes. Add lemon juice and serve at once with steamed rice.

NUTRITIONAL VALUE: 26 g protein, 9.5 g fat, 8.5 g carbohydrate, 8 g dietary fibre, 950 kJ (225 Cals). An excellent source of vitamin C, a good source of iron, zinc, magnesium and potassium, and also provides some riboflavin, vitamin A and calcium.

OKRA SOUP

If you prefer a soup with less heat, remove the seeds and membranes from the chilli. Peel and dice the sweet potato just before adding to soup.

1 tbsp vegetable oil
1 medium-sized onion, chopped
1 clove garlic, chopped finely
1 small chilli, chopped finely
400 g okra, sliced
3 cups chicken stock
1 cup tomato juice
2 white-fleshed sweet potatoes, peeled
*   and diced*
½ red capsicum, seeded and sliced
½ green capsicum, seeded and sliced
2 tomatoes, skinned and diced

SERVES 4

Heat oil in saucepan and add onion. Cover and allow to sweat for 5 minutes, stirring once or twice. Stir in garlic and chilli, cook for 2 minutes and then add the okra, stock and tomato juice. Bring to the boil, add sweet potato and simmer for 10 minutes. Add capsicum and continue cooking for 3 minutes. When ready to serve, add the tomato (do not continue cooking after this).

NUTRITIONAL VALUE: 8.5 g protein, 5.5 g fat, 35 g carbohydrate, 9 g dietary fibre, 950 kJ (225 Cals). An excellent source of vitamin C, a good source of iron, magnesium, potassium, vitamin A and niacin, and also provides some calcium and zinc.

Onions

Possibly the most widely used of all vegetables, onions grow in almost all climates and appear in cuisines throughout the world. They belong to the Allium family (as do leeks and garlic) and probably originated in Asia, but different types of onions grow naturally in Afghanistan, Iran, India, around the Mediterranean and in North America. Onions have been cultivated for at least 5000 years. Egyptian mummies were given a supply of onions, carefully wrapped in bandages, to take into the afterlife. The Chaldeans and frugal Egyptian peasants valued onions for the boost they gave to the flavour of somewhat monotonous diets. The Bible also records that the children of Israel longed for the onions (as well as the cucumbers, melons, garlic and leeks) they had enjoyed in Egypt.

The onion is a bulb. Its concentric layers are the swollen bases of the leaves from the previous year and contain the food reserves for the following year's growth. Modern science is verifying the health benefits of onions, but the major reason for their popularity is their flavour and the aroma they give off during frying. When onions are cut, an enzyme called alliinase is released and acts on

99

various sulphur compounds in onions. The aroma is due to propyl disulphide and methyl propyl disulphide. Another substance called thiopropanal sulphoxide in onions dissolves in the fluids of the eye, forming weak sulphuric acid and stimulating the eyes to water. During cooking, the aroma of onions changes as some sulphur compounds are driven off by heat and others are converted to a sugar that is much sweeter than sucrose (table sugar).

Dry onions provide some vitamin C and small amounts of other vitamins and minerals. White onions have more potassium than brown and a little more sugar, but the differences are negligible. An average sized onion has virtually no fat, 2 g of dietary fibre and 160 kJ.

Green onions have a higher level of nutrients than other onions, are an excellent source of vitamin C and provide more iron. The green sections also provide folate and beta carotene, which the body can convert to vitamin A. An average serving of ½ cup of chopped green onions provides almost no fat, 1 g of dietary fibre and 60 kJ. Welsh onions have a similar level of nutrients to green onion tops.

As well as their contribution of nutrients, onions also supply some important antioxidants that may be protective against coronary heart disease. Their sulphur compounds may also have anti-cancer effects. While the heart-healthy protective effects of onions are disputed by some who claim that most people will not consume enough onions to have any effect, a major European study found that onions were one of the three most significant sources of antioxidants. (The other two were tea and apples.)

VARIETIES • The types of onions can be divided into two main categories: those that have been left in the ground until the foliage dies down and the skin surrounding the onion bulb is dry, and those that are pulled up while still green. Pickling onions are small white or brown onions grown close together so that they do not have the opportunity to grow any larger.

White onions are available all year and have a mild but definite flavour, with some sweetness.

Brown onions are also available all year and have a slightly stronger flavour.

Red onions are also called purple or Spanish onions and are available mainly in summer, autumn and winter. They vary in shape, some being spherical and others more oval. The flavour varies, but is usually sweeter than that of white or brown onions. Red onions are often used when raw onion is called for, as they are supposed to leave less flavour in the mouth after eating them.

Yellow Spanish onion are available in summer and autumn. Their brown skin peels off easily and these mild-flavoured onions are often sold with little or no skin attached. They soften quickly and cannot be stored as long as other dry onions.

Shallots, which are occasionally called eschalots, are small brown-skinned bulbs lightly joined at the base. They have been used in Asian cooking and also in France where their mild, delicate flavour is greatly appreciated, and are now widely used in many other countries including Australia. They also cook quickly and if it were not for the tediousness of peeling the small bulbs they might well be the principal onion used.

Green onions are fresh or 'wet' onions pulled from the soil while their tops are still green. They include spring onions, bunching onions and green shallots or scallions, with immense confusion about these names.

In different states of Australia, people are adamant that their choice of name is the correct one. In New South Wales, a spring onion is a small white bulb with a green stem attached. In Victoria, this product is called a salad onion and the term 'spring onion' is used for an immature onion pulled from the soil before any bulb has formed, with the bottom white section the same diameter as the green stem. In New South Wales the latter is called a green onion or, occasionally, a green shallot or incorrectly, a 'shallot'. In the United States it is called a scallion. To complicate things further, this onion is also occasionally referred to as a bunching onion. Others use the term 'bunching onion' when a number of these bulbless green onions are grown close together and appear to be joined at the base.

Welsh onions are widely used in China and Japan. They are a bit like wide chives and although they look like a green shallot (spring onion), they have hollow stems. They may be green, bluish-green or red in colour, and are usually harvested in autumn.

Calcots, the famous onions that give rise to a yearly festival each February (end of winter) in Tarragona in Spain are blanched by piling earth around their stems. They are picked and eaten on the same day, barbecued outside restaurants over a fire of vine prunings until the outside is blackened. The calcots are then packed into a concave roof tile and left to cook through from the heat of the surrounding onions. Diners don a huge bib and pick up the hot blackened calcots in the fingers, stripping off the black skin to reveal the steaming white-based onion. A quick dip in a romesco sauce and you have one of the world's truly great dishes. Messy, but worth every bit of it.

CHOOSING AND STORING • White and brown onions are available year round, and have the best flavour during summer and autumn. Red onions are best at this time too. For dry onions, make sure they are firm and the papery skins are dry. Reject any that have begun to sprout as the inside will have softened. Dry onions should be kept in an airy dry place and will keep for several months. If they begin to sprout, either plant them in your garden or add to the compost.

Green onions are also available all year round, although the bulbed onions are available only in spring. Select specimens with crisp green ends. If the ends have been trimmed, it may indicate that they were drooping and the onions are past their best. For bulbed onions, the bulb should be shiny. Green onions (alias scallions or spring onions without a bulb) should be stored in a plastic bag in the refrigerator and will keep for about a week.

PREPARATION AND COOKING • For dry onions, remove root and stem ends and the dry, papery skin. Do not peel onions until you are ready to use them, as their flavour deteriorates without their skin. Onions can be eaten raw, although you will be able to taste raw onion for many hours afterwards and this can interfere with the pleasure of other foods. Red onions tend to have a milder oral effect and blanching raw onion slices in boiling water for 1 minute will reduce the effect without destroying the onion's crunchiness. When cooked, the flavour of onions does not linger in the mouth to the same extent. Onions can be left whole and steamed or baked, or diced, sliced or cut into wedges and fried or added to other foods.

Handy-hints columns often publish ways to prevent the tears that flow freely when peeling and chopping onions. Some recommend wearing glasses (or swimming goggles!). Others suggest putting the onion in the freezer to slow down the release of the tear-jerking substances. There are also recommendations to peel onions in the draught of a fan. I find the only thing that really helps is to leave cutting off the root end until the last moment.

With green onions, remove the stem end and trim off the green tops, as much as you wish or according to the recipe (they are edible and nutritious). With green onions that include the bulb, usually only the bulb and the first part of the stem is eaten, although the whole stem can be used. Green onions are eaten raw or cooked briefly, usually by stir-frying, although they can be cooked on the barbecue.

CARAMELISED ONIONS

One of the most popular ways to cook onions. The long cooking allows compounds present naturally in onions to be converted to sweeter sugars. Serve with grilled meats or on top of baked potatoes, or combine with mushrooms or red capsicums to serve with pasta or use as a pizza topping. You can add a little brown sugar, but onions caramelise with their own sugars.

1 tbsp olive oil
2 large onions, sliced finely
2 tbsp balsamic vinegar (optional)

SERVES 4

Heat oil in a saucepan and add onions. Cover and allow to sweat over a low heat for 30 minutes, stirring occasionally. Remove lid, add balsamic vinegar and raise heat to allow onions to brown. Stir constantly at this time until onions are a rich brown.

NUTRITIONAL VALUE: 1.5 g protein, 5 g fat ('good' fat), 4.5 g carbohydrate, 1.5 g dietary fibre, 280 kJ (65 Cals). Provides some vitamin C.

FRENCH ONION SOUP

A meal in itself, this soup brings out the natural sweetness of onions. A good stock is essential.

1 tbsp butter or olive oil
4 onions (about 750 g), sliced finely
1 clove garlic
2 sprigs rosemary
4 cups good-quality stock, preferably
  beef or veal
2 tbsp sherry
4 thick slices of wood-fired or
  Italian-style bread
¹/₂ cup grated gruyère cheese

SERVES 4

In a large saucepan, melt butter and add onions, garlic and rosemary. Cover and cook over a low heat for 20 minutes, stirring occasionally. Remove rosemary and cook, uncovered, until onion is brown. Add stock, bring to the boil and simmer for 5 minutes. Add sherry.

Toast bread on both sides and sprinkle one side with the cheese. Ladle soup into ovenproof bowls, place bread on top and place bowls under a hot grill until cheese is melted and bubbling. Serve at once.

NUTRITIONAL VALUE: 10 g protein, 10 g fat, 25 g carbohydrate, 4 g dietary fibre, 1015 kJ (245 Cals). A good source of vitamin C, niacin and calcium, and provides some iron.

Barbecued green onions with romesco sauce

A true romesco sauce is made with dried sweet peppers, but this version is excellent.

3 bunches green shallots (spring onions)

Sauce
1 medium-sized onion, cut in half
4 large cloves garlic
1 tsp olive oil
2 red capsicums
2 tbsp almonds
2 large tomatoes
1 tsp paprika
1 thick slice of wood-fired or Italian-style
  bread, crusts removed
freshly ground pepper
2 tbsp red-wine vinegar

Serves 6

Preheat oven to 250°C.

To make the sauce, place onion and garlic on one half of an oven tray and drizzle with olive oil. Place capsicums directly on an oven shelf and put the oven tray on the shelf below so that the capsicums sit over the empty part of the tray (which will catch any juices). Reduce oven heat to 220°C and cook for 35 minutes. Transfer capsicums to a bowl and place the bowl inside a plastic bag. Leave until cool enough to handle, then peel fine skin from capsicums, collecting any juice. Strain out the seeds, but keep the juice.

While capsicums are roasting, toast almonds on a dry frying pan, shaking over moderate heat until almonds are brown (take care not to burn them). Set aside. To skin the tomatoes, remove core and cut a small cross in the end of each tomato. Place in a bowl, cover with boiling water, leave for 30 seconds and drain. The skin will then peel off easily.

In a food processor place the capsicum flesh, onion halves, the flesh squeezed from the garlic cloves, the almonds, chopped tomatoes, paprika, pepper, broken-up bread and vinegar. Process until smooth, adding the reserved capsicum juices to thin the sauce. Store in refrigerator until required.

When ready to serve the dish, cook green onions on barbecue until soft and blackened on the outside (this usually takes about 10 minutes). To eat, peel back the outside skin and dip onion into romesco sauce.

NUTRITIONAL VALUE: 5.5 g protein, 4 g fat ('good' fat), 14 g carbohydrate, 5.5 g dietary fibre, 475 kJ (115 Cals). An excellent source of vitamin C, a good source of vitamin A and provides some iron, magnesium and vitamin E.

Parsnips

Parsnips originated somewhere between the Mediterranean basin and the western Caucasus region. They were cultivated by the Greeks and Romans, although there is some doubt about whether the writings of Hippocrates and Pliny were referring to parsnips or their relatives, carrots. Parsnips seem to have escaped from cultivation and spread themselves around Europe and western Asia. They were recorded as being grown in Germany in the sixteenth century and were valued for their sweetness and ability to survive in frozen ground during winter. They were also eaten as a substitute for potatoes because of their high carbohydrate content.

The sweet flavour of the parsnip depends on exposure to cold weather, preferably with frosts, as this allows some of the starches to be converted to the sugars for which parsnips are known and loved—at least by those who have had them cooked well. Parsnips were once a commonly used vegetable, but they are obviously not well known by everyone these days. I recently heard a supermarket check-out operator ask his neighbouring worker how he should enter 'white carrots'.

Parsnips provide some vitamin C, folate and vitamin E, plus a sprinkling of other vitamins and minerals. Their greatest claim to fame comes from their high level of fibre, some of it present as gums which are a valuable form of soluble fibre. An average-sized cooked parsnip has virtually no fat, 10 g of carbohydrate, 4.5 g of dietary fibre and 200 kJ.

CHOOSING AND STORING • Parsnips are available all year, but those sold in winter and spring are much sweeter. Choose smooth, fresh-looking, crisp parsnips of medium size, without a long skinny end section. Avoid large parsnips, as they may have a woody core, and also give damaged specimens a miss.

Parsnips will keep for about a week in the refrigerator in one of the plastic bags supermarkets offer for vegetables. Avoid cling wrap as parsnips will sweat if wrapped tightly.

PREPARATION AND COOKING • Remove the spindly tail, trim off the root end and peel using a potato peeler. Parsnips can be steamed or boiled (and mashed, if desired), fried, baked or made into chips. They are also excellent in casseroles and soups. For baking, leave parsnips whole or halve them lengthwise. Their natural sugar content will ensure they brown well in the roasting pan.

PARSNIP AND ORANGE SOUP

The sweetness of parsnip is excellent with the subtle flavour of orange in this easy soup.

2 tsp olive oil
1 medium-sized onion, diced
2 tsp curry powder
2 tsp finely grated orange peel
750 g parsnips
4 cups chicken or vegetable stock
4 bay leaves
½ cup orange juice

SERVES 4

Heat oil in a large saucepan and cook onion, without browning, for 5 minutes. Sprinkle curry powder over onion, stir well and cook for a further 2 minutes. Add orange peel, parsnips, stock and bay leaves and simmer for 20 minutes or until parsnips are tender. Remove bay leaves and purée soup in batches. Return to saucepan, add orange juice and bring to the boil. Serve at once.

NUTRITIONAL VALUE: 5 g protein, 3.5 g fat ('good' fat), 27 g carbohydrate, 6 g dietary fibre, 670 kJ (160 Cals). An excellent source of vitamin C, a good source of niacin, potassium, magnesium and iron, and also provides some calcium and zinc.

PARSNIP SOUFFLÉS

Delightful with roast beef or serve as a simple lunch dish with a green salad and crusty bread.

2 or 3 parsnips (about 400 g)
2 tbsp butter
2 tbsp flour
1 cup skim milk
2 tsp Dijon-style mustard
2 eggs, separated
2 extra egg whites
1 tbsp dried breadcrumbs

SERVES 6

Peel parsnips, slice and steam for about 10 minutes, or until tender. Set aside. Preheat oven to 190°C and brush or spray 6 individual soufflé dishes (10 cm diameter) with oil.

Melt butter in saucepan, add flour and stir over a gentle heat for 1 minute. Add milk and bring to the boil, stirring constantly. Remove from heat. Add mustard.

In food processor, purée parsnips. Add white sauce and egg yolks, and process again. Beat egg whites until stiff, fold one quarter into the parsnip mixture and then gently fold in the remainder. Spoon into soufflé dishes and sprinkle breadcrumbs on top. Bake for 20 minutes, or until well risen. Serve at once.

NUTRITIONAL VALUE: 6.5 g protein, 7 g fat, 13 g carbohydrate, 2 g dietary fibre, 580 kJ (140 Cals). Provides some vitamins A and C.

Peas

Shelling peas was once a familiar family activity and many peas didn't make it to the pot because various family members succumbed to their sweetness. Peas in the pod are still available, but are not often used because they have been largely replaced by frozen peas. Sugar-snap peas and snow peas have also replaced traditional green peas because they do not need to be shelled. The pods of green peas are not edible because they have a hard parchment layer of lignified cells. The pods of snow and sugar-snap peas do not have this layer.

Green peas, also known as English peas, common peas or garden peas, belong to the same family as beans, peanuts, chick peas and lentils. There is some difference of opinion about their origins. Pea seeds have been found in remains of Neolithic settlements in Jericho and from areas in central Turkey dating back to 5700 BC and some experts have dated seeds from even earlier times. Many believe peas originated in the eastern Mediterranean region, growing in rocky places and then as weeds in ancient fields of barley and wheat. Others favour central Asia or Ethiopia as the pea's native habitat. Whatever their true origin, peas are one of the most ancient of vegetables, having been grown and used dried for many thousands of years.

The green peas we eat today were probably first grown in Turkey, but their cultivation soon spread to India and China. Fresh green peas were grown by the Romans in England, but their use died out until they were re-introduced in the sixteenth century. Peas were among the first plants used to determine the characteristics of genes, the work of Thomas Andrew Knight in 1787 being followed 70 years later by the famous studies of Gregor Mendel. Mendel started out trying to improve the qualities of peas grown in some monastery gardens in Czechoslovakia. His work gave birth to modern genetics.

Snow peas, sometimes called sugar, China or mange-tout peas, were mentioned by late-sixteenth-century writers, but did not become universally popular until much later. These flat podded peas are now regularly used by those who appreciate their sweet flavour, attractive colour and texture. The fact that they need little preparation has made them even more popular.

Sugar-snap peas are a modern variety developed from the snow pea. Their edible pods encase plump, sweet-flavoured peas that are delicious raw or cooked.

Peas are among the most nutritious of all vegetables, providing an excellent source of dietary fibre and some protein as well as iron, carbohydrate, vitamin C, folate and thiamin. Half a cup of cooked green peas has 4.5 g of protein, 0.5 g of fat, 8 g of carbohydrate (including some sugars known as oligosaccharides, which are beneficial for 'good' bacteria in the large intestine), 5 g of dietary fibre and

165 kJ. Snow peas have similar nutritional value to green peas, but more vitamin C and less dietary fibre, protein and carbohydrate. An average serving of snow peas has 2.5 g of protein, virtually no fat, 3.5 g of carbohydrate, 2 g of dietary fibre and 105 kJ. Sugar-snap peas have nutritional values midway between green peas and snow peas.

CHOOSING AND STORING • Peas are available all year. The best and sweetest green peas are available in late spring and early summer. Green peas are at their best immediately after picking and there is no pea as sweet as the one that has just been picked. If that is not possible, look for crisp, bright-green pods. Green peas and sugar-snap peas are usually shiny, snow peas are not. Avoid any with damaged or spotted pods. Snow peas are best during late winter and early spring, and sugar-snap peas are available in spring.

Store all types of peas in a plastic bag in the refrigerator for 3 or 4 days. Green peas left at room temperature lose their sweetness rapidly. When peas are commercially frozen, they are processed within an hour or so of being picked and freezing slows down any loss of sweetness.

PREPARATION AND COOKING • For green peas, split the pods and remove the peas. Top and tail snow peas and sugar-snap peas, and pull off any strings running down the sides. The best way to do this is by snapping off the stem end and gently pulling downwards so that the strings on both sides peel off.

If you are buying green peas in their pods, 1 kg of peas will provide about 400 g of shelled peas. To cook, steam or boil for 10–12 minutes. Snow peas and sugar-snap peas need only about 2 minutes cooking and are excellent to stir-fry. Do not overcook sugar-snap peas or they lose their colour and burst from their pods.

SNOW PEAS WITH LIME PRAWN SALAD AND MANGO

A simple dish. Steaming the prawns over lime-infused water adds a delightful flavour.

1 mango
1 small chilli, chopped finely
2 tbsp lime juice
6–8 lime leaves
450 g green prawns
200 g snow peas, topped and tailed
2 Lebanese cucumbers, sliced
freshly ground pepper
2 kaffir lime leaves

SERVES 2

Peel mango and dice flesh. Combine with the chilli and lime juice, and set aside for flavours to blend. Peel prawns, leaving the tails attached, and devein.

Place boiling water in the bottom part of a steamer and add the lime leaves. Arrange prawns in top of steamer and steam for about 2 minutes, or until they turn pink (do not over-cook). Cook snow peas in boiling water for 1 minute, drain and run under cold water.

Arrange snow peas, cucumber and prawns on plates. Top with mango and sprinkle with pepper. Remove centre rib from lime leaves and slice very finely. Scatter over salad.

NUTRITIONAL VALUE: 28 g protein, 1 g fat, 21 g carbohydrate, 8 g dietary fibre, 885 kJ (210 Cals). An excellent source of vitamins A and C, a good source of iron, zinc, thiamin, niacin, potassium, magnesium and calcium, and also provides some riboflavin.

FRESH PEA SOUP

This soup is good hot, but even better served chilled in summer. If desired, substitute natural yoghurt for the cream, but the flavour and texture will not be as good.

3 cups chicken stock
1 kg fresh peas, podded (or use 500 g frozen peas)
1 small onion, diced
3 cups shredded lettuce
1 tsp sugar
4 sprigs fresh mint leaves
3 tbsp cream

SERVES 4

In a saucepan, bring stock to the boil. Add peas, onion, lettuce, sugar and mint, and simmer with the lid on for 10 minutes. Remove mint and then purée soup, adding the cream. Reheat to serve, or refrigerate until well chilled. Serve with plenty of black pepper.

NUTRITIONAL VALUE: 9 g protein, 7.5 g fat, 12 g carbohydrate, 8.5 g dietary fibre, 615 kJ (145 Cals). A good source of vitamins A and C, iron and zinc, and also provides some thiamin and niacin.

Peppers (see **Capsicums**)

Potatoes

Whole books have been written about the important role the potato has played in human history. It originated in the Andes mountains in Peru and Bolivia, and was used by the ancient Incas. Carbon-dating shows potatoes were in use at least 8000 years ago. Remains of potatoes have also been found near Lima in Peru, dating from 4000 BC. The Incas, in a brilliant piece of food technology, even devised a method to freeze-dry them. Neolithic farmers of Bolivia dipped their potatoes into cold water and left them to freeze in the cold air at altitudes of 3000–3500 metres. They then defrosted the potatoes by the fire, crushed the pulp and exposed them once again to the freezing cold mountain air. If left to freeze in full sunshine, the potatoes turned black, but if left to freeze away from any light, they stayed white. The freeze-dried potatoes kept for long periods, were easy to transport and could be traded for other goods.

The name potato probably comes from the Peruvian word *papas*, meaning an edible stone, although it was also called little *bappa* or *bappatas*, which became *patatas* in Spanish and 'potato' in English. Some also suggest the name derives from *batata*, the Carribean Indian name for sweet potato. The colloquial term 'spud' for potato appears to have its origins in nineteenth century Scotland, where spuds are potatoes roasted in their skins in the embers of a fire.

According to reports from La Sangre Hospital in Seville, potatoes were taken from South America to Spain in 1573. Initially, they were regarded with suspicion, partly because their leaves resembled those of the deadly nightshade and partly because of a rumour that they would cause leprosy. Gradually these ideas were put to rest, and within 100 years potatoes were widely accepted as a food for humans and animals and were being grown in every European country. By the seventeenth century they had spread to India, with China and Japan adopting them by the eighteenth century. Potatoes are now the fourth most important food crop in the world, after wheat, corn and rice.

White potatoes are also known as Irish potatoes, because of their immense popularity in Ireland. They were supposedly brought to Ireland by Sir Walter Raleigh around 1590 and have played a major role in Ireland's history. The Irish population grew rapidly in the late eighteenth century and many people had little food. The potato grew well in the Irish countryside and became the dietary staple. For large poor families, it was often virtually the only food they had, apart from some milk. Several times when disaster struck the potato crop, hundreds of thousands of Irish people died. The worst blow came in 1845 and 1846, when potatoes throughout the country were affected by blight, and more than a million people who relied on them for most of their energy and nutrients starved to death. The failure of the potato crop also led to a vast exodus of Irish people to the United States and Australia. After this terrible period in Ireland's history, new varieties of potatoes were brought from Chile. These were less susceptible to fungal disease and replaced the previously grown Andean potatoes.

Potatoes are members of the same Solanaceae family as nightshade, tomatoes, capsicums and eggplants. They grow as underground tubers, each with many 'eyes' that are the buds for future plants. Because it is difficult to peel or clean the eyes, some modern cultivars have fewer and more shallow eyes. The flesh of some potatoes is white, in others it is yellow and there are some modern cultivars with purple flesh. These look dramatic, but few would rate them highly for flavour or texture.

Potatoes are an important source of vitamin C and dietary fibre. They also supply small amounts of potassium, thiamin and folate. The fact that they are eaten often, and in quantities of 150–200 g in a typical serving, increases the value of their nutrients in the whole diet. A typical 150 g cooked potato has 0.5 g of fat, 24 g of carbohydrate, 1.5–2.5 g of dietary fibre (waxy potatoes have the higher levels) and 400 kJ.

TYPES OF POTATOES AND THEIR USES • Different types of potato contain varying amounts and types of carbohydrate, and this governs how well the potato will serve for different uses. Those with a high starch and low water content are officially referred to as 'high dry matter' potatoes or, in lay terms, 'floury' potatoes. They will bake well, mash well and make good chips. Where the carbohydrate content is a little lower and some of the carbohydrate is in the form of sugars, the potato has a more waxy texture. These will be good to steam, microwave or boil, won't break up and make excellent potato salad, but will never give smooth mash or make a good soup. Waxy potatoes are delicious brushed with a little olive oil and baked, but are not good at absorbing liquid. In making dishes where layers of potatoes are baked with milk or stock, waxy potatoes are often specified but will take long baking times to absorb the liquid and may still be firm after an hour or more. Varieties with a less waxy texture will absorb the liquid and cook much faster.

The major types of starch in potatoes are amylose and amylopectin. Amylose consists of long straight strings of glucose molecules whereas amylopectin has a branched chain structure. Within the body, amylopectin is totally broken down to glucose by enzymes in the small intestine. Amylose can also be digested by these enzymes, but some of it passes to the large intestine, where it is broken down by the same 'good' bacteria that break down dietary fibre. The amylose that passes to the large intestine is called 'resistant starch' and is thought to be highly beneficial, especially where the diet is low in dietary fibre. Different types of potatoes vary in their ratio of amylose to amylopectin. Waxy potatoes, including pink fir apple, kipfler, patrone, ratte and roseval, tend to have more amylose. Some modern potatoes, developed as all-purpose varieties, have roughly similar quantities of amylose and amylopectin and can usually be used for baking, boiling, chips, frying, microwaving and steaming, or in salads.

When any kind of potato is cooked and then left to cool, more of its starch is converted to amylose and will become 'resistant' starch in the digestive sense. Even if the potato is reheated after cooling, the level of resistant starch remains high. This may explain why cold potato salads are traditionally eaten, even in winter, in Scandinavian countries. In these areas there are few sources of dietary fibre during winter, so although the potato itself does provide some fibre, the effective quantity would be boosted by resistant starch if the potatoes were allowed to cool. Such traditions would have developed without the benefit of modern biomedical science, but may have been adopted because, over long periods, people came to see those who ate cold potatoes in potato salad as being healthier than those who ate them hot. The advantages of cold potatoes are less relevant in countries where there is a plentiful supply of sources of dietary fibre during winter, but may still be useful for good bowel health.

VARIETIES • There are many hundreds of varieties of potatoes, developed to be ready for harvest at different times of the year and to have various flavour or cooking characteristics. Some all-purpose potatoes can be used for any cooking method, although they are not all equally good. In general, you need to distinguish between waxy, floury and all-purpose potatoes for the best results. Waxy potatoes include delaware, Jersey royal, kipfler, lasoda, nadine, Nicola, patrone, pink eye (when new), pink fir apple, ratte and roseval. Floury potatoes include King Edward, purple congo, russet Burbank and spunta. All-purpose potatoes include bintje, bison, coliban (may disintegrate if boiled), desirée, kennebec, latona, pink eye (older), pontiac, royal blue, saxon, sebago, sequoia, symfonia and Toolangi delight.

Some of the more commonly available potato varieties are listed below.

Bintje, developed in the Netherlands in 1910 and now a major seller in many countries, has a long, oval shape, smooth, cream-coloured skin and pale-yellow waxy flesh. It is often small, but is versatile and has a good flavour. Good to steam, boil, mash, microwave, roast or bake whole.

Bison is a red-skinned, round potato with shallow eyes. It looks like a pontiac and can be used in the same way, although the flavour is not as good. Suitable to boil, steam, microwave, roast or bake. Not good for frying.

Chats are small smooth-skinned potatoes, usually colibans. Useful for potato salad (hot or cold), or to boil, microwave or halve and sauté in a frying pan with a little olive oil.

Coliban, one of the most common potatoes sold, is round, white and smooth-skinned with no special flavour. A fair all-round performer, although not good for boiling and makes a watery mash. Usually sold as a washed 'new' potato.

Delaware is a white-skinned oval potato with white flesh. Suitable to bake, steam, microwave or boil (usually whole), but not particularly good to mash.

Desirée, an oblong potato developed in the Netherlands in 1961, has cream-coloured flesh and a pink skin that often looks as if it has been polished. A good all-round performer to mash, bake, steam, boil, roast or microwave, and to use in soups and sliced potato dishes. Not recommended for chips.

Jersey royal is a small kidney-shaped potato with white skin and creamy-coloured flesh, developed in Britain in the 1870s. Jersey royals are sold for a few weeks in early summer as genuine new potatoes, with a superb flavour, waxy flesh and a skin you can rub off with your fingers. Suitable to roast, steam, boil, microwave or bake whole, and excellent for potato salad. Not suitable to mash.

Kennebec is a cream-skinned, white fleshed potato without much flavour. Suitable to steam, boil, mash, microwave, roast, bake whole or fry as chips.

King Edward was developed in Northumberland, England, in 1902 but is a relatively new arrival in Australian shops. Small, round or oval-shaped, it has yellowish flesh and skin that is cream with pink patches around the eyes. An excellent roasting or baking potato and also good to steam and mash. Not good for salads.

Kipfler is a smallish, slightly curved sausage-shaped potato with thin skin, yellow waxy flesh and an excellent flavour. Best scrubbed and baked or steamed whole, or halved lengthwise and cooked in a frying pan with a little olive oil. Can also be used for chips or wedges, or for salad but may fall apart if boiled and therefore not suitable to mash.

Lasoda is an all-purpose potato to steam, boil, mash, microwave, roast, bake whole, fry as chips or use for salad.

Latona is a yellow-skinned, yellow-fleshed potato to steam, boil, microwave, roast or use in a salad. Less suitable to fry and does not make good chips.

Nadine, a variety developed in Scotland, has round tubers and moist, waxy, pale cream-coloured flesh. Suitable to boil, steam, microwave or bake. Can be mashed, but does not fry well.

Nicola is a medium-sized, oval to long German potato with yellow flesh and a slightly buttery flavour. Good to steam, boil, mash, roast, bake and use for potato salad.

Patrone (sometimes spelt petrone) has creamy-coloured skin and yellowish flesh with a firm waxy texture. Excellent to steam, boil, bake or make into salad.

The texture of cooked patrone is so firm that you can grate this potato after cooking, making it excellent for potato pancakes or Swiss roesti.

Pink eye, as the name suggests, is a small creamy-coloured, knobbly potato with deep pink-purple eyes. Similar to the Champion potato developed in England in 1862, the pink eye is now grown in Tasmania. The flavour is excellent, almost nutty, and the texture is slightly floury. Good to steam, boil, microwave, roast, bake whole, or, best of all, slice or dice and cook in a frying pan with a little olive oil.

Pink fir apple is a potato developed in 1850 and now popular once more for the superb flavour of its pale-yellow, waxy flesh. Shaped like a sausage, usually knobbly and its creamy skin tinged with pink, it is excellent for potato salad or to bake whole. Its shape makes it impossible to peel, so don't try. Also good to cut in half lengthwise and cook in a frying pan with sliced onion and a little olive oil. Can be used in 'smashed' potato, sometimes described as mashed potatoes with the skins still on.

Pontiac is a pink-skinned, round potato that sometimes looks as though someone has polished it. A good all-round potato to boil, steam, mash, microwave, roast or bake whole, it can also be made into chips or used in soup.

Purple congo is a sausage-shaped potato with dark-purple skin and purple flesh occasionally streaked with white. Looks dramatic, but more for show than good taste. It doesn't perform well for many cooking methods, though its doughy texture produces excellent purple gnocchi and it also makes interesting chips. Can be mashed, if necessary.

Ratte, a French potato developed in 1872, is small and sausage-shaped but with a smoother surface than the pink fir apple. The yellow flesh has an excellent flavour and waxy texture. Ideal for potato salad or to bake or steam, boil whole or fry or halved in a little olive oil. Not yet widely available, but may be seen on restaurant menus and well worth buying if you come across it.

Royal blue is similar to Toolangi delight, with purple skin and yellowish flesh. Excellent to steam, boil, mash, microwave, roast, bake whole or fry in a little olive oil. Also good for making potato gnocchi.

Roseval is a small, oval-shaped potato with pink skin and creamy-coloured firm flesh. Developed in 1950 in France, it has excellent flavour. If available as a 'new' potato, rub off the outside skin but leave the inner skin. Use whole and steam, boil, bake or microwave. It also makes a good potato salad and is excellent to slice and then fry with a little olive oil, but it is not suitable for mashing or soups. Not always available, but worth buying if you see it.

Russet Burbank (also called Idaho) is a medium–large, long, cream-fleshed potato developed in America in 1875 by Luther Burbank. Usually sold unwashed, it bakes well, is excellent for stuffed potatoes and also good for chips. Used by major fast-food chains because it can be cut into small thin French fries that soak

up a lot of fat (fat is generally cheaper than potato and high-fat chips are more profitable). Unfortunately, this variety of potato needs more water, fertilisers and fungicides to grow and so is not an environmentally friendly potato.

Saxon was developed from the desirée. Oval or round, with white skin and pale-yellow flesh, it is good to steam, boil, microwave, roast, bake whole or fry. Makes good chips.

Sebago is the most common variety, sold as an all-purpose potato. No special problems for any use, but no special flavour either. Suitable to steam, boil, mash, roast, bake whole or use for soups or chips.

Sequoia is an oval, flattish potato with creamy skin and white flesh. Available in late summer and early autumn, it is good to boil, steam, mash or bake. Not good for frying or chips.

Spunta is an oval, medium to large potato originally from the Netherlands but commonly grown in Cyprus. It has yellowish skin, firm, cream-coloured flesh and good flavour. Excellent to steam, boil, microwave, roast, bake whole or slice and cook in a frying pan in olive oil. Also makes excellent chips.

Symfonia is similar to a desirée, with red skin and yellowish flesh. Another all-rounder suitable to steam, boil, microwave, roast, bake whole or fry as chips.

Toolangi delight has dark-purple skin but the flesh is white and this potato should not be confused with the purple-fleshed varieties. It is a great potato to steam and mash, and is also suitable to boil, microwave or roast. It makes good chips and excellent gnocchi, but is not as good for potato salad as the waxy potatoes.

CHOOSING AND STORING • Some varieties of potatoes are available all year round; others are not. The best supplies are during autumn, winter and spring, although new Jersey royals appear only in summer. Choose potatoes that are firm. Avoid those that are starting to soften, wrinkle or are beginning to sprout.

If left exposed to light, the skin of potatoes begins to develop a greenish hue which can extend into the flesh. The green colour is due to chlorophyll, itself harmless, but as the chlorophyll forms, other toxic substances are also synthesised. Two of these, solanine and chaconine, are bitter-tasting glycoalkaloids that are not destroyed by cooking. These are always present in potatoes, but at such low doses that they usually cause no symptoms or harm. Glycoalkaloids develop as an in-built toxin against attack by insects. High quantities form when potatoes start to sprout or are exposed to light and the green colour that develops at the same time is a good indicator of higher quantities being present. (Potatoes with pink skin tend to have some resistance to the adverse effects of exposure to light, although they are still sensitive.) Eating a potato with green skin may cause no more than a stomach ache or slight queasy feelings in an adult, but may be enough to produce severe stomach cramps and vomiting in a child. There is no lasting or cumulative damage from solanine because the body gets rid of it (by vomiting) if the quantity is high. Potatoes that are sold ready-washed or in clear plastic bags are especially likely to develop solanine and chaconine. Try to buy potatoes unwashed or those packed in paper. If you buy them bagged in plastic, tip them out as soon as you get home. Do not wash potatoes until ready to use.

To some extent, the size and shape of potatoes depends on the particular type, the growing period and soil conditions. Before planting, however, farmers can influence the size of the tubers eventually produced by storing potatoes at different temperatures with varying amounts of light. Exposing some types to light before planting can cause many small tubers in the subsequent harvest, whereas dark storage at slightly higher temperatures can cause a potato plant to produce fewer, bigger potatoes. With most people wanting potatoes that will cook in less time, smaller potatoes are now preferred by many growers. Many of these— kipfler, patrone, ratte, roseval, pink eye and pink fir apple—also have excellent flavour.

Many potatoes sold as 'new' are actually washed or smaller colibans. A genuine new potato is dug while the top of the plant is still green, rather than waiting until its foliage dies away (the usual time to harvest the potato crop). You can tell if a potato is genuinely new because the papery skin will rub off between your fingers when the potato is wet. Some varieties have a double skin and the top layer rubs off, leaving another layer than prevents the nutrients in the potato from being lost when the potato is cooked. The flavour of genuine new potatoes has a greater intensity and some degree of sweetness compared with other potatoes, and the texture is quite waxy. Old potatoes are left in the ground and stored in dark conditions before being sold. They have low sugar levels, less water and a higher starch content—wonderful for mashed potatoes. Many people assume that potatoes sold unwashed are old potatoes, but this is now rarely the case. Storage costs (in and out of the ground) are too high for most farmers to hold on to potatoes until they are old.

To store potatoes, tip them out of plastic bags and keep in a cool, dark, well-ventilated place. Do not refrigerate. At cold temperatures, the starches in potatoes are converted to sugars (known as 'reducing' sugars) which cause the flesh to darken when the potato is cooked, especially during frying, creating an 'off' flavour. If you have come across a black chip, you will know that they look and taste horrible. Commercially, some potatoes are kept at cold temperatures and then 'reconditioned' at room temperature to allow the sugars to convert back to starches before being sold. The flavour of potatoes treated in this way is never as good as those kept at uniform cool, but not refrigerator, temperatures. Some of the newer potato varieties have a better flavour because they do not accumulate as much sugar. Keep potatoes out of the light to prevent the skin becoming green, and throw them into the compost if they start to sprout. The sprouts, and the areas around where the sprout begins, have a high content of solanine (see above).

PREPARATION AND COOKING • Do not peel potatoes and leave them in water, as they will lose vitamins and some of their valuable starch.

Boiling or steaming

Choose either a waxy potato or an all-purpose one. Good choices for flavour include desirée, kipfler, Nicola, pink eye, pink fir apple, pontiac, ratte, roseval, Jersey royal, spunta and symfonia.

When boiling or steaming potatoes, give them a faint hint of extra flavour by adding a cut clove of garlic and a few sprigs of mint or some lemon thyme to the water. This is especially good with new potatoes.

Mashing

Ideal mashing potatoes include desirée, King Edward, Nicola, pink eye, pontiac, pink fir apple (don't peel), royal blue, sebago, sequoia, spunta, symfonia and Toolangi delight. A couple of these are slightly waxy, but they still mash well. The best of all mashing potatoes are spunta, pink eye, King Edward, royal blue and Toolangi delight.

To make good mashed potatoes, start by steaming scrubbed, unpeeled potatoes. The skin retains nutrients and flavour during cooking. Once cooked, pick up each potato on a fork and remove the skin (leave it on for varieties such as pink fir apple or King Edward). Keep the peeled potatoes warm while you peel the remainder. Using a potato masher, mash the peeled potatoes with hot milk and a good dollop of butter. Add salt, pepper and a pinch of nutmeg to taste. If you are concerned about the fat from butter, use a butter/oil mix. You can also compromise by using hot low-fat milk, which doesn't have such an adverse effect on the final flavour and texture as omitting the butter. I always avoid using margarine. Some people mash potatoes without butter but they never achieve the creaminess of good mashed potato. The exact amount of hot milk will depend on the potato. In general, for 800 g of potatoes heat ¾–1 cup of milk, although you may not need it all. The very creamy mashed potatoes served in many restaurants are often mashed with cream and a large quantity of butter— totally decadent, but wonderful for a treat.

If potatoes are cut into small pieces and then boiled, they will absorb too much water and produce a watery mash. It is best to use a standard potato masher, followed by a good beating with a fork or a wooden spoon rather than a food processor, which will break down the starch granules and produce a gummy result.

BAKING

Use bintje, King Edward, kipfler, Nicola, patrone, pink fir apple, ratte, roseval, russet Burbank or symfonia.

Either place potatoes straight on the oven shelf (if they are big enough) or warm 2–4 teaspoons of olive oil on a hot baking tray, add the potatoes and shake vigorously to coat them. Bake at 190°C for 20–40 minutes for small potatoes, and up to 1½ hours for large whole ones.

ROASTING

Use any of those listed for baking whole, plus desirée, pontiac, royal blue, saxon or Toolangi delight.

For crispy roast potatoes, make sure all the pieces are approximately the same size. Boil for 10 minutes, drain thoroughly and then shake to roughen up their surfaces a little. Heat 1–2 tablespoons of olive oil in a baking dish, add semi-cooked potatoes and shake vigorously. (Alternatively, you can use an olive oil spray to coat each piece of potato.) Bake at 190°C for 20–30 minutes or until crisp, turning once.

FOR POTATO SALAD

Use bintje, kipfler, pink eye, patrone, pink fir apple, ratte, roseval or small Nicola. Steam in their skins, then peel.

FRYING AS CHIPS

Use bintje, desirée, kennebec, King Edward, Nicola, pink fir apple, pontiac or russet Burbank. Of these, the pick would be russet Burbank, bintje or King Edward.

POTATO SALAD WITH WALNUT DRESSING

A delightfully healthy potato salad.

500 g potatoes (bintje, desirée, kipfler, Nicola,
  pink eye, pink fir apple, ratte, roseval)
½ cup white wine
2 tbsp finely chopped chives
2 tbsp chopped parsley
2 hard-boiled eggs, chopped

DRESSING
¼ cup walnuts
1 cup natural fat-reduced yoghurt
1 tbsp lemon juice
1 tsp finely grated lemon peel
1 tbsp fresh lemon thyme

SERVES 4

Steam or microwave potatoes until tender. Drain and cut in halves (or quarters, depending on size) while still hot. Place immediately in a bowl, pour wine over, cover and leave for 5 minutes. Add chives and parsley, and toss lightly.

To make dressing, place walnuts, yoghurt, lemon juice and peel, and thyme into blender or food processor and mix well. Pour over potatoes and mix gently so as not to break up potatoes. Top with the chopped eggs.

NUTRITIONAL VALUE: 11 g protein, 8 g fat ('good' fat), 21 g carbohydrate, 3 g dietary fibre, 935 kJ (225 Cals). A good source of vitamin C and also provides some iron, potassium, magnesium, calcium, zinc and riboflavin.

SAUTÉED HERBED POTATOES

Excellent with any roasted or barbecued meats, fish or chicken. Or serve simply with scrambled eggs. Suitable potato varieties include bintje, desirée, King Edward, kipfler, patrone, pink eye, pink fir apple, pontiac, roseval, royal blue, russet Burbank or symfonia.

600 g potatoes, cut into 1.5 cm dice
2 tbsp olive oil
2 cloves garlic, crushed
1 tbsp finely chopped fresh rosemary
2 tbsp finely chopped fresh mint
1 tbsp finely chopped chives
2 tbsp finely chopped parsley
freshly ground pepper

SERVES 4

Steam potatoes for 3 minutes. Heat olive oil in a large heavy-based pan, add potatoes and garlic, and cook over medium heat, stirring often, until potatoes are brown and tender. Add herbs and pepper, and toss thoroughly to combine. Serve piping-hot.

NUTRITIONAL VALUE: 4 g protein, 9.5 g fat ('good' fat), 20 g carbohydrate, 3 g dietary fibre, 780 kJ (185 Cals). A good source of vitamin C and also provides some iron and potassium.

BAKED POTATO FRITTATA

This is a handy dish, excellent for a simple lunch or picnic or to serve when visitors call in unexpectedly. Use a food processor to slice the onions and potatoes. Any all-purpose potatoes can be used.

1 tbsp olive oil
2 large onions, sliced thinly
2 cloves garlic, crushed
1 tbsp balsamic vinegar
1 tsp brown sugar
750 g all-purpose potatoes (see page 112), peeled
4 eggs plus 2 extra egg whites
½ cup fat-reduced milk
½ tsp ground black pepper
½ cup finely chopped parsley

SERVES 4

Heat a heavy-based pan, add oil and onions, cover and sweat for about 5 minutes, stirring several times. Remove lid, add garlic, vinegar and sugar, and cook for a further 2 minutes. Spoon mixture into a 20 cm cake tin.

While onions are cooking, steam or microwave potatoes until tender. Preheat oven to 180°C. Slice potatoes and arrange on top of onions.

Beat eggs, egg whites, milk, pepper and parsley. Pour over potatoes and onions, and bake for 20 minutes or until egg is set. Turn out of tin and serve hot, or refrigerate until required.

NUTRITIONAL VALUE: 15 g protein, 11 g fat, 31 g carbohydrate, 5 g dietary fibre, 1210 kJ (290 Cals). A good source of vitamin C, potassium and iron, and also provides some magnesium, zinc and vitamins A, riboflavin and thiamin.

POTATO PANCAKES

Much healthier than chips and children love them. Delicious served with home-made apple sauce. Russet Burbank are the best potatoes to use, but if they are unavailable, use desirée, pontiac, royal blue or spunta instead.

750 g potatoes, unpeeled but scrubbed
½ cup green shallots (spring onions), sliced
¼ cup self-raising flour
1 tbsp fresh lemon thyme
1 egg plus 1 extra egg white
freshly ground pepper
2 tsp olive oil

MAKES 8 PANCAKES, SERVING 4

Grate the potatoes using a food processor or coarse grater. Using your hands, squeeze potatoes to extract as much moisture as possible. Combine grated potato with onions, flour, thyme, egg, egg white and pepper. Mix well, adding a little more flour if mixture seems to be too wet (this depends on how much water you have been able to squeeze from the potatoes).

Heat a heavy-based frying pan and brush with olive oil. Cook tablespoons of potato mixture over a moderate heat, turning to brown both sides. Keep pancakes warm while cooking the rest.

NUTRITIONAL VALUE: 8 g protein, 4 g fat, 31 g carbohydrate, 3.5 g dietary fibre, 820 kJ (195 Cals). A good source of vitamin C and also provides some iron, potassium and magnesium.

HEALTHY POTATO WEDGES WITH
CHIVE YOGHURT DRESSING

Always popular, this is a healthier way to make wedges than the traditional deep-fried method. Use bintje, desirée, patrone, pink eye, pontiac, russet Burbank, sebago, spunta or symfonia potatoes.

2 tbsp plain flour
1 tbsp dry breadcrumbs
1 tbsp wheatgerm
3 tsp dried salad herbs
1 tsp paprika
½ tsp ground black pepper
2 tbsp olive oil
1 kg potatoes, scrubbed

DRESSING
200 g natural yoghurt
1 tbsp chopped chives
1 tbsp lemon juice

SERVES 6

Preheat oven to 220°C. Place flour, breadcrumbs, wheatgerm, herbs, paprika and pepper in a plastic bag and shake well to combine. Heat olive oil in a large shallow baking tray.

Cut potatoes into wedges about 2.5 cm thick. Add half the potatoes to the plastic bag and shake to coat with the flour mixture, then place on oven tray. Repeat with remaining potatoes. Bake for 25 minutes, or until crisp and brown, turning once during cooking.

To make dressing, combine yoghurt, chives and lemon juice. Serve separately.

NUTRITIONAL VALUE: 6.5 g protein, 8 g fat ('good' fat), 28 g carbohydrate, 3 g dietary fibre, 885 kJ (210 Cals). A good source of vitamin C and also provides some iron, potassium and magnesium.

POTATOES WITH PESTO

Potatoes are often served with butter or cream. Try using a healthy parsley pesto (or a traditional basil pesto) instead.

6 large russet Burbank potatoes (or use
*   desirée, pontiac, spunta or symfonia)*
coarse sea salt

PARSLEY PESTO
2 tbsp pine nuts (or use flaked almonds)
large bunch continental parsley
2 cloves garlic
2 tbsp lemon juice
2 tbsp extra-virgin olive oil
2 tbsp grated parmesan

SERVES 6

Preheat oven to 190°C. Prick potatoes in several places with a skewer. Wash and then rub the wet skin with a little coarse sea salt. Place potatoes directly on oven shelf and bake for 1–1$\frac{1}{2}$ hours, or until skin is crunchy and potato is tender inside (pierce with a skewer to test).

To make the pesto, toast pine nuts or almonds on a dry frying pan until golden-brown (take care not to burn). Tip onto a plate to cool. Remove coarse stems from the parsley and process in a blender or food processor until finely chopped. Add garlic, lemon juice, olive oil and nuts, and process again until finely ground. Stir in the parmesan.

When the potatoes are cooked, slash the top, squeeze to open slightly (use a clean tea-towel and oven mitts) and place a good dollop of pesto in the slash. Serve at once.

NUTRITIONAL VALUE: 7.5 g protein, 11 g fat ('good' fat), 27 g carbohydrate, 5 g dietary fibre, 990 kJ (235 Cals). A good source of vitamin C and potassium and also provides some iron, zinc, magnesium, calcium and vitamins A, niacin, thiamin and folate.

POTATO GRATIN

This is one dish where you need the right kind of potatoes—desirée, kennebec, King Edward, pontiac, royal blue, russet Burbank, spunta, sebago or Toolangi delight—to soak up the liquid. You could use a well-flavoured stock instead of the milk. You can either peel the potatoes or leave them whole: a food processor makes slicing easier.

1 tbsp olive oil
2 medium-sized onions, sliced thinly
1 clove garlic, crushed
1 kg potatoes, sliced thinly
1 cup fat-reduced milk
1 slice bread
½ cup parsley sprigs
½ cup grated cheddar

SERVES 6

Heat olive oil in a wok or frying pan, add the onions, cover and sweat over a gentle heat, stirring occasionally, for 10 minutes. Add garlic and cook for a further 2 minutes.

Preheat oven to 180°C. In a shallow greased ovenproof dish, arrange one-third of the sliced potatoes. Cover with half the onions, then another third of the potato, the rest of the onions and the remaining potato slices. Pour milk over, and cook in preheated oven for 45 minutes.

Place bread and parsley in food processor and process into crumbs. Add the cheese and mix well. Remove potatoes from oven, sprinkle with crumb mixture and bake for a further 20 minutes, or until potatoes are tender.

NUTRITIONAL VALUE: 9.5 g protein, 7.5 g fat, 29 g carbohydrate, 4 g dietary fibre, 935 kJ (225 Cals). A good source of vitamin C and also provides some iron, potassium, magnesium, calcium, zinc and thiamin.

POTATO AND LEEK SOUP

This warming winter soup is excellent served with a spoonful of parsley pesto (see page 122). Or chill it and serve with a dollop of natural yoghurt mixed with finely chopped mint. Suitable potatoes include desirée, kennebec, pontiac, royal blue, saxon, sebago, spunta, symfonia or Toolangi delight.

1 tbsp butter or olive oil
2 leeks, washed and sliced
750 g potatoes, cut into chunks
4 bay leaves
3–4 sprigs mint
2 cups chicken or vegetable stock
2 cups fat-reduced milk
a pinch of nutmeg
freshly ground pepper

SERVES 4

In a large saucepan, heat the butter and cook the leeks over a gentle heat, stirring often, for 5 minutes. Add potatoes, bay leaves, mint and stock, bring to the boil, cover and simmer for 20 minutes, or until potatoes are tender. Remove bay leaves and mint, and discard. Purée soup in batches, adding milk, nutmeg and pepper. Reheat or chill.

NUTRITIONAL VALUE: 11 g protein, 6 g fat, 35 g carbohydrate, 4.5 g dietary fibre, 1010 kJ (240 Cals). A good source of vitamin C and potassium, and also provides some iron, magnesium, calcium, zinc and vitamins A, thiamin, riboflavin, folate and niacin.

CURRIED POTATOES

An easy yet full-flavoured curry which is always popular. Nigella seeds are available in Asian food stores and many delicatessens. Use bintje, desirée, kennebec, kipfler, nadine, Nicola, patrone, pontiac, royal blue, sebago, spunta, symfonia or Toolangi delight potatoes. Blue flowered nigella (love-in-the-mist) is easily grown in the garden.

1 tbsp mustard oil (or use macadamia oil)
$\frac{1}{2}$ tsp black mustard seeds
1 tsp nigella seeds
1 small red chilli, chopped finely
$\frac{1}{2}$ tsp fenugreek seeds
1 tsp cumin seeds
3 cardamom pods, cracked
1 tsp ground cinnamon
a pinch of ground cloves
1 tbsp ground coriander
$\frac{1}{2}$ tsp ground turmeric
$\frac{1}{4}$ cup natural yoghurt
750 g potatoes, cut into 2 cm cubes
$\frac{1}{2}$ cup water
2 tbsp lemon juice

SERVES 4

In a saucepan, heat the oil and add the mustard and nigella seeds. Cook until the mustard seeds begin to pop, then add the fenugreek, cumin, cardamom, cinnamon, cloves, coriander, turmeric and yoghurt, and stir for 1 minute. Add potatoes, water and lemon juice, bring to the boil, cover and simmer over low heat until potatoes are cooked (about 15 minutes). If necessary, add a little more water, but try to keep the curry dry. Serve at once.

NUTRITIONAL VALUE: 5.5 g protein, 5.5 g fat ('good' fat), 27 g carbohydrate, 3 g dietary fibre, 775 kJ (185 Cals). A good source of vitamin C and also provides some iron, potassium, magnesium and vitamins A and thiamin.

POTATO AND ROSEMARY PIZZA

If desired, use a large purchased pizza base.

7 g dried yeast
2 tbsp lukewarm water
1 tsp sugar
2½ cups plain flour
1 tbsp gluten flour
½ tsp salt
1 cup lukewarm water

TOPPING

½ cup pesto (purchased or see page 122)
500 g potatoes (e.g. bintje, desirée, King
*   Edward, pink eye, pontiac, roseval)*
olive oil spray (or 2 tsp olive oil)
2 tbsp finely chopped fresh rosemary

SERVES 4

To make the pizza base, combine yeast, water and sugar in a large bowl. Leave to stand for 10 minutes. Add flours, salt and enough of the water to make a smooth dough. Knead until smooth and elastic, then place in an oiled bowl and enclose this in a plastic bag. Leave in a warm place for an hour, by which time the dough should have doubled in bulk. Punch down, knead for 2 minutes, then roll out to fit a pizza tray.

Preheat oven to 200°C. Spread dough with pesto. If desired, peel potatoes (most varieties can be left unpeeled). Slice potatoes as thinly as possible (a food processor slicing blade makes this easy) and arrange in overlapping layers on the pizza. Spray or brush with olive oil, sprinkle with rosemary and bake for 15–20 minutes, or until crust is cooked.

NUTRITIONAL VALUE: 15 g protein, 14 g fat ('good' fat), 83 g carbohydrate, 7 g dietary fibre, 2200 kJ (525 Cals). A good source of vitamin C and also provides some iron, potassium, calcium, zinc, magnesium and vitamins A, thiamin, and niacin.

POTATO, PUMPKIN AND APPLE BAKE

Excellent on a cold night, and goes well with barbecued chicken or roast lamb. If desired, make in individual dishes. Suitable potatoes include bintje, desirée, King Edward, Nicola, pink eye, pontiac, pink fir apple, royal blue, sebago, sequoia, spunta, symfonia or Toolangi delight.

400 g potatoes, scrubbed
400 g pumpkin, peeled and cut into chunks
2 Granny Smith apples, peeled, cored
  and quartered
1 cinnamon stick
¾ cup low-fat natural yoghurt
2 tsp Dijon-style mustard
freshly ground black pepper
2 tbsp chopped fresh mint
3 egg whites
1 tsp butter
1 clove garlic, cut in half

SERVES 4

Steam potatoes, pumpkin and apples for 15 minutes, or until tender, adding the cinnamon stick to the water beneath the steamer. Mash vegetables, adding yoghurt, mustard, pepper and mint.

Preheat oven to 180°C. Butter a shallow ovenproof dish, rub the base and sides with the garlic halves and then discard the garlic. Beat egg whites until stiff, fold one quarter into the potato mixture, and then the remainder. Spoon into the ovenproof dish and bake for 15–20 minutes, or until brown.

NUTRITIONAL VALUE: 10 g protein, 2 g fat, 31 g carbohydrate, 4.5 g dietary fibre, 780 kJ (185 Cals). A good source of vitamins A and C and potassium, and also provides some iron, magnesium, calcium and vitamins A and riboflavin.

SPINACH-STUFFED SPUDS

A great way to encourage reluctant little spinach-eaters. Use true spinach, not silverbeet. Cooking potatoes in the oven will produce a crunchy skin, whereas microwaving them will give a soft skin.

4 medium–large potatoes (desirée, pontiac, russet Burbank, sebago or spunta), scrubbed
½ bunch spinach
½ cup ricotta
a pinch of nutmeg
2 tbsp chopped green shallots (spring onions)
1 tbsp lemon juice
1 tbsp grated parmesan

SERVES 4

Preheat oven to 180°C. Bake potatoes on oven shelf for about 1¼ hours, or until tender when pierced with a skewer. (Alternatively, microwave on High for 12–15 minutes.) Remove, cut a lid from each potato and scoop out the flesh.

While potatoes are baking, wash spinach and steam until just wilted. Cool, squeeze tightly to remove as much water as possible, then chop finely. Mash potato flesh, adding spinach, ricotta, nutmeg, onions and lemon juice. Pile back into potato shells, top with parmesan and bake for 20 minutes, or microwave on High for 4–5 minutes.

NUTRITIONAL VALUE: 9.5 g protein, 4.5 g fat, 25 g carbohydrate, 4 g dietary fibre, 760 kJ (180 Cals). A good source of vitamin C and potassium, and also provides some iron, magnesium, calcium, zinc and vitamin A.

Pumpkin

There is no precise botanical distinction between squash and pumpkins—what some call a pumpkin, others call a winter squash. And what some consider to be a delicious vegetable, others think is best hollowed out as a decorative lantern to hold a candle. Pumpkins have low status in some parts of the world, possibly because they grow on vines at a sometimes rapid rate (often adding 300 g to their weight each day), and develop a watery, fibrous texture, making them more suitable as a food for animals, especially those housed inside over the winter months. To some extent, these differences of opinion may arise from the type of pumpkins grown. Some, like Queensland blue and butternut, are full of flavour, whereas the large orange pumpkins usually used for carving at Halloween in the United States have little flavour.

Pumpkins are members of the Cucurbita family, which also includes cucumbers, marrows and zucchini, and the inedible, but highly decorative, gourds. The word 'pumpkin' may have been derived from the Greek word *pepon* (which refers to a large, ripe melon-like fruit) and then modified to 'pampion' and 'pomkin' by the English and finally to 'pumpkin' by settlers in North America. Pumpkins are native to South and Central America, and there is evidence they were cultivated as far back as 8000 BC. They were not introduced to Europe until 1591, and even then were regarded as a food for animals or very poor peasants—a situation which still persists in some areas.

The hard skin on pumpkins may be orange, red, deep grey-blue, green, yellow or striped. The edible and highly nutritious seeds can be white, green, brown or black. Roasted green pumpkin seeds are called pepitas.

Pumpkins are an excellent source of beta carotene, which the body converts to vitamin A: the highest quantities are found in those with the brightest orange flesh. Varieties such as Queensland blue are also a good source of vitamin C. Pumpkin has a little more carbohydrate than many vegetables, but the level is not high and is much less than in potatoes. Queensland blue has the highest carbohydrate content, more than half of which is in the form of sugars rather than starch. A typical serving of cooked pumpkin has virtually no fat, 4.5–9.5 g of carbohydrate, 1.5–4 g of dietary fibre and 100–195 kJ, depending on the variety. The kilojoule level varies inversely with the water content. Watery pumpkins, commonly used in the United States, have the lower level and the full-flavoured pumpkins with a high-dry matter content, such as Queensland blue or butternut, also more. However, no pumpkin could be classified as high in kilojoules. Pumpkin seeds are highly nutritious and a good source of vitamin E.

VARIETIES • *Baby blue* is related to the familiar Queensland blue, but is smaller, usually weighing only 2–3 kg. With its thick grey-blue skin and yellow-orange flesh, it is good eating, bakes well and is excellent for pumpkin soup.

Butternut is one of the earliest species cultivated in Mexico, where evidence suggests it was used in about 3400 BC. Its botanical name is *Cucurbita moschata* and the pear-shaped fruits have a smooth, pale, orange-brown skin and orange flesh. The seeds lie in a bulbous section at the bottom and most butternut pumpkins have a longish neck. A good eating pumpkin because it has a lower water content than some varieties, it is excellent in salads, or sliced and sautéed. Also good for pumpkin soup or scones.

Golden nugget is a small pumpkin that grows on a bush rather than a vine. It has bright-orange skin and orange flesh, and is usually 10–12 cm in diameter. Good for stuffing, but does not have much flavour.

Jap, also known as Kent, is a little bigger than the golden nugget and has glossy dark-green skin with light-brown splotches. The flesh is deep yellow and sweet.

Jarrahdale is a large round pumpkin with fluted appearance. It has a grey skin that is easier to slice than the Queensland blue, although the flesh does not quite match the flavour of the tougher-skinned pumpkins.

Queensland blue is an Australian pumpkin with a blue-grey, fluted shell and bright-orange flesh. Its flavour is good and it has a lower water content than many of the pumpkins rejected as tasteless. The most common variety in Australia, the Queensland blue usually weighs about 5 kg, but specimens weighing more than 180 kg have been recorded.

Sweet dumpling is a small, ribbed pumpkin usually about 10 cm in diameter, with white skin dappled dark-green. The skin sometimes turns orange, making it very attractive. Good for stuffing, although more as a container because its flesh has little flavour.

CHOOSING AND STORING • Pumpkins are available all year, but those with the best flavour ripen during winter and autumn. Select pumpkins that feel heavy for their size and still have the stump of their stalk. Avoid those with any damage to the skin. If the pumpkin has already been cut, check that the cut edges look fresh and there is no slime among the seeds.

Whole pumpkins will keep in a cool dark place for several months. Cut pumpkin should be wrapped in plastic and refrigerated for up to 5 days.

PREPARATION AND COOKING • It is relatively easy to remove the skin from pumpkins such as butternut. Queensland blue can cause more problems, because its skin is hard enough to break the blade of a weak knife. It may be easier to steam or bake pumpkin in its skin and remove it when the pumpkin is cooked. You can eat baked pumpkin skin, or diners can remove it at the table.

Remove the seeds before cooking pumpkin. They can be roasted and salted, although the commonly available varieties of pumpkin do not produce the tasty green pumpkin seeds sold as pepitas.

Pumpkin can be steamed and mashed with butter and a pinch of nutmeg or cinnamon, or baked or stir-fried. It is also delicious in salads (peel and slice it and cook in a little olive oil, or try long strands of grated raw pumpkin). Smaller pumpkins, such as golden nugget or sweet dumpling, look attractive if hollowed out and stuffed with a rice or cracked-wheat mixture. Pumpkin does not take well to boiling, as much of the flavour dissolves into the cooking water and many types become stringy and lose their texture. It can, however, be microwaved successfully.

CURRIED PUMPKIN SOUP

This slightly spicy pumpkin soup is excellent in winter.

1 tbsp mustard oil
1 large onion, chopped
2 tsp good-quality curry powder
2 tsp ground coriander
1/2 tsp ground cardamom
800 g peeled pumpkin (any type), cut into chunks
3 cups stock
1 cup fat-reduced milk
1 cup evaporated skim milk
1/3 cup natural yoghurt

SERVES 4

In a large saucepan, heat oil and gently cook onion for 2 minutes. Add curry powder, coriander and cardamom, and cook for 2 minutes, stirring continuously. Add pumpkin and stock, bring to the boil, cover and simmer for 15 minutes, or until pumpkin is tender. Purée soup, adding both types of milk. Reheat, and serve piping-hot, adding a dollop of yoghurt to each bowl.

NUTRITIONAL VALUE: 15 g protein, 7.5 g fat ('good' fat), 31 g carbohydrate, 4.5 g dietary fibre, 1050 kJ (250 Cals). An excellent source of vitamins A and C, a good source of calcium, iron, potassium and riboflavin, and also provides some zinc, magnesium and niacin.

PUMPKIN LOAF

A healthy moist cake that is excellent on its own, or sliced and spread with light cream cheese.

1 cup soy and linseed bran cereal
1 cup skim milk
1/2 cup raisins
1/2 cup sultanas
2 tbsp honey
1 cup cold mashed pumpkin
2 eggs, beaten
1 tsp vanilla
1/2 cup walnut pieces
1 cup wholemeal plain flour
2 tsp baking powder
2 tsp cinnamon

MAKES 16 SLICES

Place cereal, milk, raisins, sultanas and honey in a bowl and leave to stand for at least an hour. Preheat oven to 180°C. Line a 14 × 21 cm loaf tin with baking powder.

Add pumpkin, eggs, vanilla and walnuts to bran mixture. Sift flour, baking powder and cinnamon, add to cake mixture, stir well and spoon into loaf tin. Bake for 50 minutes, or until a skewer inserted comes out clean. Leave to cool.

NUTRITIONAL VALUE PER SLICE: 4 g protein, 3.5 g fat, 19 g carbohydrate, 3 g dietary fibre, 510 kJ (120 Cals). Provides some calcium.

PASTA WITH PUMPKIN, PINE NUTS
AND POPPY SEEDS

Use butternut, Queensland blue or golden nugget for this easy dish.

1 tbsp pine nuts
375 g pasta (fettuccine or spirals)
1 tbsp extra-virgin olive oil
2 cloves garlic, crushed
500 g peeled pumpkin, sliced thinly
½ cup chicken or vegetable stock
3 tsp poppy seeds
2 tbsp chopped fresh basil

SERVES 4

Cook pine nuts in a dry frying pan, tossing frequently until brown (take care they do not burn). Tip onto a plate.

Cook pasta according to packet directions, and drain well. While pasta is cooking, heat oil in a heavy-based pan and cook garlic and pumpkin in batches until brown on both sides. Do not overcook pumpkin—the slices should be firm. Add chicken stock and simmer for a couple of minutes so that pumpkin is tender but slices do not break up. Add poppy seeds.

Place pasta in warmed serving bowls, top with pumpkin and sprinkle with pine nuts and basil.

NUTRITIONAL VALUE: 14 g protein, 9.5 g fat ('good' fat), 76 g carbohydrate, 7.5 g dietary fibre, 1885 kJ (450 Cals). A good source of vitamins A and C, and also provides some iron, zinc, potassium, magnesium, thiamin and riboflavin.

PUMPKIN SALAD WITH SESAME DRESSING

Butternut pumpkin is surprisingly good in this salad.

1 tbsp olive oil
750 g butternut pumpkin, peeled, seeded and
*   thinly sliced*
1 bunch watercress
150 g mung-bean sprouts

DRESSING
2 tbsp sesame seeds
1 tbsp olive oil
1 tbsp cider vinegar
1 tbsp orange juice
1 tsp honey
1 tsp whole-grain mustard

SERVES 4

Heat olive oil in a large heavy-based frying pan. Add pumpkin slices and cook over a high heat for 2 minutes, turning once. Do not overcook: pumpkin should still have some bite. Place watercress around the edge of a salad platter. Inside, arrange overlapping pumpkin slices and then pile the beansprouts in the centre.

To make dressing, toast the sesame seeds in a dry frying pan over a gentle heat until golden-brown (take care they do not burn). In a small saucepan, combine olive oil, vinegar, juice, honey and mustard, stirring over a low heat until the ingredients are blended. Drizzle warm dressing over pumpkin and sprinkle with sesame seeds.

NUTRITIONAL VALUE: 7.5 g protein, 12 g fat ('good' fat), 16 g carbohydrate, 5 g dietary fibre, 830 kJ (200 Cals). An excellent source of vitamins A and C, a good source of potassium and also provides some iron, zinc, magnesium and vitamins E, thiamin and riboflavin.

PUMPKIN SCONES

Delicious served with cumquat or orange marmalade, or with pumpkin marmalade (see next recipe). The secret is to steam the pumpkin and mash it thoroughly, keeping it as dry as possible: if it is too wet, the scones will be heavy.

2½ cups plain white flour
3 tsp baking powder
2 tsp mixed spice
1 tbsp sugar
1 tbsp butter, melted
1 cup cold mashed pumpkin,
    preferably butternut
¼ cup milk

MAKES 12

Preheat oven to 200°C. Sift flour, baking powder and spice, add sugar and mix thoroughly. Make a well in the centre and add butter, pumpkin and milk, adding a little more flour if necessary to form a soft dough (the exact amount of flour and milk depends on the moisture level of the pumpkin). With floured hands, pat the dough out to about 2.5 cm thick and cut into rounds using a small glass (dipped in flour to stop the dough sticking).

Place close together on a flat, greased baking tray, brush tops with a little extra milk and bake for 15 minutes, or until golden-brown. Enjoy while warm, split and topped with jam or marmalade.

NUTRITIONAL VALUE PER SCONE: 3.5 g protein, 2 g fat, 24 g carbohydrate, 1.5 g dietary fibre, 540 kJ (130 Cals). Provides some calcium and vitamin A.

PUMPKIN MARMALADE

If you have pumpkins growing, use some to make this bright-orange marmalade.

1.5 kg pumpkin
5 cups water
2 grapefruit, sliced finely
1 orange, sliced finely
2 lemons, sliced finely
3 cinnamon sticks
1½ kg sugar

MAKES ABOUT 8 MEDIUM-SIZED JARS

Peel pumpkin, remove seeds and use a food processor to grate the flesh. In a large heavy-based saucepan, place water, grapefruit, orange, lemon and cinnamon. Bring to the boil, cover and simmer for 15 minutes. Add the pumpkin and continue cooking for another 20 minutes, or until the citrus peel is quite soft.

Remove cinnamon sticks and stir in the sugar until it is dissolved. Boil, uncovered, until mixture gels (about 30 minutes). To test whether the marmalade is ready, drop about a teaspoonful onto a saucer and place in the freezer for a couple of minutes: if it sets, the marmalade is ready. Remove from stove, allow to rest for 2 minutes, then stir and bottle into sterilised jars.

NUTRITIONAL VALUE PER TABLESPOON: 0 g protein, 0 g fat, 7 g carbohydrate, 0.5 g dietary fibre, 115 kJ (25 Cals).

Purslane (see **Other vegetables**)

Radicchio (see **Lettuce**)

Radishes

Most experts claim that radishes are native to eastern Europe and wild radishes still grow near the Caspian Sea. Others believe they originated in China. The radish had spread to Egypt by at least 2700 BC, where it formed part of the diet given to the slaves building the Pyramids. Radishes were also recorded in China in 500 BC and have been used in Japan for more than 1300 years. The first cultivated radishes had a black skin and were valued partly because they kept well during the winter months. By the late sixteenth century, long white radishes with red skins were being cultivated in Spain and Italy. Small round radishes first appeared in the eighteenth century. Green, yellow, red, white, purple or black radishes are now available. Most have white flesh, although a red-fleshed variety is used in China.

In Europe the radish is used as a salad vegetable, whereas oriental radishes are often cooked. The hotness of radishes comes from a substance in their skin and is removed if you peel them. Radishes are closely related to cabbages and all types contain similar valuable compounds known as isothiocyanates, now recognised as having anti-cancer action within the body. Young radish leaves are also edible, and radish sprouts are delicious.

Radishes are a good source of vitamin C and also contain some iron, folate and dietary fibre. Oriental radishes have less iron and vitamin C, but are usually eaten in larger quantities so the absolute amount consumed may be greater. An average serving of 4 small red radishes has no fat, 0.5 g of dietary fibre and 25 kJ. A typical serving of $^1/_2$ cup cooked oriental radish contributes almost no fat, 1 g of dietary fibre and 60 kJ.

Radish leaves are an excellent source of vitamin C and beta carotene and one of the richest vegetable sources of iron. Half a cup of cooked radish leaves has 65 kJ.

VARIETIES • *Oriental radishes* (known as daikon in Japan and loh baak in China), long white radishes, are especially popular in Korea. They are sometimes grated and eaten raw, or they may be sliced and cooked in soups, added to stir-fried dishes and pickled or dried. Fresh large radishes are also carved into elaborate shapes to decorate Japanese and Chinese feast dishes. In China, the oriental radish is added to a type of rice-flour 'pudding', either sweet or savoury, which is steamed and cooled, then fried just before serving.

Horseradish is not always considered a vegetable. Native to south-eastern Europe, its rhizomes are eaten and enjoyed for their pungency, which comes largely from allyl isothiocyanates. These are valuable compounds with anti-carcinogenic action, although it is difficult to eat enough horseradish to take in significant quantities.

CHOOSING AND STORING • Radishes are available all year, with the best supplies in spring and early summer. Select crisp, bright ones with fresh-looking leaves. Avoid those where the leaves look slimy. Choose oriental radishes that feel heavy, and avoid very large ones as they may be hollow inside.

To store radishes, remove leaves and keep in a plastic bag in the refrigerator for 2–3 days.

PREPARATION AND COOKING • Red radishes are usually eaten raw. In Europe and elsewhere, people often sit down to a plate of radishes (usually with the green stems still attached) and enjoy them with fresh bread, butter and salt. The radishes are dipped in salt and eaten with bread and butter, or the butter is spread onto the radishes and they are then dipped in the salt.

To prepare radishes, scrub away any dirt and trim off the leaves and roots. If you want to reduce their hotness, peel them thickly. Any kind of radish can be steamed or boiled, and they usually cook in 5–10 minutes. If sliced and steamed, they turn a pretty pink. The oriental radish can be cooked in soups without disintegrating.

RADISH, CUCUMBER AND PUMPKIN SALAD

A refreshing summer salad that goes well with barbecued lamb. Grated raw pumpkin is delicious.

1 bunch radishes, trimmed of roots and leaves
250 g raw butternut or Queensland
    blue pumpkin
3 Lebanese cucumbers
200 g natural yoghurt
2 tbsp lemon juice
2 tsp finely grated lemon peel
1 tbsp finely shredded fresh mint leaves

SERVES 4

Grate radishes, pumpkin and cucumbers (the coarse grating blade on a food processor is ideal), and toss lightly together. Combine yoghurt, lemon juice, peel and mint. Add to the grated vegetables and mix gently to combine. Serve in lettuce cups.

NUTRITIONAL VALUE: 4.5 g protein, 2.5 g fat, 9.5 g carbohydrate, 2.5 g dietary fibre, 335 kJ (80 Cals). An excellent source of vitamin C, a good source of vitamin A and also provides some iron, calcium, magnesium, potassium and riboflavin.

RAW RADISH RELISH

Try this with Chinese roast chicken or duck.

1 bunch radishes
2 tbsp salt-reduced soy sauce
2 tbsp mirin or rice vinegar
1 tbsp sesame oil
2 tsp sugar

SERVES 6

Trim leaves and roots from radishes, reserving the leaves. Slice radishes finely (a food processor makes this easy). Combine soy sauce, mirin, sesame oil and sugar, and stir until sugar is dissolved. Pour over radishes and leave to stand for 1–2 hours. Just before serving, shred the radish leaves and add to salad. Toss well and serve.

NUTRITIONAL VALUE: 0.5 g protein, 3.5 g fat, 2 g carbohydrate, 0.5 g dietary fibre, 170 kJ (40 Cals).

WHITE RADISH CREAM

A delicious accompaniment for roast beef or potatoes baked in their jackets.

1 oriental radish
2 tsp salt
200 g natural yoghurt
1 tbsp lemon juice
1 tsp fennel seeds
freshly ground black pepper

SERVES 4

Grate radish coarsely into a colander, sprinkle with salt and leave for 20 minutes. Rinse thoroughly under the tap and squeeze radish as dry as possible, using your hands or a clean tea-towel. Combine radish with yoghurt, lemon juice, fennel and pepper.

NUTRITIONAL VALUE: 3 g protein, 2 g fat, 4.5 g carbohydrate, 1 g dietary fibre, 200 kJ (45 Cals).
A good source of vitamin C and provides some calcium.

Rape

Now known most commonly for a modified variety called canola, and grown mostly for its seeds and the valuable oil they contain, rape is also a highly nutritious green vegetable. Rape leaves are sometimes purchased as 'broccoli de rabe', 'broccoli raab' or 'rapini' and are popular in parts of Italy. With its mustard flavour, and dark-green leaves, rape belongs to the cabbage or Brassica family. Like its relatives, rape is a potent source of isothiocyanates, which act as antioxidants and have anti-cancer action. These compounds do not survive processing into canola oil, but mustard oil contains small quantities.

Rape is an excellent source of vitamin C and a good source of beta carotene and various other carotenoids. It also supplies iron and vitamins E, K and folate.

CHOOSING AND STORING • Generally available in spring. Look for fresh leaves that have not wilted and are not damaged.

Store leaves in a plastic bag in the refrigerator for 3–4 days.

PREPARATION AND COOKING • Wash rape leaves before cooking. As their flavour is strong, they are often shredded and steamed briefly, or sautéed in a little olive oil with garlic and a squeeze of lemon just before serving. The best way to serve them is with pasta (see recipe).

PASTA WITH RAPE LEAVES

Ideally, this dish should be made with orecchiette—little ear-shaped pasta which originated in Puglia in Italy—but you could use penne, shells or spirals instead. If rape leaves are unavailable, substitute Chinese broccoli or turnip tops.

¼ tsp salt (optional)
375 g pasta
500 g rape leaves
2 tbsp olive oil
1 medium-sized onion, sliced finely
3 cloves garlic
1 small red chilli, chopped finely
freshly ground black pepper

SERVES 4

Bring a large pot of water to the boil, add salt (if using) and pasta. While pasta is cooking, trim away coarse stems from rape leaves and cut any large leaves in half lengthwise.

Heat olive oil and gently cook onion, garlic and chilli for 5–6 minutes, without browning. When pasta is almost cooked, add rape leaves to the pasta pot and continue boiling for 1 minute. Drain pasta and leaves, and place in a heated serving bowl. Add onion mixture and toss well. Serve with plenty of ground pepper.

NUTRITIONAL VALUE: 16 g protein, 11 g fat ('good' fat), 74 g carbohydrate, 10 g dietary fibre, 1940 kJ (465 Cals). A good source of vitamins A, C and folate, calcium, iron and magnesium and also provides some potassium.

Rocket

Also known as arugula (occasionally spelt arrugula), rocket is another cruciferous vegetable, like the Brassicas. It originated in southern Europe and the western parts of Asia and was used by the ancient Romans. The oil from its seed has a reputation (unproven) as an aphrodisiac.

Once it's planted, you have rocket for a long time, as it self-seeds in winter and new plants emerge in cracks, paths and flower beds. The dark-green leaves look a bit like those of radishes and have a sharp mustard flavour. Varieties sold in shops tend to have shorter leaves and a milder flavour than naturalised garden specimens.

Rocket is a good source of antioxidants and of beta carotene, which is converted to vitamin A in the body. Rocket also supplies vitamins E and K, and some C. An average serving (50 g) of rocket has no fat, 1 g of dietary fibre and 50 kJ.

CHOOSING AND STORING • Rocket is available all year, but best supplies are in spring and summer. Choose leaves that look fresh and have not wilted.

Keep rocket in a plastic bag in the refrigerator for 2–3 days, but it is best used as soon as possible after purchase.

PREPARATION AND COOKING • Rocket is usually eaten raw in salads, although it can be steamed briefly or stir-fried. It is also good torn and sprinkled on pizza, either before or after cooking.

ROCKET AND GOAT'S CHEESE SALAD

Light lunches don't come better than this. Rocket seems to have a particular affinity with goat's cheese.

1 bunch (about 200 g) fresh asparagus
100 g goat's cheese, sliced
4 thick slices wood-fired or Italian-style bread
2 tbsp extra-virgin olive oil
1 tbsp raspberry vinegar
2 tsp Dijon-style mustard
4 cups rocket leaves, washed
2 cups baby spinach leaves
4 cooked baby beetroot, halved
½ cup torn basil leaves

SERVES 4

Cook asparagus in boiling water for 2 minutes, drain and run under the cold tap. Drain again.

Preheat oven to 180°C.

Place a quarter of the cheese on each slice of bread and bake for 10 minutes or until edges of bread are crusty and cheese is melted. In a screw-top jar, combine the oil, vinegar and mustard, and shake well.

Arrange rocket, spinach and beetroot on four individual plates. Top with asparagus and drizzle dressing over leaves. Top each serving with a slice of the goat's-cheese toast and some basil. Serve at once.

NUTRITIONAL VALUE: 12 g protein, 18 g fat, 24 g carbohydrate, 4.5 g dietary fibre, 1290 kJ (310 Cals). An excellent source of vitamin C, a good source of calcium, vitamin A and folate, and also provides some potassium, iron, zinc, magnesium, thiamin and riboflavin.

ROCKET PESTO

This pesto is bright green. Although it has a milder flavour than you might expect, walnuts stand up to its flavour better than the milder pine nuts used in a traditional pesto. Serve it with pasta, spread on baguettes filled with salad, use as a healthy alternative to butter on potatoes, or dollop it into minestrone.

1 bunch rocket
2 cloves garlic
2 tbsp extra-virgin olive oil
2 tbsp ricotta
¼ cup walnuts
2 tbsp grated parmesan

MAKES ¾ CUP

Place rocket and garlic in blender or food processor and blend until smooth. Add oil, ricotta and walnuts and process again. Stir in the cheese.

NUTRITIONAL VALUE PER TABLESPOON:
1 g protein, 5.5 g fat ('good' fat), 0.5 g carbohydrate, 0.5 g dietary fibre, 230 kJ (55 Cals).

Rutabaga (see **Swede**)

Salsify and scorzonera (see **Other vegetables**)

Scallions (see Green onions under **Onions**)

Shallots (see Dry onions under **Onions**)

Silverbeet

Known as Swiss chard in most parts of the world, silverbeet is sometimes mistakenly called spinach in Australia. In fact, its flavour is much coarser than spinach and many children who dislike silverbeet might be more favourably disposed towards the milder flavour of the real thing. Some people consider its botanical name, *Beta vulgaris*, appropriate possibly because they have only ever tasted boiled silverbeet.

Closely related to beetroot, silverbeet originated around the Mediterranean and is probably popular because it grows fast and easily. The outer, dark-green crinkled leaves can be picked and the plant will have produced more within a few days. Newer cultivates have a red or green rib and are often grown as ornamental garden plants.

Generations of children have been encouraged to eat their silverbeet for its iron content. Silverbeet, like spinach, is indeed an excellent source of iron, but unfortunately—again like spinach— it is also high in oxalic acid which 'ties up' the iron (and the calcium) so that it cannot be absorbed by the body. This does not mean there is no nutritional reason to eat silverbeet as it is a good source of vitamin K, folate and vitamin C, provides beta carotene (which the body converts to vitamin A), and has more dietary fibre than most vegetables. It also provides some vitamin E. A cup of cooked silverbeet has 0.5 g of fat, 4 g of dietary fibre and 75 kJ.

CHOOSING AND STORING • Silverbeet is available all year. Select crisp, glossy deep-green leaves with heavy white stems. Avoid bunches that are limp or where the leaves have lost their gloss. To store, remove the white stalk below each leaf, wrap the leaves in plastic and refrigerate for 2 or 3 days.

PREPARATION AND COOKING • Wash silverbeet thoroughly, as dirt is often trapped in its curly leaves. The white stalk is edible, but is usually removed. With red-ribbed varieties, the rib is smaller and looks attractive, so it is usually retained. The ribs can be sliced and stir-fried as a vegetable in their own right, or added to mixed stir-fries.

Silverbeet can be used in any recipes that use spinach. It can be steamed, microwaved, sliced and stir-fried, or rinsed and then cooked with the water that clings to its leaves before being added to a dish. A large saucepan of spinach will wilt to a smallish pile after a few minutes of cooking. Keep cooking time short as the bright-green colour darkens unattractively after more than 2–3 minutes. If the coarse stalk is removed, silverbeet leaves can also be blanched briefly and used to roll around stuffing or to line a terrine. One of the nicest ways to eat silverbeet is to cook it briefly in water, then purée and reheat it with a tablespoon or two of cream and a pinch of nutmeg.

SILVERBEET AND SALMON PANCAKE STACK

A great way to encourage reluctant vegetable-eaters to consume silverbeet. If desired, make this ahead and warm it in the microwave when needed.

PANCAKES
1 cup plain flour (wholemeal or white)
2 eggs, separated
1 cup fat-reduced milk
a pinch of nutmeg
1 tsp butter

FILLING
1 large bunch silverbeet
1/2 cup sliced green shallots (spring onions)
220 g canned red salmon, drained and mashed
1 cup fat-reduced ricotta
1/2 cup chopped parsley
freshly ground pepper

SERVES 4

Place flour, egg yolks, milk and nutmeg in blender and process to a smooth batter. Beat egg whites until stiff and gently fold into batter. Melt half the butter in a heavy-based pan, add a sixth of the pancake mixture, swirl to spread and cook until bubbles appear. Turn and brown other side. Repeat to make 6 pancakes.

Now make the filling. Wash silverbeet and place in a large saucepan with any water clinging to its leaves. Cook for 2 minutes, drain and, when cool enough, squeeze out as much water as possible and chop finely. Combine silverbeet with onions, salmon, ricotta, parsley and pepper.

Place one pancake in the bottom of a pie dish, top with one fifth of the silverbeet filling. Repeat layers, finishing with a pancake. Cover with plastic and heat in microwave for about 10 minutes, or cover with foil and heat in a moderate oven for about 15 minutes. Cut into wedges to serve.

NUTRITIONAL VALUE: 30 g protein, 14 g fat, 32 g carbohydrate, 6 g dietary fibre, 1585 kJ (380 Cals). An excellent source of vitamin C, a good source of calcium, iron, iodine and vitamin A, riboflavin and folate, and also provides some potassium, zinc, magnesium, niacin and thiamin.

SILVERBEET STIR-FRIED WITH GINGER

Although not a traditional Asian vegetable, silverbeet is excellent stir-fried and stands up well to the flavour of sesame oil. You can leave the ribs in this dish, or remove them.

2 tsp sesame oil
1 small onion, sliced
1 clove garlic
2 tsp finely sliced fresh ginger
1 bunch silverbeet, washed and cut into coarse
  shreds
1 tsp sugar
2 tbsp mirin or dry sherry
1 tbsp salt-reduced soy sauce
1 tbsp toasted sesame seeds

SERVES 4

Heat a wok or large frying pan and add oil and onion. Stir-fry, without browning, over a gentle heat for 3 minutes. Add garlic and ginger, and toss well. Add silverbeet and stir-fry for about 2 minutes, or until leaves are wilted. Combine sugar, mirin and soy sauce, and stir into silverbeet. Serve at once, topped with sesame seeds.

NUTRITIONAL VALUE: 3.5 g protein, 4.5 g fat ('good' fat), 4 g carbohydrate, 5 g dietary fibre, 320 kJ (75 Cals). An excellent source of vitamin C, and provides some vitamins A, folate and riboflavin.

CREAM OF SILVERBEET SOUP

A quick recipe, and you can use any all-purpose potato. The flavour and texture are improved by the addition of a small amount of cream, but omit it if you are concerned about saturated fat.

4 cups chicken or vegetable stock
2 medium-sized potatoes, peeled and cut
  into cubes
1 leek, washed and sliced
1 bunch silverbeet, washed and chopped
  roughly
¼ cup parsley leaves
½ cup skim-milk powder
2 tbsp cream
a pinch of nutmeg

SERVES 4

In a large saucepan, bring the stock to the boil. Add potatoes and leek, cover and simmer for 10 minutes. Add silverbeet and continue cooking for 5 minutes. Purée soup in batches, adding parsley and milk powder. Reheat, stir in cream and nutmeg and serve hot.

NUTRITIONAL VALUE: 10 g protein, 5.5 g fat, 22 g carbohydrate, 6.5 g dietary fibre, 740 kJ (175 Cals). An excellent source of vitamin C, a good source of calcium, potassium and vitamins A and riboflavin, and also provides some zinc, magnesium, niacin and folate.

Snow peas (see **Peas**)

Sorrel

Long popular as a vegetable in France, sorrel is being used increasingly in other countries. Large-leafed wild sorrel (*Rumex acetosa*), also known as dock, is native to Britain and Europe. Its arrow-shaped leaves are a little like those of some types of rocket, or a slightly longer and slimmer baby spinach, and it has a sour, lemony flavour. The word sorrel is derived from a Germanic word meaning sour. French sorrel (*Rumex scutatus*) grows wild in mountainous areas of Europe, Turkey and northern Iran. It has small squarish leaves and a more intense lemon flavour than dock. French sorrel is easily grown in the home garden and the varieties with reddish stalks make attractive plants.

Like all green vegetables, sorrel is an excellent source of vitamin C and also provides folate and beta carotene as well as potassium and small quantities of other minerals. Half a cup of sorrel has 0.5 g of fat, 2 g of dietary fibre and 60 kJ.

CHOOSING AND STORING • Sorrel is available in late spring and summer. Choose bright-green, fresh-looking leaves. Avoid bunches where the string has cut into the leaves and caused them to break and wilt, or where the leaves are starting to turn yellow. If you grow sorrel, pick only young tender leaves.

Place in a plastic bag and store for 1–2 days. Even better, pick it straight from the garden.

PREPARATION AND COOKING • Wash sorrel just before use, and remove any large tough stems. Shred large leaves before use, as the flavour can be very strong. If steaming, cook only for 1 minute or sorrel will lose its colour and become bitter. Small sorrel leaves can be added to salads.

Sorrel is ideal to use in sauces to serve with roast pork, game meats or poultry as its acid flavour cuts their richness. It is also good in soups and goes well with potato.

SORREL-STUFFED CHICKEN

Roast chicken is always a favourite and this stuffing is both easy and healthy. For a vegetarian alternative, fill pumpkins instead of chicken. Double the quantity of all the stuffing ingredients, take 4 small golden nugget pumpkins and cut a 'lid' from each. Remove the seeds and blanch the pumpkins in boiling water for 3 minutes. Drain away any water, fill with stuffing mixture and bake for 30 minutes.

1 roasting chicken
2 tbsp chopped hazelnuts
1 lemon
1 cup fresh wholemeal breadcrumbs
1 cup shredded sorrel leaves, coarse stems
  removed
½ cup sliced green shallots (spring onions)
freshly ground black pepper

SERVES 4

Preheat oven to 180°C.

Using your hands, pull out the fat pads from under the chicken skin and discard. Toast hazelnuts in a dry frying pan, shaking frequently, until they brown (take care not to burn). Cut lemon into quarters and remove seeds. Place lemon in blender and process until finely chopped.

Combine half the chopped lemon with the hazelnuts, breadcrumbs, sorrel, onions and pepper, and mix well to combine. Pack into chicken cavity, tie chicken legs together with string and place chicken in roasting pan. Rub chicken skin with remaining lemon. Bake for 1–1¼ hours, or until cooked. (To test if chicken is cooked, insert a skewer into the area between leg and thigh. The juices should be clear: if they are still pink, cook a little longer.)

Serve with roast potatoes and green vegetables or a green salad.

NUTRITIONAL VALUE: 38 g protein, 22 g fat, 6 g carbohydrate, 2.5 g dietary fibre, 1615 kJ (385 Cals). If you remove all skin, the fat content will be 7 g and kJ will fall to 975 (235 Cals). A good source of vitamin C, iron, zinc and niacin, and also provides some potassium and vitamins A, thiamin and riboflavin.

SORREL TIMBALES

An excellent accompaniment for roast lamb, veal or chicken. Or serve with a green salad and crusty bread as a lunch dish.

2 medium-sized potatoes
2 tsp butter
1 medium-sized onion, chopped finely
1 bunch sorrel, washed, coarse stems removed
¼ cup milk
½ cup grated parmesan
freshly ground black pepper
2 eggs, beaten
2 extra egg whites

SERVES 6

Preheat oven to 190°C. Grease 6 individual soufflé dishes.

Peel potatoes, steam until tender and mash while hot. While potatoes are cooking, heat butter and cook onion over a gentle heat for 5 minutes. Add sorrel and cook until it wilts, stirring to combine with the onion. Tip mixture into a bowl and chop roughly. Add mashed potatoes, milk, parmesan, pepper and the two beaten eggs, mixing well.

Beat extra egg whites until stiff. Add a quarter of the egg whites to the sorrel mixture, then fold in the remainder. Spoon mixture into dishes, put dishes in a larger baking pan and add water to come halfway up the soufflé dishes. Bake for 25–30 minutes, or until puffed and golden-brown.

NUTRITIONAL VALUE: 9.5 g protein, 7 g fat, 9.5 g carbohydrate, 2 g dietary fibre, 580 kJ (140 Cals). A good source of vitamin C and also provides some zinc, magnesium, iron and vitamins A and riboflavin.

Spaghetti squash (see **Squash**)

Spinach

In Australia, spinach is sometimes called 'English spinach' to distinguish it from silverbeet. It has a milder flavour than silverbeet. The baby spinach leaves now widely available and are an excellent way to encourage reluctant spinach-eaters to enjoy this delicious and nutritious vegetable.

Spinach originated either near Iran (formerly Persia) or in the western Himalayas. It was first cultivated in Iran around 1000 BC. It spread from Nepal to China in the seventh century, was cultivated in North Africa and taken to Spain by the Arabs in the eleventh century, reaching England in the sixteenth century. Other forms of wild spinach are found in Africa, India (Malabar spinach), and Australia and New Zealand (see Warrigal greens under **Other vegetables**).

Popeye the Sailor Man used to down a can of spinach when he needed instant energy for some heroic feat. Presumably the writers of the comic strip did not know that spinach contains oxalic acid, which prevents iron in spinach being absorbed. Modern cultivars have lower levels of oxalic acid, which reduces the bitterness and also means that a little of the iron (and calcium) in spinach may be available to the body. In general, however, the high iron levels present in spinach are not as useful as many people have been led to believe. Spinach is, however, an excellent source of vitamin C, beta carotene and folate, and also supplies some vitamin E, as well as contributing a high level of fibre. A cup of cooked spinach has 0.5 g of fat, 11.5 g of dietary fibre and 140 kJ.

CHOOSING AND STORING • Spinach is available from autumn to early spring, with the best supplies from winter to early spring. Select bunches that have fresh, bright-green leaves. Avoid those with damaged or yellowing leaves.

Spinach will keep for a day or two in a plastic bag in the refrigerator, but is best used soon after purchase. It freezes well and commercially frozen spinach is useful and nutritious.

PREPARATION AND COOKING • Wash spinach well and trim off roots and the end parts of the stalk. The remaining parts of the stalks are usually eaten, but can be removed by folding the leaf back and cutting away the stalk down the centre. This is important when spinach is to be puréed, as the stalks will leave stringy bits.

The best way to cook spinach is to place it into a saucepan with the water still clinging to its leaves after washing. Cover and cook over a moderate heat until it wilts—usually about 2–3 minutes. Spinach cooks down a lot and 6 cups of raw leaves will yield 1 cup cooked. Spinach puréed with a pinch of nutmeg and a spoonful of light sour cream is delicious. If using frozen spinach, defrost in the microwave or cook from frozen.

Baby spinach leaves have usually been washed ready for salads and need no preparation other than tossing with some dressing. Regular spinach leaves can also be used in salads, but have a stronger flavour than the baby ones.

SPINACH WITH CURRANTS AND PINE NUTS

This is served everywhere in Spain and in Italy is often piled into a crusty bread roll as a morning snack. Half this recipe will serve 2 and leave a little over to have on toast later.

2 tbsp pine nuts
2 bunches spinach
2 tbsp extra-virgin olive oil
2 tbsp currants

SERVES 6

Toast pine nuts in a dry frying pan, shaking frequently, until golden-brown. Wash spinach, remove roots and cook leaves in their own juice in a saucepan until just starting to wilt. Drain well and press out as much water as possible.

Heat olive oil and cook currants for 2 minutes. Add spinach and pine nuts, and toss well together. Serve hot, or allow to cool a little.

NUTRITIONAL VALUE: 4 g protein, 9.5 g fat ('good' fat), 3.5 g carbohydrate, 4 g dietary fibre, 480 kJ (115 Cals). An excellent source of vitamin C, a good source of vitamin A and folate, and also provides some potassium, iron and zinc.

SPINACH SALAD

You can use a bunch of regular spinach in this recipe, but the baby spinach leaves are much nicer.

2 slices white bread, crusts removed
2 tsp olive oil
350 g baby spinach leaves
½ large red capsicum, seeded and
    sliced finely
2 hard-boiled eggs, shelled and diced

DRESSING
1 tbsp extra-virgin olive oil
1 tbsp tarragon vinegar
2 tsp Dijon-style mustard
a pinch of sugar
freshly ground black pepper

SERVES 4

First make the croutons. Preheat oven to 190°C. Cut the bread into 1 cm cubes. Heat a shallow baking dish in the oven, add oil and bread, and toss cubes to coat them with the oil. Bake for 10 minutes, or until croutons are golden, shaking several times. Allow to cool.

Place spinach and capsicum in salad bowl. Combine all dressing ingredients, pour over the vegetables and toss to mix. Top with the hard-boiled eggs and the croutons, and serve at once.

NUTRITIONAL VALUE: 6.5 g protein, 10 g fat ('good' fat), 9 g carbohydrate, 3 g dietary fibre, 630 kJ (150 Cals). A good source of iron and vitamins A and C, and also provides some magnesium, riboflavin and folate.

SPINACH PARCELS

Wonton wrappers are available from Asian food stores or some delicatessens.

2 bunches spinach
150 g ricotta cheese
2 tbsp grated parmesan
2 tsp finely grated lemon peel
1 tbsp fresh lemon thyme
freshly ground black pepper
16 round wonton wrappers

FRESH TOMATO SAUCE
2 tsp olive oil
1 small red onion, chopped finely
1 cup chopped canned tomatoes
500 g ripe fresh tomatoes, skinned and diced finely

SERVES 4

Wash spinach and trim off the roots and stalks. Cook spinach in a large saucepan until it wilts. Drain, cool, squeeze out as much water as possible, and chop finely.

Combine spinach, ricotta, parmesan, lemon peel, thyme and pepper. Put out 4 wonton wrappers and place 1 tablespoon of the spinach mixture on each. Moisten edges and fold in half, ensuring filling is completely enclosed. Cover with a clean tea-towel while you repeat with the remaining wrappers. Allow to stand for 30 minutes.

To make tomato sauce, heat oil in a saucepan and gently cook onion, without browning, for 5 minutes. Add canned tomatoes and bring to the boil. Remove from heat and add diced fresh tomato.

Bring a large saucepan of water to the boil. Add 4 wontons and cook for 3–4 minutes, or until they float to the surface. Remove with a slotted spoon and keep warm while cooking the remaining parcels. Serve hot, with the tomato sauce.

NUTRITIONAL VALUE: 16 g protein, 8.5 g fat, 27 g carbohydrate, 9 g dietary fibre, 1065 kJ (255 Cals). An excellent source of vitamins A and C and magnesium, a good source of potassium, thiamin, riboflavin and folate, and also provides some iron, zinc, calcium and niacin.

SPINACH WITH FRESH CHEESE

The best cheese to use for this recipe is home-made fresh cheese, but firm ricotta is a good substitute (creamed ricotta is not suitable). Those who avoid dairy products can substitute silken firm tofu for the cheese.

200 g firm ricotta
1 tbsp mustard oil (or use cold-pressed canola oil)
1 bunch coriander, washed thoroughly
1 tsp ground cumin
1 tsp chopped fresh ginger
1 tbsp ground coriander
1 tsp dried fenugreek leaves
2 tsp grated fresh turmeric (or use ½ tsp dried)
2 bunches spinach
¼ cup hot water
½ tsp sugar
½ cup natural yoghurt

SERVES 4

Cut ricotta into 16 cubes and place on paper towels to absorb the excess moisture. Heat half the oil in a frying pan and brown the cheese cubes. Set aside.

Separate roots and stalks from coriander leaves. Set leaves aside and chop the roots and stalks finely. Heat remaining oil in a wok or large frying pan and fry the coriander roots and stalks with the cumin, ginger, coriander, fenugreek and turmeric for 2–3 minutes, stirring constantly.

Wash spinach, discard roots and bottom section of stalks, then chop leaves. Add spinach to spice mixture in wok and cook over a moderate heat until spinach starts to wilt. Add water and sugar, cook for a further 5 minutes, then stir in the yoghurt and add the cheese cubes. Serve piping-hot.

NUTRITIONAL VALUE: 13 g protein, 13 g fat, 5.5 g carbohydrate, 10 g dietary fibre, 795 kJ (190 Cals). An excellent source of vitamins A and C, a good source of calcium, iron, zinc, potassium, magnesium and zinc, and also the B vitamins folate and riboflavin.

Spring greens (see **Cabbage**)

Sprouts

Almost any bean can be sprouted, but those usually sold as 'bean sprouts' are mung-bean sprouts. Other sprouts, such as alfalfa, fenugreek and snow-pea are usually named as such.

Alfalfa is a type of lucerne. It probably originated in the Middle East and was taken to the United States by Chilean gold-seekers at the time of the California gold rush. It was known as Chilean clover and became a popular and nutritious crop for dairy cows, beef cattle and horses. We eat sprouted alfalfa seeds, though more as a garnish than as a source of nourishment. Alfalfa can cause an allergic reaction, often called 'farmer's lung' and usually seen in farmers exposed to large fields of alfalfa. The small quantities consumed do not usually cause any adverse reaction.

The *mung bean* probably originated in the region around India and Myanmar and grows wild in the foothills of the Himalayas. Mung beans are a major crop in India and are eaten fresh and dried, used as a pulse or sprouted. One gram of beans gives 6–8 g of sprouts.

Fenugreek sprouts come from fenugreek seeds, native to both Europe and Asia and a common ingredient in Indian curries. Fenugreek seeds are also soaked in water to produce a jelly-like mucilaginous mass used with bitter herbs in the Middle East.

Snow-pea sprouts are available as flat-stemmed sprouts with soft sweet leafy tips, or as snow-pea shoots, the tender growing tips of snow-pea plants and long regarded as a delicacy in many parts of Asia.

A typical serving of 20 g of alfalfa sprouts contributes a small amount of folate, insignificant quantities of other nutrients, virtually no fat, and 20 kJ. Fenugreek sprouts are a good source of iron and vitamin C; a serving of 20 g provides no fat and 30 kJ. Mung-bean sprouts are a good source of dietary fibre and provide some vitamin C, folate and iron; an average 50 g serving has no fat, almost 3 g of fibre and 65 kJ. Pea sprouts provide some folate; a typical serving of 30 g has no fat and 160 kJ.

CHOOSING AND STORING • Most sprouts are available year-round. If they are in punnets, select crisp-looking, fresh-smelling, green-coloured sprouts with white stalks or roots. With alfalfa sprouts, the colouring varies depending on their exposure to light, but the greener sprouts have higher levels of antioxidants. Some mung-bean sprouts still have the green cap of the original bean attached; others are cream from head to tip because the green skin has been removed. The shorter and fatter the mung-bean sprout, the better its flavour. For all sprouts, make sure they are firm. Avoid those that look brown, droopy or slimy, have broken ends, have begun to discolour or have a strong or sour smell or where there is any moisture in the bottom of the container.

There have been cases of salmonella contamination of alfalfa sprouts in the United States and health authorities there have issued warnings to avoid them. This is not necessary in Australia.

Keep sprouts refrigerated in their punnet for up to 3 or 4 days. For mung-bean sprouts, refrigerate unwashed in the bag or container in which they are purchased. Use as soon as possible, preferably within a day or two.

PREPARATION AND COOKING • No preparation is needed for alfalfa, fenugreek or snow pea sprouts, although they can be rinsed and drained if desired. These sprouts are not suitable for cooking and are best used raw on sandwiches or in salads.

Place mung-bean sprouts in a colander and rinse just before cooking. If the green caps are still present, remove them if desired: they need very little cooking and go soggy if cooked for more than a few minutes.

LAKSA WITH BEAN SPROUTS

An authentic laksa can take a lot of preparation, but using one of the good-quality laksa pastes now available makes it easy. For vegetarians, use vegetable stock in place of prawn stock and use 2 cups sliced mushrooms and 300 g cubed silken tofu in place of the prawns.

16 king prawns

3¹/₂ cups water

2 tsp sesame oil

1 medium-sized onion, chopped

2 tsp dried shrimp paste

2 tsp very finely sliced lemongrass (white part only)

2 tsp chopped fresh galangal

1 red chilli, finely chopped

1–2 tbsp laksa paste

3 cups prawn stock

200 g mung-bean noodles

1 cup coconut milk

2–3 kaffir lime leaves, finely shredded

250 g mung-bean sprouts

1 cup fresh coriander leaves

1 Lebanese cucumber, cut into long strips

SERVES 4

Shell and devein the prawns. Place shells in a saucepan, add the water, bring to the boil, cover and simmer for 15 minutes. Strain stock and discard the prawn shells.

In a large wok or frying pan, heat oil and cook onion, shrimp paste and lemongrass over a medium heat for 3–4 minutes. Add galangal, chilli and laksa paste, and continue to stir-fry for another 2 minutes. Add strained stock and simmer for 5 minutes more.

Meanwhile, pour boiling water over the noodles and leave to stand for 5 minutes. Drain.

Add coconut milk, prawns and lime leaves to wok, bring back to the boil and simmer for 1–2 minutes, or until prawns are pink.

Divide bean sprouts between 4 deep bowls. Top with one quarter of the noodles and then ladle the hot soup over. Garnish with coriander and cucumber.

NUTRITIONAL VALUE: 23 g protein, 17 g fat, 49 g carbohydrate, 5 g dietary fibre, 1820 kJ (435 Cals). Also provides iron, zinc, calcium, magnesium, phosphorus and potassium, as well as vitamins of the B complex and vitamin C.

SPRING ROLLS

An easy version that is messy to eat, but worth it. For a vegetarian version, add an extra ½ cup of peanuts instead of the prawns.

1 cup mung-bean or fenugreek sprouts
1 cup sliced snow peas
½ cup grated carrot
1 cup cooked rice noodles
4 kaffir lime leaves, finely shredded
1 tbsp lime juice
2 tsp fish sauce
1 cup chopped cooked prawns
2 tbsp chopped peanuts
2 tbsp coriander
12 rice-paper sheets

DIPPING SAUCE
1 tbsp boiling water
1 tsp sugar
2 tbsp lime juice
1 tbsp salt-reduced soy sauce
1 tbsp chopped coriander
1 small red chilli, finely chopped (optional)

SERVES 4

Combine sprouts, snow peas, carrot, noodles, lime leaves and juice, fish sauce, prawns, peanuts and coriander. Fill a basin with moderately hot tap water and dip in each rice-paper sheet for about 1 minute to soften. Lay rice-paper on flat surface, place on it about 2 dessertspoonfuls of filling mixture and roll up, tucking the ends in as you go (the moist rice paper will stick to itself and seal the parcel). Place on serving platter, seam-side down.

For the dipping sauce, pour water over sugar and stir to dissolve. Add lime juice, soy sauce, coriander and chilli, and stir well.

NUTRITIONAL VALUE: 16 g protein, 4.5 g fat ('good' fat), 20 g carbohydrate, 5 g dietary fibre, 770 kJ (185 Cals). An excellent source of vitamin A and also provides some niacin, iron and folate.

SPROUT AND AVOCADO BURGERS

These healthy burgers are popular with teenagers and can be made in minutes.

FOR EACH BURGER

1 flat bread roll, preferably whole-grain
1 tbsp grainy mustard
2 tsp mayonnaise
2 slices tomato
2 slices cooked or canned beetroot
½ small avocado, peeled and sliced
1 slice cheddar cheese
½ cup alfalfa or snow-pea sprouts
1 leaf of butter or coral lettuce

SERVES 1

Split roll and toast inside surfaces under the griller. Combine mustard and mayonnaise, and spread over roll. On one half roll place the tomato, beetroot, avocado and cheese slices, then grill until cheese melts. Top with the sprouts, lettuce and remaining toasted half roll. Serve at once.

NUTRITIONAL VALUE: 19 g protein, 41 g fat ('good' fat), 36 g carbohydrate, 8 g dietary fibre, 2450 kJ (585 Cals). A good source of essential fat, calcium, iron, vitamins A, E, C, folate and fibre.

Squash

Squash, marrow and pumpkin all belong to the same family, along with zucchini and gourds. They originated just north of Mexico or in South America, and the word 'squash' comes from a native American word.

In the United States, what Australians call pumpkins (hard skins) are known as winter squash and what Australians call squash are known as summer squash (soft skins). Just to complicate matters further, the vegetable called spaghetti squash in Australia has a hard skin, and should therefore be classified as a pumpkin! It is known as vegetable spaghetti in other parts of the world. Soft-skinned squash and marrow were introduced to Europe in the sixteenth century.

Squash are a good source of vitamin C and brightly coloured varieties (either yellow or green) also provide some beta carotene. Marrow also provide vitamin C, but spaghetti squash have lower levels of vitamins. All types provide small quantities of a range of minerals. A serving of 3 or 4 button squash provides no fat, 2 g of dietary fibre and 80 kJ. One cup cooked marrow has no fat, 1 g of dietary fibre and 120 kJ. For spaghetti squash, 1 cup of cooked strands has 0.5 g of fat, 3.5 g of dietary fibre and 150 kJ.

VARIETIES • *Button or patty pan squash* were developed as garden vegetables in England. These small, squat, fluted squash are 4–6 cm in diameter and have

156

yellow, light-green or dark-green or mottled green and yellow skins. Scallopini is a dark-green variety with cream flesh and is slightly larger in diameter.

Marrow, also called bush marrow, are white or light-green squash which range in length from 20–40 cm. In the garden, some will go from small to large within a day. Larger marrows develop tough seeds and have much less flavour than younger, smaller ones, so if you grow marrows try to pick them when they are small. The large ones are probably best stuffed with a mixture of cooked spiced minced pork and veal, plus rice or cracked wheat.

Spaghetti squash is one of the most unusual vegetables. It is about the size of a small honeydew melon, with pale-yellow, hard skin and flesh with a striking resemblance to long strands of spaghetti (hence its name). It originated in Manchuria and is widely used in Japan, often pickled in a salad.

Zucchini are dealt with separately on page 185.

CHOOSING AND STORING • Squash are available all year, but especially prevalent in summer, as the name 'summer squash' suggests. Select firm, medium-sized specimens with glossy skin. Avoid those with soft spots or any damage.

Refrigerate squash in a plastic bag for up to 4 or 5 days.

PREPARATION AND COOKING • Wash and trim the ends of squash and marrow. Steam button squash whole, or slice or quarter them for stir-fries. They can also be halved and cooked on a barbecue.

Slice marrow and barbecue or fry it in a little olive oil. To stuff marrows, either cut in half lengthwise and hollow out seeds or, with smaller marrows, cut off one end and remove the middle section using an apple corer. Steam whole spaghetti squash for about 30 minutes. Cut open and fork out the strands, which can be used as regular pasta and topped with a sauce.

HONEYED SQUASH KEBABS

Pick out the smallest squash for this recipe. If cooking for vegetarians, substitute 400 g cubed firm tofu for the lamb.

8 yellow button squash, halved
8 green button squash, halved
2 zucchini, each cut into 4 chunks
8 button mushrooms
1 red capsicum, seeded and cut into 16 squares
400 g skinless lamb fillets, cut into
    16 2.5 cm cubes

MARINADE
1 tbsp honey
2 tbsp balsamic vinegar
2 tbsp orange juice
2 tsp finely chopped fresh ginger
1 clove garlic, crushed
2 tsp sesame oil

SERVES 4

Soak 8 wooden skewers in water for 30 minutes to prevent them burning during cooking (or use metal skewers). Combine all the ingredients for the marinade and place in a shallow dish. Add lamb, turn to coat, then leave for 15 minutes.

On each skewer thread 2 yellow and 2 green squash halves, 1 zucchini chunk, 1 mushroom, 2 squares of capsicum and 2 lamb cubes. Brush skewers with marinade and grill or barbecue for 5 minutes, turning often and brushing with marinade.

NUTRITIONAL VALUE: 29 g protein, 4.5 g fat ('good' fat), 15 g carbohydrate, 6.5 g dietary fibre, 905 kJ (215 Cals). An excellent source of vitamin C, a good source of iron, zinc and niacin, and also provides some potassium, magnesium and vitamins A and riboflavin.

SPAGHETTI SQUASH SAUTÉ

This delicious vegetable goes well with Asian flavours.

1 medium-sized spaghetti squash
2 tsp sesame oil
2 cloves garlic, crushed
1 small chilli, finely chopped
½ red capsicum, seeded and sliced
½ green capsicum, seeded and sliced
2 tbsp salt-reduced soy sauce
1 cup fresh coriander leaves
1 tbsp toasted sesame seeds

SERVES 4

Steam spaghetti squash for 30 minutes (if it does not fit into the steamer, boil it for 25 minutes). It is cooked when a skewer pierces the skin easily. Taking care not to burn yourself, cut squash in half, remove and discard seeds in the centre. Using a fork, pull out the strands of flesh.

In a wok, heat sesame oil and cook garlic, chilli and capsicum for 2–3 minutes. Add spaghetti squash strands and toss to combine. Sprinkle with soy sauce, add coriander and toss well. Serve at once.

NUTRITIONAL VALUE: 3.5 g protein, 5.5 g fat ('good' fat), 11 g carbohydrate, 7 g dietary fibre, 430 kJ (105 Cals). An excellent source of vitamin C, a good source of vitamin A and also provides some iron.

Swedes

Also known as rutabaga, or turnip-rooted cabbages, the swede or Swedish turnip is known for its green tops (a type of rape) as much as for the yellow-orange root. Its seed is also a popular commercial crop grown mainly for oil and its bright-yellow flowers are beautiful in spring. The bulbous root is usually yellow or light orange-brown with purple emanating from the leaf end. Some varieties also have green or bronze colours.

Swedes were first cultivated in Sweden, as the name suggests, and were a cross between a turnip and a cabbage. They arrived in England in the late eighteenth century and became popular in Scotland, possibly because they grew well in the cold climate there. Their flavour improves if they are harvested after a light frost, when some of their starches turn to sugar. Swedes have a sweeter flavour than turnips, and are best if not left to grow too large—7–10 cm in diameter is ample.

Swedes are a good source of vitamin C and fibre, but provide only small amounts of other nutrients. Half a cup of cooked swedes has no fat, 2 g of dietary fibre and 65 kJ.

CHOOSING AND STORING • Available all year, but best during the winter months. Select firm swedes, not too large. Avoid any with soft spots. The green swede tops can also be eaten but have usually been removed before they reach the supermarket.

Store swedes in a cool, dry place with good air circulation. They can also be stored in the refrigerator for a month.

PREPARATION AND COOKING • Peel swedes before using. They can be steamed, boiled, microwaved, baked or stir-fried. Some people also like them mashed. Puréed swedes can be incorporated into a sweet pie, in much the same way as pumpkin.

MINESTRONE

There are many recipes for the popular Italian soup. This one is packed with vegetables and is good topped with a spoonful of rocket pesto (see page 142). For a vegetarian version, omit the bacon and use 1 tablespoon olive oil instead.

1 cup dried black-eyed beans

6 cups water

2 rashers bacon, chopped

1 large onion, chopped finely

2 cloves garlic, crushed

extra 2 litres water

4 bay leaves

2 carrots, peeled and sliced

3 swedes, peeled and diced

800 g canned tomatoes

125 g macaroni

2 stalks celery, sliced

1/2 red capsicum, seeded and sliced

3 cups shredded cabbage

1 cup frozen peas

2 tbsp finely chopped parsley

6 tsp grated parmesan

SERVES 6

Place beans in a large saucepan, add the 6 cups of water, bring to the boil, cover and turn off heat. Allow beans to stand for 1 hour then drain.

Place bacon, onion and garlic in a large saucepan and cook over gentle heat for 5 minutes, stirring occasionally. Add drained beans, the extra water and the bay leaves. Bring to the boil, cover and simmer for 30 minutes. Add carrots, swedes and tomatoes, and cook for a further 15 minutes. Remove and discard bay leaves.

Add macaroni, celery, capsicum, cabbage and peas to pot and continue cooking for 15 minutes, or until macaroni is tender. Serve sprinkled with parsley and parmesan.

NUTRITIONAL VALUE: 17 g protein, 5 g fat, 38 g carbohydrate, 15 g dietary fibre, 1130 kJ (270 Cals). An excellent source of vitamins A and C, a good source of potassium, magnesium, zinc, iron and folate, and also provides some calcium, niacin and thiamin.

LAMB SHANKS WITH SWEDES AND PRESERVED LEMON

A hearty meal that is good for cold nights. Preserved lemons are easy to make, but are available from delicatessens and food stores. For a vegetarian alternative, in place of the lamb shanks use 2 cups cooked drained red kidney beans and 2 cups cooked drained black-eyed beans, and reduce initial baking time to 30 minutes.

4 lamb shanks, left whole
1 large onion, sliced
1 medium-sized eggplant, cut into cubes
150 g mushrooms, sliced
1 cup white wine or water
3–4 sprigs fresh rosemary
1 lemon, sliced
2 medium-sized swedes, peeled and cut
  into cubes
1 red capsicum, seeded and sliced
2 tbsp finely chopped parsley
1 tbsp chopped preserved lemon skin

SERVES 4

Preheat oven to 180°C.

Heat a large casserole on top of stove and brown lamb shanks on all sides. Remove shanks and add onion, eggplant and mushrooms to casserole. Cook, stirring occasionally, for 5 minutes, then replace the shanks and add the wine and rosemary. Place lemon slices on top of shanks, cover and bake for 1½ hours.

Remove rosemary and lemon, add swedes and capsicum to casserole and bake for another 30 minutes. Serve topped with parsley and preserved lemon.

NUTRITIONAL VALUE: 35 g protein, 3 g fat, 10 g carbohydrate, 7 g dietary fibre, 885 kJ (210 Cals). A good source of potassium, zinc, iron and vitamin C, riboflavin and niacin, and also provides some magnesium, vitamin A and thiamin.

Sweetcorn

A variety of maize, sweetcorn came originally from a mutation in corn grown for grain. Sweetcorn has been commercially cultivated for more than 200 years and much of the world's production is in the United States. The ear of corn is made up of a cob enclosed by kernels and surrounded by long silky strands and encased by the leafy husk. The corn kernels initially accumulate sugars, but these turn to starch at higher temperatures and as the corn ages.

Certain varieties of corn maize are grown in some countries primarily as food for animals and poultry. Oil extracted from corn is used as a polyunsaturated cooking oil or processed into margarines or frying fats. The sugars in corn are used to produce corn syrup solids, widely used as a substitute for cane sugar. Corn therefore plays a vital role in the food economy of some countries. It has a smaller role in places like Australia, where corn is not widely used as feed and there are other sources of fat and sugar. Some corn, known as flint corn (*indurata*) because its kernels have very hard skins, is grown for use as polenta. Another variety (*amylacea*) is used for making cornflour and is also good for making corn tortillas. Most of what we buy as cornflour is actually made from wheat starch. The corn grown for popcorn (*everta*) has very hard husks.

The types of corn grown to produce sweetcorn have less starch and more sugar. In grain corn, the starch content increases in the growing kernels until it reaches 75 per cent of the dry weight of the kernels. By contrast, the starch in sweetcorn increases slowly to maturity and then stops when it reaches about 60 per cent of the dry weight. The lower starch content also means that sweetcorn kernels have lower keeping qualities than grain corn. Modern sweetcorn cultivars have been bred with genes that act as sugar enhancers within the kernels and the sugar content can go as high as 50 per cent of the dry weight in some of those that taste especially sweet. These types of corn stay sweet for longer once picked, but all corn tastes sweeter if consumed soon after picking. The sugars consist mainly of sucrose, with some glucose, fructose and maltose. The starch contains both amylose and amylopectin. Corn pollen readily interbreeds, so many environmental scientists are concerned about the advent of genetically modified corn.

Sweetcorn has some vitamin C, some folate and a variety of carotenoids that function as antioxidants in the body, especially one called cryptoxanthin. On a weight basis, baby corn has four times more folate and over five times as much vitamin C as its grown-up relatives, but similar levels of most other nutrients. An average cob of cooked corn has 1 g of fat, 19 g of carbohydrate, 2 g of dietary fibre and 350 kJ. Six coblets of baby corn have 0.5 g of fat, 12 g of carbohydrate, 1.5 g of dietary fibre and 215 kJ.

CHOOSING AND STORING • Sweetcorn is best during the summer months. It is available at other times of the year, but will not have the sweetness or flavour of summer corn. Select fresh-looking ears with green husks and some glistening silk visible. Some shop-owners or supermarkets will peel back a cob or two so you can see the condition of the kernels. They should be full, round and bright yellow, and if you press a kernel with your fingernail it should produce a spurt of milky (rather than clear) juice. Avoid cobs with dried husks. You can also take a look at the stem: if it is pale green, the corn is very fresh. The stalk turns opaque after 24 hours, and then it goes brown.

Baby corn, when available, have usually been taken from their husks. They have pale, small kernels and much less sweetness. Occasionally, corn cobs with multi-coloured kernels are for sale, especially in nurseries. These are for decoration and are too tough to eat.

Use sweetcorn cobs as soon as possible after purchase. If not using straight away, leave the husks on, wrap in damp paper towels and refrigerate. Cobs will keep in the refrigerator for a day or two, but the sweet flavour deteriorates for every day after harvest. Do not leave corn sitting at room temperature. Corn cobs that have already been stripped of the husk and are wrapped in plastic may be more convenient, but will not have the sweetness or flavour of corn still in its husks. Frozen cobs have usually been frozen soon after picking and so retain their sweetness.

PREPARATION AND COOKING • If cooking corn on the barbecue, strip the husk down but leave it attached at the base. Remove the silk and wrap the husk back up around the corn. Dip the cob briefly in water before putting on the barbecue, where it will take about 15 minutes to cook. Serve with butter, pepper and sea salt, or a dob of pesto (the rocket pesto on page 142 is good).

For steaming or boiling, remove the husk and silk. The length of steaming time depends on the age of the cobs: straight from the garden, a cob needs only 5–10 minutes, if it is older it may take 15–20 minutes. Do not add salt to the water when cooking sweetcorn, as it will toughen the kernels.

If you want to remove corn from the cob, use a sharp knife and cut down the length of the cob to remove the kernels as close as possible to the cob.

BARBECUED CORN ON THE COB WITH
AVOCADO CHILLI SALSA

This recipe is simple but excellent with a summer barbecue. It is also good using mint instead of coriander.

4 corn cobs
1 small avocado, peeled and diced
1 red chilli, chopped finely
2 tbsp lime juice
2 ripe tomatoes, skinned and diced
½ cup chopped fresh coriander

SERVES 4

Pull back the corn husks (do not break them off), remove silk and wrap the husks back up. Tie with a piece of string (it will burn off, but the corn will be almost cooked by that time). Dip each cob into a bowl of water, place on the barbecue and cook for 15 minutes, turning often. Strip off burnt husks before serving.

To make the salsa, combine avocado, chilli, lime juice, tomatoes and coriander. Toss gently together and serve with the cooked corn.

NUTRITIONAL VALUE: 6 g protein, 9.5 g fat ('good' fat), 19 g carbohydrate, 6.5 g dietary fibre, 790 kJ (190 Cals). An excellent source of vitamin C, and provides some potassium, zinc, iron and vitamins A and thiamin.

CORNBURGERS

These burgers taste good, are popular with children and, with their high-fibre, low-fat content, are a much healthier alternative to fatty hamburgers. Use a food processor blade to grate the vegetables quickly. Spread buns with mango chutney, if desired.

3 zucchini, grated
2 medium-sized carrots, grated
1 cup cooked corn kernels
1 stalk celery, sliced finely
1 cup mashed potato
1 egg
½ cup wheatgerm
2 tsp dried salad herbs
2 tsp olive oil
4 flat burger buns
4 leaves butter lettuce
2 tomatoes, sliced
4 large (or 8 small) slices canned beetroot

SERVES 4

Place grated vegetables in a clean tea-towel and squeeze out as much moisture as possible. Combine grated vegetables with the corn, celery, potato, egg, wheatgerm and salad herbs. Form into 4 patties and refrigerate for about 30 minutes.

Heat olive oil in a heavy-based frying pan and cook the patties for about 5 minutes on each side. Split and toast buns and divide lettuce and tomatoes between the bottom halves of the buns. Layer in the corn patties and beetroot, and top with the remaining toasted buns.

NUTRITIONAL VALUE: 14 g protein, 4.5 g fat, 51 g carbohydrate, 9.5 g dietary fibre, 1250 kJ (300 Cals). An excellent source of vitamins A and C, a good source of potassium, magnesium, iron and thiamin, and also provide some riboflavin, niacin, calcium and zinc.

Sweet potatoes

Different varieties of sweet potatoes are available, with skin colour ranging from brown to red and flesh that is white, yellow or orange. When cooked, some of the white-fleshed sweet potatoes have a sweet moist texture produced when enzymes convert much of their starch to sugar during cooking. Other varieties are quite fibrous or have dry flesh, where the starch stays as starch and the texture after cooking is more like that of a potato.

Sweet potatoes are not true tubers, but rather the roots of a vine belonging to the morning glory family. They are not related to yams (see **Other vegetables**). They are native to South America and there is evidence they were cultivated by the Mayans in Central America and pre-Inca peoples in Peru. They were introduced to Spain and the rest of Europe before regular potatoes and were also widely grown in Polynesia. They were cultivated in New Zealand hundreds of years before white settlement and James Cook and Sir Joseph Banks recorded their use there in 1769. The seeds of sweet potatoes have extremely hard coats and they could easily have survived long periods of travel in the sea. They were also taken to China by the sixteenth century and became popular in India, western Africa and Japan.

Sweet potatoes are now one of the most important crops in developing countries, occupying one-fifth of all land devoted to root and tuber vegetables. They are ranked as the ninth most important world food crop.

Sweet potatoes are high in starch and have more sugar than any other vegetable. They are a good source of vitamins C and E, and provide potassium. Orange-fleshed varieties are also an excellent source of beta carotene, which the body converts to vitamin A. An average piece of cooked sweet potato has no fat, 18 g of carbohydrate, 2 g of dietary fibre and 350 kJ.

Kumara is an excellent source of vitamin C and also provides a range of carotenoids, as well as some potassium, a little vitamin E and some starchy carbohydrate. An average serving of cooked kumara has 0.5 g of fat, 28 g of carbohydrate, 3 g of fibre and 115 kJ.

CHOOSING AND STORING • Sweet potatoes are available all year, being brought from the warm climates where they grow best (they need eleven hours of sunlight a day). Choose smooth, firm specimens free from blemishes. Avoid those that are broken, have damaged ends or any soft spots.

Store in a cool dry place out of sunlight. Do not keep sweet potatoes in the refrigerator as the flesh of the white varieties may darken in the cold. Eat within 5 days of purchase.

PREPARATION AND COOKING • Scrub sweet potatoes to remove dirt. They can be peeled, but the white flesh discolours quickly, so drop peeled pieces into a bowl of water containing some lemon slices. Alternatively they can be cooked in the skin, which is especially appropriate for baked sweet potatoes. Heat a small quantity of olive oil in a baking dish and roll pieces in the oil before baking. When steamed or microwaved, they are usually peeled first. They can also be boiled, but tend to absorb too much water and become unsuitable for mashing. A mash of orange-fleshed sweet potatoes is excellent, and though it is also possible with white fleshed varieties the mash tends to be greyish and can be watery. If mashing sweet potato, add a knob of butter but do not add milk. Sweet potato can also be added to soups and casseroles.

Kumara is usually peeled, although you can bake it unpeeled after scrubbing the skin. A slight darkening of the flesh occurs after peeling or cutting, although this is not as much as in many other varieties of sweet potato. However, it is best to prepare just before using. Kumara is delicious baked and can be steamed and mashed. It is also good in soups and makes excellent crisps or chips. If overcooked or boiled, it can be mushy. If roasting pieces of kumara, they will cook faster than similar-sized pieces of potato.

SWEET POTATOES WITH APPLES

This recipe is delicious with roast pork.

750 g sweet potatoes, scrubbed
½ cup water
1 tbsp honey
2 tsp finely chopped fresh ginger
1 cinnamon stick
¼ cup lemon juice
2 Granny Smith apples, peeled, cored
  and sliced

SERVES 4

Steam sweet potatoes for 10 minutes (they will be only partially cooked). Meanwhile, place water, honey, ginger and cinnamon in a small saucepan, bring to the boil, cover and simmer for 5 minutes. Remove and discard cinnamon stick, and add lemon juice.

Preheat oven to 190°C. Butter a shallow ovenproof casserole, overlap sweet potato and apple slices in it and pour spiced honey mixture over. Bake for 20 minutes or until sweet potatoes are tender.

NUTRITIONAL VALUE: 3 g protein, 0.5 g fat, 47 g carbohydrate, 5.5 g dietary fibre, 855 kJ (205 Cals). A good source of vitamin C and also provides some iron, zinc and vitamin E.

SWEET POTATO CURRY

This curry can be made with either orange- or white-fleshed sweet potato.

2 tsp mustard oil (or use cold-pressed canola
  oil) or macadamia oil
1 medium-sized onion, chopped
2 tbsp Thai red curry paste
½ bunch fresh coriander, washed
2 medium-sized sweet potatoes
2 cups cubed eggplant
3 cups cauliflower pieces
1 cup water
½ cup coconut milk
2 tbsp lime juice

SERVES 4

Heat oil in a saucepan, add onion and cook over a medium heat for 3 minutes, stirring occasionally. Remove leaves from coriander and set aside. Chop roots and stems finely, add to onion, stir in curry paste and cook for 2 minutes.

Peel sweet potato and cut into cubes. Add sweet potato, cauliflower, eggplant and water to onion. Bring to the boil, cover and simmer for 10 minutes, or until vegetables are tender. Stir in coconut milk and lime juice. Serve with steamed rice, topped with the reserved coriander leaves.

NUTRITIONAL VALUE: 7 g protein, 12 g fat, 38 g carbohydrate, 8 g dietary fibre, 1180 kJ (280 Cals). An excellent source of vitamin C, a good source of iron and also provides some zinc, potassium and vitamins A, E, thiamin and riboflavin.

CURRIED KUMARA AND GREEN BEANS

Take care not to overcook the kumara. If you cannot find pea eggplants, use cubes of regular eggplant. If you have access to kaffir lime leaves, shred 4 or 5 very finely and scatter over the curry.

1 tbsp macadamia nut oil (or use olive oil)
1 large onion, cut into wedges
2 tbsp Thai red curry paste
250 g pea eggplants, stems removed
2 medium-sized kumara (approximately
   700 g), peeled and cut into 2 cm dice
400 g green beans, topped and tailed
½ cup water
¾ cup light coconut milk
2 tbsp lime juice
1 tbsp fish sauce
½ cup fresh coriander leaves

SERVES 4

Heat a wok and add oil and onion. Stir-fry onion over a moderate heat, without browning, for 3 minutes. Add curry paste and cook for about 2 minutes, stirring. Add eggplants, kumara, beans and water, bring to the boil and cook for 3–4 minutes, stirring several times. Add coconut milk and cook for a further 5 minutes, or until kumara is just tender. Stir in lime juice and fish sauce and sprinkle with coriander. Serve with steamed rice.

NUTRITIONAL VALUE: 8.5 g protein, 9.5 g fat, 34 g carbohydrate, 8.5 g dietary fibre, 1055 kJ (250 Cals). An excellent source of vitamins A and C, a good source of potassium and iron and also provides some zinc, calcium, magnesium and riboflavin.

KUMARA AND ORANGE MASH

A winter favourite that holds its heat and flavour. Those concerned about using butter can mash kumara without it, but the flavour will not be as good.

750 g kumara, peeled and cut into chunks
1 cup orange juice
1 cinnamon stick
1 tbsp butter

SERVES 4

Place kumara, orange juice and cinnamon stick in a saucepan and cook, covered, for 10 minutes. Remove lid and continue cooking until liquid is evaporated and kumara is soft (take care it does not burn). Remove and discard cinnamon stick. Mash kumara, adding butter, and serve hot.

NUTRITIONAL VALUE: 4 g protein, 4 g fat, 31 g carbohydrate, 3.5 g dietary fibre, 720 kJ (170 Cals). An excellent source of vitamins A and C, and provides some potassium.

Swiss chard (see **Silverbeet**)

Taro

Also known as dasheen, taro may have originated 7000 years ago in parts of India where rice is now grown. The starchy tuber with hairy dark-brown skin has been cultivated for more than 2000 years in Africa, Asia and Polynesia. Its bland-flavoured flesh is usually white, but may be purple. Taro flesh contains calcium oxalate, which is toxic if the taro is eaten raw, but newer varieties grown now have been developed to have much lower oxalate levels. All taro is safe after cooking.

Taro is a good source of starchy carbohydrate and of vitamin C and dietary fibre. It has some vitamin E and zinc, but is low in iron. Taro leaves are high in beta carotene and vitamin C, and contribute folate, vitamin E, potassium and iron. One cup of cooked taro has virtually no fat, 4.5 g of dietary fibre, 30 g of carbohydrate and 500 kJ.

Taro leaves are edible and are eaten as a vegetable or wrapped round other foods. Taro corms can be kept in the dark, which forces them to send out shoots that are also edible.

A variety of taro known as the elephant foot yam is often grown as an ornamental plant or around the edges of swimming pools. The large tuberous root of this variety is edible, but you may get more pleasure from admiring the attractive, large, glossy green leaves.

CHOOSING AND STORING • Taro is available all year. Choose firm tubers without soft spots, and store in a dry, cool, dark place.

PREPARATION AND COOKING • Taro must be peeled as the skin can contain high levels of calcium oxalate, which is toxic. In Polynesia, taro is boiled, boiled and fried, or wrapped in its own leaves and cooked in the embers of a fire. The thick, very smooth texture (which is due to its very small starch granules) may not appeal to those not used to eating it, and roasted taro or fried taro cakes may be the best way to introduce this vegetable. In Asia, taro is made more interesting by cooking it with pork and plenty of soy sauce and garlic.

A gluey paste made from cooked taro corms is known as 'poi' in Hawaii. A similar product in Africa is called fufu (although this is often made from tannia, a related product). In both areas, it is often fermented and is more popular with those who have grown up eating it than it is with others.

TARO VEGETARIAN SPRING ROLLS

As I am not a fan of taro, this recipe comes from Henk de Jong, who also supplied the breadfruit recipes.

50 g mung-bean noodles
1/2 cup green split peas
4 cups water
1 small taro (about 400 g), peeled and grated
1 medium-sized carrot, grated
300 g fresh tofu
3 tbsp soy sauce
1 tbsp sugar
16 spring-roll pastry sheets
1 egg, beaten
olive oil for frying
16 leaves iceberg lettuce
1/2 cup chopped fresh basil
1/2 cup chopped fresh mint
1/2 cup fresh coriander leaves

SAUCE
3 tbsp boiling water
1 tbsp sugar
3 tbsp white vinegar
1/4 cup soy sauce
1 hot chilli, chopped finely

MAKES 16

Place noodles in a bowl and cover with boiling water. Leave to soften for about 10 minutes, then drain and cut into 5 cm lengths. Place split peas in saucepan with the water, bring to the boil and simmer for 45 minutes or until soft. Drain and cool.

Combine peas, taro, carrot and tofu, and mix well. Place in a clean tea-towel and squeeze out excess liquid. Tip mixture into a bowl, add noodles, soy sauce and sugar, and mix well. Place about a tablespoon of mixture on each pastry sheet and roll up, tucking ends in. Brush edges of pastry with egg to form a parcel.

For the sauce, combine water and sugar and stir until sugar dissolves. Add vinegar, soy sauce and chilli, and stir well.

Heat olive oil and deep-fry spring rolls in batches, taking care not to crowd them. To eat, take a lettuce leaf, sprinkle with a little basil, mint and coriander, top with a spring roll and roll up. Dip into sauce.

NUTRITIONAL VALUE PER ROLL: 6 g protein, 7.5 g fat, 20 g carbohydrate, 3 g dietary fibre, 720 kJ (170 Cals). Provides some vitamins A, C, E and thiamin, and also calcium and iron.

Tomatoes

South Americans claim the tomato as their own, probably correctly, and wild tomatoes are found in Ecuador, Peru and parts of northern Chile. But wild bush tomatoes were also a valuable part of indigenous people's diets in outback parts of Australia. Which came first? If we go back far enough, there was once a land bridge between South America and Australia, so the presence of tomatoes in both places is less strange than it would appear. Australian bush tomatoes were ignored for years—as were many items that Aboriginals ate. With a modern gourmet interest in some of the strongly-flavoured bush tomatoes, they may yet reach greater prominence and be cultivated more widely. Not all bush tomatoes have the same wonderful flavour, so it is important to seek out good ones. Some are used commercially for making chutneys.

Tomatoes were taken from Mexico to Europe in the sixteenth century, the earliest records being those of the Italian botanist Matthiolus, in 1544. They were originally considered poisonous in Europe, presumably because they were unfamiliar and a member of the Solanaceae family, along with deadly nightshade (eggplant, capsicums and potatoes). The French called them *pommes d'amour* ('love apples') and the Italians dubbed them *pomodoro* ('golden apple'), presumably because the first tomatoes taken to Europe were yellow. For some years, tomatoes were grown as an ornamental fruit, although the Italians soon discovered their culinary possibilities. Others decided, possibly from their name, that they had aphrodisiac qualities. The term tomato came into use in 1695. It is now difficult to imagine Mediterranean cuisines without the tomato, and indeed, its flavour is important in countries around the Mediterranean. The hard, pale, watery, tasteless specimens commonly sold in other parts of the world show how far this wonderful product has fallen.

Tomatoes are an excellent source of vitamin C, and also provide beta carotene (which the body converts to vitamin A), potassium and vitamin E. Cherry tomatoes have almost twice as much vitamin C as other tomatoes. Tomatoes have recently risen to nutritional fame because they are excellent sources of carotenoids, a class of plant chemicals whose best-known member is beta carotene. Tomatoes are one of the few rich sources of a carotenoid called lycopene, which is being extensively studied for its possible protective role against prostate cancer and some eye disorders in elderly people. Lycopene and other carotenoids are more available to the body when vegetables are cooked than when they are eaten raw. This has led to considerable publicity for tomato sauce, pizza with tomato and other popular tomato-based products. There is no doubt that lycopene is valuable, and that it is more available from cooked tomatoes, but this should not be taken to imply that there is anything wrong with eating tomatoes raw. Much of the lycopene and many of the other carotenoids are available from raw tomatoes, as well as a higher level of vitamins.

An average-sized tomato has virtually no fat, 2 g of dietary fibre and 85 kJ. Half a punnet of cherry tomatoes has 1.5 g of fibre and 75 kJ.

VARIETIES • The main varieties of tomatoes are common tomatoes, cherry tomatoes and the egg-shaped roma tomatoes. Within each of these categories, there are dozens of different varieties, some with more flavour than others. Unfortunately, many tomatoes have been bred to make them suitable for mechanical harvesting, long transportation or longer shelf life, usually at the expense of flavour. However, some new, and revived old, flavoursome varieties are now available. Grosse lisse, rouge de marmande, costaluto de mande (all favoured by home gardeners), oxheart (also known as beef heart) and little Tommy toe have loads of flavour, as do some of the cherry tomatoes. Tomatoes grown hydroponically, sometimes labelled as truss tomatoes, are halfway between cherry and regular tomatoes in size and some have good flavour. For a while, tomatoes with their green calyx attached and called 'vine-ripened' had excellent flavour, but many of the tomatoes now sold in this way have no more flavour than others. Long strands of tomatoes seen in southern European countries tend to have superb flavour, similar to that of the Tommy toe.

The colour of tomatoes is a reflection of their carotenoid content. Red tomatoes have a high level of beta carotene and lycopene; yellow varieties have a different set of carotenoids.

CHOOSING AND STORING • Tomatoes are available all year round and this is part of the problem in getting good-flavoured tomatoes. Those available in winter and spring rarely have good flavour. Those left to ripen naturally in late summer and autumn taste much better and it might be best if we concentrated on eating tomatoes at these times. The flavour of roma tomatoes is better than other varieties during the winter months as they are transported from warmer areas.

Choose tomatoes that feel heavy for their size and are bright red. It may mean buying tomatoes more often, but most of us shop for bread and milk every few days and we should consider tomatoes also as purchases that need to be made often. There is no reason why tomatoes should all be the same size or perfectly smooth—many of the bumpy varieties have more flavour. I also find that tomatoes sold as 'cooking' tomatoes have better flavour value, as long as you avoid those with split skins or other physical damage. With cherry tomatoes, or the yellow tear-drop varieties, check that the bottom of the punnet is dry. Avoid any that are split.

Do not store tomatoes in the refrigerator or their flavour will not develop. Place them, stem-side down, or a window sill but not in direct full sun. If you have more fully ripe tomatoes than you can use, they can be refrigerated, but they will lose some of their flavour. Remove them from the fridge an hour or so before serving to restore some flavour.

PREPARATION AND COOKING • Tomatoes are the ultimate fast food and need no preparation other than removing the stalk and core. Sliced on toast, topped with a few torn basil leaves and some freshly ground black pepper, a well-flavoured tomato becomes a delicious and simple meal.

Skinning tomatoes

Tomatoes used raw do not need to be skinned, but when cooked the skins separate into long unpleasant strands. To skin tomatoes, remove the core and make a shallow cross on the bottom of the tomato with a sharp knife. Place tomatoes into a bowl and cover with boiling water. Leave for 30 seconds, then drain and pull the skin off with your fingers. To remove the seeds, cut the skinned tomato in halves or quarters and squeeze gently.

Drying and oven-roasting tomatoes

If drying tomatoes at home, use roma tomatoes. Halve tomatoes lengthwise and dry on racks in the full hot sun over 2–3 days (bring them inside each evening). To dry tomatoes in the oven, preheat the oven to its lowest setting, preferably 60°–80°C. Place halved tomatoes close together on a wire rack, topping each half with a sprig of rosemary or oregano if desired. Cook for 8–10 hours (leave overnight). Once they are dried, store tomatoes in the refrigerator, sprinkled with a little extra-virgin olive oil and dried herbs if desired.

Sun-dried tomatoes are available in supermarkets, preserved in oil or sold loose and dry (usually close to the fresh tomatoes). They are excellent to use in winter. Those in oil can be drained and used in sandwiches or salads, or with pasta. The dry ones are suitable for pasta sauces and other cooked dishes. To reconstitute them, place into a small bowl, cover with boiling water and leave for 30 minutes, then drain, reserving the full-flavoured water for pasta sauces or casseroles.

FRESH TOMATO SAUCE

Make double quantities of this sauce when tomatoes are cheap and flavoursome. It freezes well and is ideal to use with pasta or in lasagne. For a smooth texture, purée the sauce or add 2 cups chicken stock to the mixture and purée it to make a fresh tomato soup, served with a dollop of natural yoghurt.

1 tbsp olive oil
1 large onion, chopped
2 cloves garlic, crushed
1 tsp dried thyme
1 kg fresh tomatoes, skinned and diced
1 tsp sugar
½ cup white wine
4 bay leaves
2 tbsp tomato paste

SERVES 4

Heat olive oil in a wok, saucepan or frying pan and add onion, garlic and thyme. Cover and allow onion to sweat for 5 minutes, stirring occasionally. Add tomatoes, sugar, wine and bay leaves, and cook over a medium heat for 10 minutes. Remove bay leaves and stir in tomato paste.

NUTRITIONAL VALUE: 3.5 g protein, 5 g fat ('good' fat), 8.5 g carbohydrate, 4.5 g dietary fibre, 405 kJ (95 Cals). An excellent source of vitamin C and provides some vitamin A and potassium.

ROASTED TOMATO SAUCE WITH PASTA

This sauce has a rich, full flavour that is perfect with pasta. And this dish can be on the table within 30 minutes.
1 kg ripe tomatoes, quartered
2 medium-sized onions, chopped
3 cloves garlic, crushed
freshly ground black pepper
2 tsp sugar
1 tbsp olive oil
a few sprigs of rosemary
375 g pasta
½ cup torn basil leaves
shaved parmesan

SERVES 4

Preheat oven to 190°C.

In a large bowl, combine tomatoes, onions, garlic and plenty of ground pepper. Sprinkle with sugar and olive oil and toss well to combine. Spread onto an oiled oven tray, strew rosemary over the top and bake for 20 minutes. Discard the rosemary.

While tomatoes are roasting, cook pasta according to packet directions. Drain and top with tomato mixture. Sprinkle with basil and add parmesan. Serve with a green salad.

NUTRITIONAL VALUE: 18 g protein, 9.5 g fat ('good' fat), 76 g carbohydrate, 10 g dietary fibre, 1970 kJ (470 Cals). An excellent source of vitamin C, a good source of vitamin A, thiamin, potassium, calcium, iron and zinc.

OVEN-ROASTED TOMATOES

When the flavour of tomatoes is less than perfect, roasting them improves the flavour somewhat. They are good with avocado, roasted capsicum and rocket inside a baguette or on good wood-fired bread or toast.

12 tomatoes, preferably Roma, halved
2 tsp sugar
2 tsp olive oil
a few fresh rosemary sprigs

Preheat oven to 180°C.

Place tomatoes close together on an oven tray. Sprinkle with sugar and olive oil and strew rosemary over the top, and roast for 30 minutes. Cool and refrigerate, covered, until required. They will keep for several days.

NUTRITIONAL VALUE: 1.5 g protein, 1.5 g fat, 4.5 g carbohydrate, 2 g dietary fibre, 170 kJ (40 Cals). A good source of vitamin C.

TOMATO SALAD

This salad, similar to the panzanella served in Italy, makes a wonderful lunch. It goes well with barbecued lamb, fish or chicken. Italian-style wood-fired bread with some body is essential—bread sold in plastic wrapping won't work in this recipe.

800 g ripe red tomatoes
½ telegraph cucumber or
  2 Lebanese cucumbers
350 g Italian-style bread, cut into
  2.5 cm cubes
2 tbsp finely chopped chives
1 cup torn basil leaves

DRESSING
1 clove garlic, cut in half
2 tbsp extra-virgin olive oil
2 tbsp balsamic vinegar
2 tbsp orange juice

SERVES 4

Quarter the tomatoes and squeeze out the seeds (it doesn't matter if a few remain) and dice the flesh. Cut cucumber in half lengthwise and scoop out the seeds. Cut the cucumber flesh into small pieces.

Combine tomato, cucumber, bread, chives and basil. For the dressing, place garlic, oil, vinegar and juice into a screw-top jar and shake well. Remove garlic and pour dressing over tomato mixture. Toss well and allow to stand for 5 minutes so that the bread soaks up the dressing.

NUTRITIONAL VALUE: 10 g protein, 12 g fat ('good' fat), 48 g carbohydrate, 6 g dietary fibre, 1435 kJ (345 Cals). An excellent source of vitamin C, a good source of thiamin, and provides some vitamin A, calcium, iron, zinc and magnesium.

Turnips

Turnips, *Brassica rapa*, originated in eastern Afghanistan and western parts of Pakistan and may also have grown in some Mediterranean regions. Some historians believe the turnip may have been used as far back as 10000 BC. They were certainly known to the Romans in the pre-Christian era and, since many varieties of turnip had Greek names, they were presumably also known to the Greeks. The turnip was taken to North America in the sixteenth century, but has always been more popular in England and Europe. Part of their popularity may be due to the ease of growing them in northern European winters and their long keeping qualities in cool weather conditions. They can also be dug up and then kept in soil for some months during winter.

Many of the Brassicas, such as canola, are grown for the edible oil that can be produced from their seeds. These and many types of Chinese cabbage, have been developed from the humble turnip. Radishes are also a relative. The modern cultivated turnip has an enlarged fleshy form and most are round, cylindrical or flattened globular shapes. They grow quickly and easily, and their edible green leaves are sold in Europe as 'spring greens'. The smooth skin is usually white with a blush of bright purple where the leaves emerge, although some may also have green or bronze blushes. The flesh is white or cream and has a slight mustard flavour.

Turnips provide dietary fibre, vitamin C and a sprinkling of other vitamins and minerals. They have a small amount of carbohydrate, but not enough to fit the category of starchy vegetables (such as potatoes). Most of it is in the form of sugars rather than starch, but these are absorbed slowly into the body because of the associated high fibre levels. One cup of cooked white turnip, or three baby turnips, has 5.5 g of carbohydrate, 4.5 g of dietary fibre and 135 kJ. Turnip tops are an excellent source of folate, vitamin C and beta carotene (which is converted to vitamin A in the body). They are also a good source of vitamin E and iron.

CHOOSING AND STORING • Turnips are available all year, but the best supplies are in late autumn, winter and early spring. Choose small, young, firm turnips about the size of a golf ball. Even people who think they do not like turnips have been amazed at the difference in flavour if they choose small ones. Avoid any with soft spots or damaged skin, and the green tops should look fresh. The turnip greens are often removed, which is a pity because they can indicate freshness and are highly nutritious; when young, they taste delicious.

Before storing turnips, remove their leaves, which can be kept in a plastic bag in the refrigerator for 2–3 days. Turnips can be stored in a cool dry place, but if the weather is likely to be at all warm it is best to put them in the refrigerator, where they will keep for a month or more.

PREPARATION AND COOKING • Trim the green tops from turnips and cut off the root. Wash and peel turnips, using a potato peeler. They can be boiled, steamed, microwaved, stir-fried or baked, and are also good added to casseroles. Grated turnips can also be used in salads.

Turnip greens can be steamed or stir-fried. If very young, they can also be used in salads.

GLAZED BABY TURNIPS

Try this recipe if you have previously shunned turnips.

500 g young turnips (golf ball size)
2 tsp butter
2 tsp brown sugar
½ cup orange juice
1 tsp finely grated orange peel

SERVES 4

Steam turnips for 10 minutes (if using larger ones, dice them and steam for 5 minutes). Melt butter in a saucepan, add sugar and stir to dissolve. Add hot turnips and toss to coat. Add orange juice and peel, bring to the boil and toss until juice has evaporated and turnips are shiny.

NUTRITIONAL VALUE: 2 g protein, 2 g fat, 9 g carbohydrate, 3.5 g dietary fibre, 250 kJ (60 Cals). An excellent source of vitamin C.

TURNIP SALAD

I enjoyed this salad in Tunisia and realised turnips had possibilities I had not previously considered. The salad is excellent with barbecued steak. Preserved lemons are available from delicatessens.

8 small turnips (golf ball size)
2 tbsp olive oil
2 tbsp lemon juice
1 clove garlic, crushed
freshly ground black pepper
1 cup young turnip leaves (or use rocket)
1 tbsp chopped preserved lemon
1 tbsp finely chopped parsley

SERVES 4

Peel turnips and slice very thinly (a food processor makes this fast). Combine olive oil, lemon juice, garlic and pepper. Pour over turnips and toss well to combine. Cover and refrigerate for 30 minutes.

To serve, place turnip leaves or rocket on a flat plate and arrange turnips in centre. Top with preserved lemon and sprinkle with parsley.

NUTRITIONAL VALUE: 1.5 g protein, 9.5 g fat ('good' fat), 4.5 g carbohydrate, 3.5 g dietary fibre, 470 kJ (110 Cals). An excellent source of vitamin C and also provides some vitamins A, E and folate.

Vegetable oyster (see Salsify and scorzonera under
Other vegetables)

Vegetable spaghetti (see under **Squash**)

Vine leaves (see **Other vegetables**)

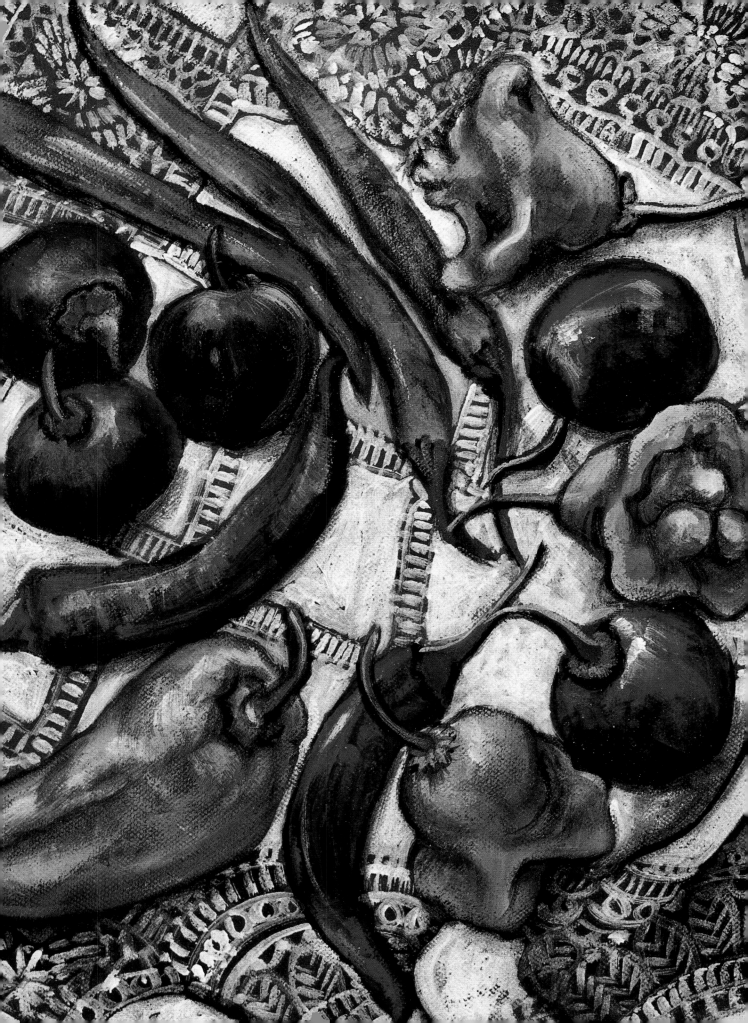

Warrigal greens (see **Other vegetables**)

Water chestnuts

The Chinese water chestnut (*Eleocharis dulcis*), also known as 'matai', is native to tropical Asia and is quite different from the true water chestnut (*Trapa bicornis*), which is an aquatic plant native to Asia and Africa.

The Chinese water chestnut looks like any other chestnut, having dark-brown skin that can be peeled to reveal white flesh. These chestnuts are often grown in rotation with rice and harvested when the tops of the plant have died down and the field has been drained of water. Chinese water chestnuts retain their crunchiness when canned, but are sometimes available fresh. They can be eaten raw and their crunchy texture adds great appeal to stir-fried dishes. Even when canned, they retain their crunchiness.

The true water chestnut grows in deep water, with the fruit appearing just below the water surface. Its green or red fruit matures to a shiny-black when ripe and it has distinct wing- or horn-like protuberances. These water chestnuts contain a toxic parasite that is destroyed after an hour's boiling.

Water chestnuts are a source of carbohydrate, with fairly similar proportions being provided by sugars and starches. They also provide some potassium. An average serving of 5 raw water chestnuts has no fat, 5 g of carbohydrate, 1.5 g of dietary fibre and 90 kJ.

CHOOSING AND STORING • Available winter, spring and early summer. Buy firm nuts with no signs of damage, and refrigerate in a plastic bag for up to a week.

PREPARATION AND COOKING • Peel water chestnuts before eating. If you happen to come across the true horned water chestnut, it must be peeled and then boiled for about an hour. Chinese water chestnuts can be eaten raw, sliced and used in salads, or added to stir-fries. They need little cooking and even if added to soups or casseroles and cooked for a longer period they retain their crunchy texture.

WATER CHESTNUT AND SEAFOOD SALAD

This is an easy salad to serve on a spring evening. If you can't buy fresh water chestnuts, use canned ones—they are almost as good. If serving to children, omit the chilli.

150 g mung-bean noodles
500 g green prawns
400 g white fish (e.g. blue eye or ling)
6 lime leaves
2 tbsp peanuts
100 g snow peas
150 g water chestnuts, sliced into fine strips
6 green shallots (spring onions), sliced

DRESSING
2 tsp sesame oil
2 tbsp lime juice
1 tsp sugar
1 small red chilli, finely chopped
1 tbsp fish sauce

SERVES 4

Place noodles in a bowl and cover with boiling water. Leave to stand for 5 minutes, drain and rinse under the cold tap. Drain again.

Peel and devein the prawns. Cut fish into 2.5 cm cubes. Put lime leaves in water in base of steamer, and steam prawns and fish until prawns turn pink and fish is opaque (do not overcook).

Toast peanuts on a dry frying pan until starting to brown. Tip onto a plate. Top and tail snow peas and cut lengthwise into fine strips.

Combine noodles, snow peas, water chestnuts and green onions. Mix together all the dressing ingredients, pour over noodles and toss well. Add seafood, stir gently and top with peanuts.

NUTRITIONAL VALUE: 42 g protein, 7.5 g fat ('good' fat), 39 g carbohydrate, 2 g dietary fibre, 1670 kJ (400 Cals). A good source of vitamin C and niacin, and also provides some magnesium, calcium, iron, zinc, potassium and vitamin A.

Watercress

Originating in the eastern Mediterranean region and nearby parts of Asia, watercress is a member of the Brassica family. Closely related varieties are also native to other parts of Asia and to the highlands of Papua New Guinea. Watercress grows in clean running water, preferably slightly alkaline, and some types can also be grown in moist soils. It has a slight peppery flavour. The younger leaves are milder and more tender, and both leaves and stem can be used. With older watercress, the stems can be tough.

An excellent source of vitamin C and a good source of beta carotene, vitamin E and folate, watercress also contributes iron, potassium and manganese. A cup of watercress leaves and stems provides no fat, 1.5 g of dietary fibre and 30 kJ.

CHOOSING AND STORING • Available all year. Select bright-green watercress that looks fresh, and avoid any where the leaves are turning yellow. To store, place stems in a glass of water, cover the glass and watercress with a plastic bag and keep in the refrigerator for 2–3 days.

PREPARATION AND COOKING • Rinse watercress just before using and dry in a salad spinner. Remove any stems that are too coarse. Watercress is usually served raw in salads, but can be stir-fried (very briefly) or used in soups or sauces.

WATERCRESS SAUCE

Make this quick sauce and serve it with fish or grilled chicken, or even with steamed potatoes. It is also good mixed into mashed potatoes.

2 cups watercress
2 cloves garlic
2 tsp Dijon-style mustard
2 tbsp walnuts
2 tbsp white-wine vinegar (or use cider vinegar)
½ cup fat-reduced ricotta

SERVES 4

Discard any coarse stems from watercress and purée in blender. Add garlic, mustard, walnuts, vinegar and ricotta, and process to a thick green paste.

NUTRITIONAL VALUE: 5 g protein, 6.5 g fat, 1.5 g carbohydrate, 1.5 g dietary fibre, 365 kJ (85 Cals). A good source of vitamin C and provides some calcium.

Winter melon (see **Other vegetables**)

Winter squash (see **Pumpkin**)

Witlof

Also called Belgian endive, French endive and witloof ('white leaf') chicory, witlof grows as an enlarged bud (*chicon* in French). It is about 15 cm long and its compact leaves are white, tinged with light green. Witlof is grown by pulling up the plant, cutting off the green leaves, trimming the root and leaving it to dry for a week and then replanting under a mound of sawdust or sand. The roots then send up shoots which are protected from the light by the mound. A farmer needs some skill in knowing when to harvest just before the witlof emerges into the light, which would turn it green and bitter. Witlof can also be grown using hydroponics and a red cultivar is now available.

Witlof supplies small quantities of many minerals and vitamins, but is not a rich source of any. One average witlof head has 1.5 g of fibre and 35 kJ.

CHOOSING AND STORING • Witlof is available all year, with best supplies during winter and spring. Choose compact heads and reject those with torn or browning leaves. Refrigerate in a brown paper bag for several days, but use as soon after purchase as possible. Witlof should not be left in the light and some greengrocers cover it with blue plastic.

PREPARATION AND COOKING • Witlof is delicious raw, in salads or the leaves used as 'boats' to hold fillings. Whole heads are also excellent braised. No preparation other than washing and trimming the base is needed. The red variety does not cook well and is best used raw.

WITLOF WITH VIETNAMESE CHICKEN

Delicious finger food.

2 or 3 witlof, depending on size
2 tsp sesame oil
1 small onion, chopped finely
1 chilli, chopped finely
2 tsp finely chopped fresh lemongrass
250 g minced chicken
1/2 cup green shallots (spring onions),
   sliced finely
2 tbsp crushed peanuts
2 tbsp fish sauce
2 tbsp lime juice
2 tbsp Vietnamese mint, shredded

SERVES 8 AS A SNACK

Separate witlof leaves (you will need about 32 leaves).

Add oil to a hot wok and stir-fry onion, chilli, lemongrass and chicken until chicken is brown. Add green shallots, peanuts, fish sauce, lime juice and mint.

When ready to serve, place 2 teaspoons of chicken mixture in each witlof leaf.

NUTRITIONAL VALUE: 5.5 g protein, 18 g fat ('good' fat), 7.5 g carbohydrate, 2.5 g dietary fibre, 890 kJ (215 Cals). A good source of vitamin C.

BRAISED WITLOF

This is a delicious accompaniment to roast chicken or pork.

2 cups chicken stock
4 witlof
2 tsp olive oil
1 lemon, cut into slices

SERVES 4

Boil chicken stock until it is reduced to 1 cup. Preheat oven to 190°C.

Halve witlof lengthwise and arrange in a shallow ovenproof dish in which they fit snugly. Drizzle with olive oil, place lemon slices on top and pour stock over. Cover with a lid or foil and bake for 20 minutes. Remove lid or foil and bake a further 5 minutes. Serve hot.

NUTRITIONAL VALUE: 1 g protein, 2.5 g fat ('good' fat), 4 g carbohydrate, 2.5 g dietary fibre, 185 kJ (45 Cals).

Yams (see Other vegetables)

Zucchini

Zucchini, also known by their French name *courgettes*, are technically squash but are usually considered as a vegetable in their own right. The skin colour may be dark green, pale green (almost striped in appearance) or yellow. The pale-green variety tends to be a little sweeter.

Before zucchini develop on the bush, a yellow flower blooms. The vegetable develops behind the flower, but when the vegetable is picked early, the flower may still be attached. Zucchini flowers are also sold on their own. They are difficult to transport, but are so highly regarded that specialist greengrocers sometimes have them in summer. Zucchini flowers are often stuffed with a creamy ricotta filling, or dipped in a light batter and deep-fried. Home gardeners can pick zucchini with the flowers attached.

Zucchini are an excellent source of vitamin C and also supply folate, some potassium and small amounts of other minerals and vitamins. The golden yellow varieties have higher levels of potassium and the dark-green ones more beta carotene. An average-sized zucchini has virtually no fat, 1.5 g of dietary fibre and 60 kJ. The flowers contain beta carotene, vitamin C and other nutrients, but as they are very light in weight the quantity consumed will not contribute many nutrients or kilojoules. Each flower has less than 5 kJ.

CHOOSING AND STORING • Zucchini are available all year, but the best supplies are in summer. Choose small firm, crisp zucchini, as these tend to have the most flavour (zucchini grow rapidly, and the flavour disappears as the size increases). Avoid those with damage to the skin or any that are softening. Store zucchini in a plastic bag in the refrigerator.

PREPARATION AND COOKING • Zucchini need little preparation, apart from trimming the stems. There is no need to peel them and they need only brief cooking. They are suitable to steam, microwave or stir-fry, either whole, sliced or cut into chunks. Sliced zucchini cook in 1 minute. I prefer not to boil them as they absorb too much water and go soggy.

You can use an apple corer to hollow out the centre of zucchini and then stuff and bake them. Or grate them and use in coleslaw or other salads. They are good sliced and cooked in olive oil with garlic, to serve with pasta, and can also be added to Asian stir-fries. Perhaps the best way to serve zucchini is to slice them lengthwise, brush with a little olive oil and grill them on the barbecue. They can also be grated and used in muffins or cakes, as you would use grated carrot, and are excellent in soups.

ZUCCHINI FRITTATA

A good way for children to enjoy zucchini.

1 tbsp olive oil
500 g zucchini, sliced
1 clove garlic, crushed
6 eggs
¼ cup water
½ cup grated cheddar
freshly ground pepper
2 tsp chopped fresh dill
1 tsp ground paprika

SERVES 4

Heat olive oil in a frying pan, add zucchini and garlic, and cook until zucchini begins to brown. Beat eggs and water, and pour over zucchini in the pan. Cook for 2-3 minutes, lifting edges to let uncooked egg mixture run underneath. Sprinkle with cheese and pepper and place under griller to melt the cheese. Sprinkle with dill and paprika, and serve hot or cold.

NUTRITIONAL VALUE: 14 g protein, 17 g fat, 2.5 g carbohydrate, 2 g dietary fibre, 930 kJ (220 Cals). A good source of vitamins A and C, and also provides some calcium, iron, zinc and riboflavin.

ZUCCHINI AND LEMON SOUP

An ideal way to use up lots of zucchini. Use any variety, but the dark-green ones give the best colour.

1 tbsp olive oil
1 onion, chopped
2 cloves garlic, crushed
1 kg zucchini, cut into chunks
4 cups chicken stock
3 bay leaves
1 lemon, cut into quarters
¾ cup natural yoghurt
2 tsp finely grated lemon peel

SERVES 4

In a large saucepan, heat oil and add onion and garlic. Cover and allow to sweat for 5 minutes, stirring occasionally so that onion does not brown. Add zucchini and cook for a further 2 minutes. Stir in chicken stock, bring to the boil, add bay leaves and lemon, and cook for 10 minutes. Remove and discard bay leaves and lemon, squeezing lemon flesh back into soup. Purée soup to a smooth or chunky consistency. Reheat. Serve topped with a dollop of yoghurt and some finely grated lemon peel.

NUTRITIONAL VALUE: 6.5 g protein, 8 g fat ('good' fat), 12 g carbohydrate, 5.5 g dietary fibre, 625 kJ (150 Cals).

GREEK-STYLE ZUCCHINI

In Greece, vegetables are not served raw or simply steamed, but are cooked in flavoursome juices that can be mopped up with plenty of good bread. Serve this dish hot or cold.

¹/₂ cup white wine
¹/₂ cup water
2 tbsp extra-virgin olive oil
2 cloves garlic, crushed
2 bay leaves
1 tsp dried thyme
2 sprigs fresh rosemary
2 tbsp lemon juice
12 baby onions, peeled
12 small zucchini, cut into chunks
6 baby eggplant, cut into chunks
1 red capsicum, seeded and sliced
1 green capsicum, seeded and sliced
200 g button mushrooms

SERVES 6

In a saucepan combine the wine, water, olive oil, garlic, bay leaves, thyme and rosemary. Bring to the boil, add onions, cover and simmer for 10 minutes. Add zucchini, eggplant, capsicums and mushrooms, and simmer for a further 10 minutes. Remove bay leaves and rosemary. Serve hot or cold.

NUTRITIONAL VALUE: 5.5 g protein, 7.5 g fat ('good' fat), 9 g carbohydrate, 6.5 g dietary fibre, 520 kJ (125 Cals). An excellent source of vitamin C and also provides some iron, vitamin A, thiamin and riboflavin.

ZUCCHINI AND APPLE MUFFINS

Best eaten while still warm. Use a food processor to grate the zucchini and apple.

2 cups self-raising flour
¹/₂ cup brown sugar
1 cup coarsely grated zucchini
1 cup coarsely grated apple
2 eggs
1 tsp vanilla
¹/₄ cup macadamia oil (or use light olive oil)
¹/₄ cup fat-reduced milk

MAKES 12

Preheat oven to 200°C and grease 12 small muffin pans.

Sift flour into a bowl. Stir in sugar, zucchini and apple. Beat eggs with vanilla, oil and milk, and mix into flour mixture, taking care not to over-mix. Spoon into muffin tins and bake for 20 minutes, or until an inserted skewer comes out clean.

NUTRITIONAL VALUE PER MUFFIN:
4 g protein, 6.5 g fat ('good' fat), 28 g carbohydrate, 1.5 g dietary fibre, 765 kJ (185 Cals).

zucchini

BARBECUED VEGETABLES WITH
RED CAPSICUM SAUCE

There is nothing wrong with barbecues—as long as they include some vegetables. Try these, with or without meat. Delicious with watercress sauce, too (see page 181).

4 small zucchini, halved lengthwise
4 baby eggplant, halved lengthwise
400 g kumara, peeled and sliced thickly
4 green shallots (spring onions)
8 mushroom cups
1 tbsp olive oil

SAUCE
1 tbsp olive oil
1 small onion, chopped
1 large (or 2 small) red capsicums, seeded
    and sliced
2 cloves garlic, crushed
1 tsp brown sugar
1 tbsp balsamic vinegar
1 tbsp tomato paste

SERVES 4

To make the sauce, heat the olive oil in a saucepan, add onion, cover and allow to sweat for 2–3 minutes, stirring once. Add capsicums and garlic, and cook for 10 minutes, stirring often. Stir in sugar, vinegar and tomato paste. The sauce can be served like this, or purée it until smooth.

For the barbecued vegetables, have the barbecue hot. Brush zucchini, eggplant and kumara with olive oil. Barbecue all vegetables until tender, turning zucchini, eggplant, kumara and spring onions. Keep hot and serve with capsicum sauce and some good crusty bread

NUTRITIONAL VALUE: 7 g protein, 10 g fat ('good' fat), 25 g carbohydrate, 10 g dietary fibre, 930 kJ (220 Cals). An excellent source of vitamin C and provides some potassium, iron, zinc, vitamin A, riboflavin and niacin.

Other vegetables

ARROWHEAD

Also called the swamp potato or Chinese potato, this vegetable is grown mainly in China, but is also common in Japan, Taiwan and is seen in Indonesia, Malaysia and India. The name 'arrowhead' comes from the shape of the plant's leaves. The plant grows in water. The starchy, aromatic corms, about 5 cm in diameter, are peeled and then cooked by steaming or frying. Their flavour is slightly bitter.

Nutritionally, arrowhead is a good source of starchy carbohydrate, potassium and iron. A 100 g portion of cooked arrowhead has 18 g of carbohydrate, virtually no fat and 385 kJ.

BITTER MELON (FOO GWA)

This vegetable, also known as bitter gourd, karella, bitter cucumber or balsam pear, looks like a warty, withered green-skinned cucumber. When the vegetable is immature, the flesh is very bitter (due to its high content of quinine) and this gives it an appeal in India, Sri Lanka, Indonesia and China where it is popular. If left to become fully ripe, the flesh turns orange and is sweeter, but less attractive.

Choose deep-green young bitter melons, but then reduce the bitterness slightly. Start by cutting the melon in half lengthwise and remove and discard the brown seeds. You can then either blanch the flesh and skin in boiling water for 2–3 minutes, or sprinkle it with about 2 teaspoons of salt, leave for about 15 minutes (as you would with eggplant) and then rinse thoroughly and squeeze the flesh dry. After this the now pleasantly bitter melon can be stir-fried (often with pork and black-bean sauce), added to curries, or fried with onion, chilli and spices to serve as a sambal. It is also good cooked in a fennel-flavoured home-made tomato sauce.

Nutritionally, bitter melon is an excellent source of vitamin C and supplies small quantities of iron and other minerals and vitamins. An 80 g portion has virtually no fat or carbohydrate, 3 g of dietary fibre and only 15 kJ.

BURDOCK

A popular vegetable that grows wild in many parts of Europe and is used widely in Japan (where it is called gobo), Taiwan and Hawaii. The large fleshy root is generally eaten, although the leaves are also edible, especially when young.

The root is sometimes boiled until tender or, more often, pickled in a soy-based sauce.

Nutritionally, burdock root provides some dietary fibre, folate and vitamin B$_6$. Half a cup provides no fat, 2.5 g of fibre and 230 kJ.

CARDOON

Looking somewhat like silvery-grey celery and tasting like a globe artichoke, cardoons are popular in Italy, France and Spain. They grow wild in Mediterranean countries. In cultivation, the stalks of the plant are tied together to reduce bitterness and increase tenderness in the inner stalks, which can then be eaten raw. The dried flowers of the cardoon plant will set junket and can be used as a substitute for rennet in making fresh soft cheese. Cardoons are available in markets in late winter and early spring, and will keep in a plastic bag in the refrigerator for up to 2 weeks. Place sliced or cut cardoons immediately in water with a few slices of lemon, to prevent discolouration.

Nutritionally, cardoons provide small amounts of folate and other vitamins, as well as selenium, potassium and magnesium. Half a cup of cooked cardoons provides 1.5 g of dietary fibre and 90 kJ.

CASSAVA

Also known as manioc, cassava is native to tropical America and was taken by Portuguese sailors to various islands in the Pacific where it grows well. It is a staple food in parts of Polynesia, where it can grow prolifically. The tuberous roots, which grow out of the base of the plant like spokes, are usually harvested when they weigh about a kilo but if left in the ground, can weigh up to 25 kg. When young, the leaves of the cassava plant are a nutritious vegetable which can be used like spinach; older leaves are used to wrap food for steaming or cooking in a ground oven.

Tapioca is made from cassava root and many of the food starches used in processed foods are also derived from it.

There are two varieties of cassava—one sweet, the other bitter. Many people prefer the bitter variety, although its skin contains poisonous cyanide. If the thick rough skin is peeled away and the cassava is soaked and then boiled, it is safe to eat. The flesh is often sold grated in Pacific Island countries and in Asian food markets and is used to make flat, rather heavy cakes. Whole tubers are available in most suburban supermarkets. After peeling thickly, boil pieces of cassava for about 15 minutes. When cooked, the pieces will split and you can remove the tough core. Fry the pieces in oil, slice to make cassava chips, or fry and serve with a mixture of grated coconut, chilli, fried onion, lime juice and salt.

Nutritionally, cassava is an excellent source of vitamin C and starch, and also provides zinc, some fibre and small quantities of other vitamins and minerals. In poor countries, its low protein content makes it inadequate as a staple food but it makes a valuable contribution to the diet. A 200 g portion of cooked cassava has very little fat, 60 g of starchy carbohydrate, 4 g of dietary fibre and 1100 kJ.

GOURDS

There are many different types of gourds. Some varieties, also known as luffas or loofahs, are long, thin, green-ridged vegetables 25–50 cm long. The bottle gourd is native to Africa, south of the Sahara desert, but there is also evidence it was cultivated in South America around 7000 BC. No other crop food was found on both sides of the Atlantic, and some believe that the gourds could have floated between the two continents. The bottle gourd is also known as a dudi or lokhi in India and may be up to 2 metres long or shaped like a waisted bottle. The snake gourd, also called chichinda, grows to a similar length, but is inedible by this stage of its twisted growth and most are picked when they reach 50–60 cm.

The bitter melon is discussed on page 189. Gourds can be sliced and added to curries, or stir-fried with meat or chicken and other vegetables. With the luffa, use a potato peeler to remove the ridges but leave the skin in between to produce a striped appearance.

LOTUS ROOT

Lotus roots look like a string of smallish, fat brown sausages, but they feel quite solid and if you cut them in half the centre is a series of lace-like tunnels. The lotus root produces beautiful pink flowers, but in Asia also serves as an important starchy vegetable. Creamy-white lotus seeds can be eaten fresh from their green pods, or dried and boiled to make sweets. The leaves of the plant are used as wrappers for steamed foods, adding a unique flavour to the ingredients inside. Dried lotus leaves are available from Asian food stores.

To cook lotus roots, scrub them thoroughly, discard the neck and peel or scrape off the thin outer skin. Fresh young lotus roots can be eaten raw; older specimens can be sliced or chopped and boiled, braised, baked or fried, or added to soups. For special occasions, Chinese cooks stuffed lotus roots with mashed mung beans and braise them with pork. They can also be candied and used as a sweet.

Nutritionally, lotus roots are an excellent source of vitamin C, provide small quantities of many of the B-complex vitamins, including some folate, as well as iron, potassium and selenium. One root has no fat, 20 g of starch, 5.5 g dietary fibre and 355 kJ.

NASTURTIUMS

The leaves, seeds and flowers of nasturtium are edible and the flowers are often added to salads to provide colour and a slight peppery flavour. The nasturtium is native to Peru and was introduced to Europe in 1576, as 'Indian cress'. The plant was given its present name in 1656. Young leaves are sometimes used as a substitute for watercress and can give a peppery flavour to stuffing. The leaves are used as an addition, more as you would use a herb. The seeds are sometimes suggested as a substitute for capers, but their flavour is not as good.

Nutritional data are not available, but the quantities likely to be consumed are so small that nasturtium leaves or seeds would make little nutritional contribution.

NETTLES

Although most people think of nettles as nasty stinging plants, they are edible and an excellent source of nutrients. The trick is to don some stout gloves and take only the top tips of the plant, preferably in early spring when it is sending out new growth. Once cooked, the prickles on nettles disappear and the sting (which is due to formic acid) disappears, so there is no danger of damaging your mouth eating cooked nettles. The main culinary use for nettles is in a soup; gently sauté onion and garlic in a little olive oil, add a good bunch of nettles, 2 cups of stock and 1 cup of milk, and cook for about 5 minutes, then purée.

Nettles are rich in vitamin C and carotenoids.

PURSLANE

A member of the Portulaca family, purslane is often considered to be a weed but has sprung into prominence recently because it is a source of an omega 3 fatty acid—the same healthy kind of fat found in linseed and fish. Purslane is often eaten in Greece and southern Italy, and some medical researchers consider it a major reason for the healthfulness of the traditional Mediterranean diet. Purslane also enters the diet indirectly through the milk and cheese of goats and sheep and the eggs of hens that eat it. In Australia, poultry farmers are feeding hens linseed and soy as a source of omega 3 fats, but an egg from a Greek hen contains larger quantities. Purslane was also consumed by indigenous people in Australia and I have seen it on sale in markets in Turkey, Morocco and Istanbul. It is also available in some greengrocers in Australia.

Purslane has fleshy green leaves with a flavour something like watercress or water spinach, and it is usually used in salads. It grows in spring and summer, but there is also a winter variety known as miner's lettuce. In Malawi, the name for purslane translates to 'buttocks-of-the-wife-of-a-chief', probably referring to its rounded fleshiness.

SALSIFY AND SCORZONERA

Native to southern Mediterranean Europe, salsify is a member of the daisy family. It is sometimes called 'goat's beard' because the plant looks a little like an edible plant called goatsbeard that grows beside the roads in much of Europe and North America. A bunch of the creamy-coloured roots, which look like dishevelled skinny parsnips, do somewhat resemble a goat's beard. Salsify is also known as 'vegetable oyster' because its flavour, which is accentuated after cooking, is said to resemble that of the succulent bivalve. Salsify is sometimes confused with scorzonera, another long slender root but with brown-black skin and known in some areas as black salsify. Scorzonera is native across southern Europe to Siberia. Both vegetables wither quickly after they are dug and this is probably why they are usually better known by home gardeners.

Salsify is usually eaten in late winter or early spring, after winter frosts have converted its stored starches to sugar. However, it is not as sweet as the parsnips it resembles and most people liken its flavour to a combination of Jerusalem artichokes, coconut and oysters. When cut, salsify exudes a white latex-like sap and both salsify and scorzonera darken as soon as they are exposed to air. While preparing them, drop cut pieces into water acidulated with a few slices of lemon to prevent the flesh discolouring. Salsify is better cooked than raw, and can be boiled or steamed and used in any recipe that calls for Jerusalem artichokes. It is also good mashed or puréed in soups, or sautéed in a little butter and dressed simply with lemon juice.

Nutritionally, salsify is a good source of dietary fibre and provides folate. Half a cup of cooked salsify has virtually no fat, 3 g of dietary fibre and 80 kJ.

VINE LEAVES

If you have a grape vine (ornamental or grape-bearing), pick some leaves in spring. Wrap them round rice stuffing (combine cooked wild and white rice with toasted slivered almonds, currants and finely grated orange peel), grilled prawns, or ricotta flavoured with chopped herbs and olives. Grape leaves can be used after blanching in boiling water for 1 minute, or you can follow this with a brief dip (for 1 minute) in a brine solution.

Nutritionally, vine leaves are a source of beta carotene, vitamin C and calcium, although the weight you eat will probably not contribute much of these nutrients. Pickled vine leaves are high in salt, but if you rinse them just before use, the salt content will be lower. Four vine leaves will contribute about 10 kJ.

WARRIGAL GREENS

Also known as New Zealand spinach or tetragon, this plant with bright-green, arrow-shaped leaves grows as a ground cover in coastal and sandy regions of Australia and New Zealand. Warrigal is an Aboriginal word meaning 'wild'. Like many other types of wild spinach, warrigal greens have a high content of oxalic acid which can give them a slightly bitter flavour (cooking the leaves reduces the oxalic acid). Their flavour is midway between that of green beans and silverbeet. Use them as you would use spinach. In the early days of white exploration of Australia and New Zealand, James Cook, who had taken measures to ensure his crews did not succumb to scurvy, encouraged his crew to eat these wild greens. They thus had an excellent source of vitamin C and beta carotene.

WINTER MELON

Also known as white gourd, ash gourd, preserving melon or don kwa, winter melon is one of the largest cultivated vegetables and looks much like its cousin, the watermelon. Winter melons may weigh 20 kg and some very large specimens may reach 50 kg. They are sold by the slice in Asian food stores. Choose melon that smells fresh and has firm white flesh. It can be stir-fried, but is usually made into soup. In India, it is treated with a heavy sugared solution to make a crystallised product called *petha*.

Winter melon is 96 per cent water and 100 g contributes vitamin C and 55 kJ.

YAM

The name yam is often given to sweet potatoes and other starchy tubers, including taro. True yams belong to the Dioscorea family and appear to have developed independently in Africa and South-east Asia, probably about 3000 BC. They then spread to South China and the Caribbean and South America, and grow well in tropical regions, where they are generally harvested after the rainy season. Best left in the ground until needed, they are suited to boiling, baking or frying—rather like sweet potatoes—and yam chips and crisps are popular. The skin of some varieties of yam contains toxic alkaloid substances that can be removed by soaking or boiling. Other types of yam contain plant hormones that resemble the female hormone progesterone. These are extracted and added to creams or sold as supplements, although there is little real proof that they are effective in improving the skin or relieving symptoms of menopause. Some yams also contain a steroid, sapogenin, which can be extracted and used to make cortisone.

Several species of yams grow wild in Australia and were widely used for food by Aboriginal people. Long yams which grow in sandy soil may be up to a metre long. They have a similar flavour to sweet potato, but a more creamy texture. Long yams were expertly gathered by Aboriginal women, who would approach them from the side and retrieve them intact. Aboriginal people always distinguished between male and female yam vines, digging the male vines first and waiting until the seeds of the female vine had dispersed before digging its produce. The cheeky yam from northern Australia contains bitter and toxic compounds, but Aboriginal people had many elaborate methods to remove these, detailed in books on Australian bush foods such as *The Bush Food Handbook* by Vic Cherikoff and Jennifer Isaacs.

Yams provide a valuable source of starchy carbohydrate (generally around 20 g per 100 g, which is one and a half times that found in potatoes). The protein content is low, but the dietary fibre is high. Studies are also showing that the carbohydrate in yams is digested and absorbed into the bloodstream very slowly, unlike many modern sources of carbohydrate which are absorbed rapidly and cause a surge of insulin. The energy content of yams varies, but most have around 320 kJ per 100 g. They also supply vitamins C and E.

Measures

Measures used in this book refer to the standard measuring cup and spoon sizes approved by the Standards Association of Australia

1 cup = 250 mL	1 teaspoon = 5 mL
¼ cup = 60 mL	½ teaspoon = 2.5 mL
⅓ cup = 80 mL	1 tablespoon = 20 mL
½ cup = 125 mL	

MASS (WEIGHT)

IMPERIAL	METRIC
½ oz	15 g
1 oz	30 g
2 oz	60 g
3 oz	90 g
4 oz (¼ lb)	120 g
5 oz	155 g
6 oz	185 g
7 oz	220 g
8 oz (½ lb)	250 g
9 oz	280 g
10 oz	315 g
11 oz	345 g
12 oz (¾ lb)	375 g
13 oz	410 g
14 oz	440 g
15 oz	470 g
16 oz (1 lb)	500 g (0.5 kg)
24 oz (1½ lb)	750 g
32 oz (2 lb)	1000 g (1 kg)
3 lb	1500 g (1.5 kg)

LIQUIDS

IMPERIAL	CUP	METRIC
1 fl oz		30 mL
2 fl oz	¼ cup	60 mL
3 fl oz		90 mL
4 fl oz	½ cup	120 mL
5 fl oz (¼ pint)		150 mL
6 fl oz	¾ cup	200 mL
8 fl oz	1 cup	250 mL
10 fl oz (½ pint)	1¼ cups	300 mL
12 fl oz	1½ cups	375 mL
14 fl oz	1¾ cups	425 mL
15 fl oz		475 mL
16 fl oz	2 cups	500 mL
20 fl oz (1 pint)	2½ cups	600 mL

RECOMMENDED DIETARY INTAKE OF SELECTED VITAMINS

The values for some of the vitamins are as follows.

VITAMIN A

AGE	RDI (micrograms retinol equivalents)
Breastfed	425
Bottle-fed	425
7–12 months	300
1–3 years	300
4–7 years	350
8–11 years	500
12–15 years	725
16–18 years	750
Adults, all ages	750
Pregnancy	750
Lactation	1200

THIAMIN

AGE	RDI (milligrams)
Breastfed	0.15
Bottle fed	0.25
7–12 months	0.35
1–3 years	0.5
4–7 years	0.7
Boys, 8–11 years	0.9
Girls, 8–11 years	0.8
Boys, 12–15 years	1.2
Girls, 12–15 years	1.0
Boys, 16–18 years	1.2
Girls, 16–18 years	0.9
Men, 19–64 years	1.1
Men, over 64 years	0.9
Women, 19–54 years	0.8
Women, over 54 years	0.7
Pregnancy	1.0
Lactation	1.2

RIBOFLAVIN

AGE	RDI (milligrams)
Breastfed	0.4
Bottle fed	0.4
7–12 months	0.6
1–3 years	0.8
4–7 years	1.1
Boys, 8–11 years	1.4
Girls, 8–11 years	1.3
Boys, 12–15 years	1.8
Girls, 12–15 years	1.6
Boys, 16–18 years	1.9
Girls, 16–18 years	1.4
Men, 19–64 years	1.7
Men, over 64 years	1.3
Women, 19–54 years	1.2
Women, over 54 years	1.0
Pregnancy	1.5
Lactation	1.7

NIACIN

AGE	RDI (milligrams)
Breastfed	4
Bottle fed	4
7–12 months	7
1–3 years	10
4–7 years	12
Boys, 8–11 years	15
Girls, 8–11 years	15
Boys, 12–15 years	20
Girls, 12–15 years	18
Boys, 16–18 years	21
Girls, 16–18 years	16
Men, 19–64 years	19
Men, over 64 years	16
Women, 19–54 years	13
Women, over 54 years	11
Pregnancy	15
Lactation	18

VITAMIN B₆

AGE	RDI (milligrams)
Breastfed	0.25
Bottle-fed	0.25
7–12 months	0.45
1–3 years	0.6–0.9
4–7 years	0.8–1.3
Boys, 8–11 years	1.1–1.6
Girls, 8–11 years	1.0–1.5
Boys, 12–15 years	1.4–2.1
Girls, 12–15 years	1.2–1.8
Boys, 16–18 years	1.5–2.2
Girls, 16–18 years	1.1–1.6
Men, 19–64 years	1.3–1.9
Men, over 64 years	1.0–1.5
Women, 19–54 years	0.9–1.4
Women, over 54 years	0.8–1.1
Pregnancy	1.0–1.5
Lactation	1.6–2.2

VITAMIN E

AGE	RDI (milligrams alpha tocopherol equivalents)
0–6 months, breastfed	2.5
0–6 months, bottle-fed	4.0
7–12 months	4.0
Children, 1–3 years	5.0
Children, 4–7 years	6.0
Children, 8–11 years	8.0
Boys, 12–15 years	10.5
Boys, 16–18 years	11.0
Girls, 12–15 years	9.0
Girls, 16–18 years	8.0
Men, all ages	10.0
Women, all ages	7.0
Pregnancy	7.0
Lactation	9.5

VITAMIN B₁₂

AGE	RDI (micrograms)
Breastfed or bottle-fed	0.3
7–12 months	0.7
1–3 years	1.0
4–7 years	1.5
Boys & girls, 8–11 years	1.5
Boys & girls, 12–18 years	2.0
Men, all ages	2.0
Women, all ages	2.0
Pregnancy	3.0
Lactation	2.5

VITAMIN C

The recommended dietary intake of vitamin C differs between countries but is generally in the range of 30 to 60 milligrams a day. The RDI in Australia is as follows:

AGE	RDI (milligrams)
Breast or bottle-fed	25
7–12 months	30
Boys, 1–15 years	30
Boys, 16–18 years	40
Girls, 1–18 years	30
Men, all ages	40
Women, all ages	30
Pregnancy	60
Lactation	75

FOLATE

AGE	RDI (micrograms)
Breastfed or bottle-fed	50
7–12 months	75
1–7 years	100
Boys & girls, 8–11 years	150
Boys & girls, 12–18 years	200
Men, all ages	200
Women, all ages	200
Pregnancy	400
Lactation	350

Index of recipes

Index

alfalfa, 152
allicin, 75–6
alliin, 75
alliinase, 99–100
alliums, 99
amaranth, 1–2
amylopectin, 111–12, 162
amylose, 111–12, 162
anaemia, and broad beans, 18
aniseed, *see* fennel
anthocyanins, 39, 65
antioxidants, vii, 2, 7, 26, 32, 39, 46, 65, 75, 81,
    100, 139, 141, 162
arrowhead, 189
artichoke, French, 3
artichoke, Jerusalem, 5–7
artichokes, globe, 2–5, 190
arugula, *see* rocket
Asian greens, 7–10
asparagus, 11–13
aubergine, *see* eggplant

balsam pear, 189
bamboo mustard cabbage, 8
bamboo shoots, 15–16
bean sprouts, *see* sprouts
beans, 16–26
beetroot, 26–9
beets, *see* beetroot
Belgian endive, 68, 181
bell peppers, 42
beta carotene, 46, 87, 129; and cancer, viii
biotin, 49, 91
bitter melon, 189
black fungus, 92
bok choy, 8; rosette bok choy, 9
Brassicas, 8, 32, 35, 139, 140, 176, 180
breadfruit, 29–32
brinjal, 65
broccoli raab, 139
broccoli, 32–5
broccolini, 32, 33, 34
burdock, 189–90

cabbage, 39–42
calabrese, 32
calcots, 101
cancer, bowel, 5
cancer, vii–viii, anti-cancer compounds, 32, 35,
    54, 100, 137, 139

canola, 8, 139
capsaicin, 57
capsicums, 42–5, 57
caraway, 45
cardoon, 190
carotenaemia, 46
carotenoids, 39, 46, 69, 87, 140, 162, 165, 171,
    172, 192
carrots, 45–9
cassava, 190–91
cauliflower, 49–52
celeriac, 52–4
celery, 54–6
celinon, 56
cepes, *see* under mushrooms
chaconine in potatoes, 115
chanterelles, *see* under mushrooms
chayote, 59
chicory, 68–9, 181
children, vii
Chilean clover 153
chillies, 42, 57–9
China peas, 107
Chinese broccoli, 8
Chinese cabbage, 8, 176
Chinese kale, 32
Chinese spinach, 2, 8
chitin, 91
chlorophyll, in potatoes, 115
choi, 7
chokos, 59–60
cholesterol, blood, 75
choy sum, 8
chrysanthemum greens, 8, 9
chuk gai choy, 8
chye sim, 8
colds, 10
collards, 81
coriander, 45
courgettes, 185
cranberry beans, 17
cryptoxanthin, 162
cucumber, bitter, 189
cucumbers, 61–3
Cucurbita, 128
cyanogenetic glycosides, 18
cynarin, 3

daai gaai choy, 8
daikon, *see* radishes